D0515375

"I was blown over by this book! I have never seen a compendium of inter-views like this, from so many different perspectives, in such rich and human detail. Not only were the interviews sensitively and honestly transcribed in a way that makes each of the interviewees feel like he or she is jumping right off the page, but the background information on each conflict, and the notes for each chapter heading, are equally moving and insightful. I wish everyone could read this book and understand that 'peace' and 'justice' are not abstract terms."

— *Melanie Greenberg, president, Alliance for Peacebuilding*

"*Speaking Their Peace* provides a glimpse directly into the lives of the women and men, the youngsters and retirees, the teachers and taxi drivers, the rebels and the conscripts who have seen the impact of war in their homes, schools, villages, and streets. They've experienced terrible things. Yet, what's most remarkable is their determination not only to survive but to thrive, not to seek revenge but to build a better life for themselves, their families, and their entire societies. It's inspiring. And it needs to be heard by everyone lucky enough to have seen modern conflict only on TV."

— *Manal Omar, author of* Barefoot in Baghdad

"A remarkable book in both big and small ways. The landscape of the book— the disturbing, scarring, but often astonishingly resilient world of souls emerging from war and violence into a tentative peace—is a cautionary tale full of urgent lessons to be learned. But the heart of the book—the specific voices of the people who suffer and survive—will stay with me. This is essential reading for all who wish to make a difference in these settings."

— *Peter T. Coleman, professor of psychology and education, Columbia University*

"In this collection of moving interviews, Colette Rausch illustrates, at the most basic level, how important peacemaking and peacekeeping are, and how difficult. Participants and victims alike reveal the trauma and the antagonisms that conflict leaves in its wake. Reconciliation comes only very gradually and often incompletely, requiring persistent local leadership and long-term international support from people like Ms. Rausch and her colleagues at the United States Institute for Peace. Readers will find a new appreciation of why this is worth doing."

— *James Dobbins, senior fellow with the RAND Corporation and special envoy for the Barack Obama, George W. Bush, and Bill Clinton administrations*

"This book should be required reading for all those involved in postconflict peace and reconciliation processes."

— *Lady Anne Greenstock, Advisory Board Member, Women for Women International*

SPEAKING THEIR PEACE

Personal Stories from the Frontlines of War and Peace

COLETTE RAUSCH

Roaring Forties Press
Berkeley, California

United States Institute of Peace
Washington, D.C.

Copyright © 2015 by the Endowment of the United States Institute of Peace.

Roaring Forties Press
1053 Santa Fe Avenue
Berkeley, CA 94706

www.roaringfortiespress.com

Printed in the United States of America. All rights reserved.

Cover design by Oliver Munday
Interior design by Nigel Quinney

Library of Congress Cataloging-in-Publication Data

Rausch, Colette.
  Speaking their peace : personal stories from the frontlines of war
and peace / Colette Rausch.
     pages cm
   ISBN 978-1-938901-38-6 (paperback) -- ISBN 978-1-938901-43-0 (pdf)
-- ISBN 978-1-938901-44-7 (kindle) 1. Peace-building--Case studies.
2. Postwar reconstruction--Social aspects--Case studies. I. Title.
  JZ5538.R38 2015
  303.6'60922--dc23
                                         2015002444

This book is dedicated to all those who have lived through violent conflict and persevered in their efforts to build a more peaceful world in the face of immense hardship, loss, and trauma.

When It Is Calm Again

The storm has ceased, but it is raining still
The thunders roar and lightnings flash
The ground is firm, but it is slippery and wet
Soon the rain will stop and it will be dry again

A storm so sudden and strangely cruel
Will one day cease, but will never die
The pain and anguish it has caused
We may forgive, but will never forget

When it is dry again, we will rise and search
For friends and families and lost loved ones
But who amongst them will be there to find?
What damages are there have we yet to know?

When it is dry again, we will build new homes
Start new families and make new friends
But to the memories of those we've lost
We will remember the storm, even when it is calm

— *Saah Charles N'Tow*

CONTENTS

FOREWORD

His Holiness the Dalai Lama

For many years, I have been stressing that if we are truly to create a better world for ourselves—a world of peace, brotherhood, and harmony—the key lies in our cultivating a sense of universal responsibility. Each of us must learn to work not just for his or her own self, family, or nation, but also for the benefit of all humankind. The world is no longer what it used to be like in ancient times. It has become more interdependent as a result of rapid technological advances and international trade, as well as increasing transnational relations. The dynamic of today's world is such that a crisis in one part of the world—whether global warming, war, injustice, suffering, poverty, etc.—invariably has ripple effects in other parts of the world, and the repercussions are felt by almost everybody. This leaves us with no option but to treat each major local problem as a global concern from the moment it begins.

I am, therefore, pleased to see the book, *Speaking Their Peace,* a compilation of voices of people from eleven conflict zones across the world. They inform us of their lives, struggles, and hopes, and also let readers gain better perspectives on the situation in these zones. It is a beautiful contribution to the promotion of peace and dialogue among different peoples of the world.

I understand that, as the associate vice president for Governance, Law, and Society at the United States Institute of Peace, Ms. Rausch is involved in various peacebuilding works in conflict zones around the world. Her work and this book are a good example of what I term "universal responsibility." I want to express my appreciation and wish her success.

March 7, 2015

ACKNOWLEDGMENTS

There are so many people to acknowledge and thank for their invaluable participation in the development of this book. It truly has been a joint creation, spanning continents, cultures, languages, and experiences.

Above all, I want to thank those who invited us into their homes, lives, and hearts and graciously agreed to be interviewed. As they shared with us their personal stories, we witnessed not only trauma and hardship, but also triumph and transformation. We learned about the resilience of the human spirit and its unquenchable desire to transcend the ravages of war and seek a lasting peace in which the individual, family, and community do not only survive, but thrive.

I would like to thank Nigel Quinney, editor extraordinaire. This book would not have been possible without him. His patience and unmatched ability to parse through text and quickly glean the gems hidden within is unparalleled. On those occasions when I could no longer string together a proper sentence and sent to Nigel a collage of words and letters, he would invariably respond, gently and always in very proper British English, with suggestions to add a bit more here, explain a bit more there. It would have been easy for him to shake his finger at my prose while shaking his head in dismay—yet, if he did, it never reflected in his always clever, always humorous, yet always supportive e-mails and phone calls to me to give it another go.

A very special thanks goes to the *Speaking Their Peace* team: Najla Elmangoush, Teuta Gashi, Erica Gaston, Khitam Al-Khaghani, Anil Kochukudy, Tim Luccaro, Leanne McKay, Morgan Miller, Lelia Mooney, Govinda Rijal, and Suzanne Wopperer. Many interviews were made possible only by their tenacity and dedication, and their willingness to help out despite already having a heavy workload to accomplish in war zones and postconflict states. The team members were not only recruited as interviewers, but also conscripted as photographers and videographers, and they performed these additional tasks with great artistic flair. Many of us in the team found that our participation resulted in our own personal growth and a transformation in how we looked at war or peace. An interview was not a one-sided affair, but a therapeutic, cathartic conversation of give-and-take that left us enriched.

Also invaluable were the contributions from numerous people in each country we visited who stepped up and helped out on many fronts, including making introductions, interpreting, transcribing, handling logistics, and providing insight into the local culture and political context. Fahd Al-Abssi, Daniel Akau, Shobhakar Budhathoki, Karon Cochran-Budhathoki, Abdulbaset Elgadi,

Leben Moro, Abul Hakim Al-Offairi, Jim Peterson, Julio Pineda, Assadullah Sahil, Fahd Saif, Jimmy Shilue, and Wallah Wilsitow all deserve recognition for their tireless efforts and invaluable contributions.

In Liberia, members of the team met Saah Charles N'Tow, who spoke about his experiences and quoted his wonderful poem, "When It Is Calm Again." I am grateful to Saah for allowing me to use that poem to set the stage for this book.

I would also like to thank and recognize Vijay Simhan, who used his video-editing skills and creativity to produce video pieces for the *Speaking Their Peace* website, and Patrick Dunn for his video footage and behind-the-scenes photography, as well as for his word-smithing. Thanks go, too, to Bethany McGann for her vision and creative energy in building the website and Kay Spencer for spearheading the development of the discussion guides.

Appreciation goes to all those who contributed to the conflict profiles through their research, drafting, and reviewing of completed drafts. It was important that each profile not only give readers a succinct yet informative background to a given conflict but also avoid presenting a black-and-white history, for every conflict involves different narratives and myriad nuances. So thank you to those who worked so hard to make this happen: Johnnie Carson, Priscilla Clapp, Erica Gaston, Paul Hughes, Khitam Al-Khaghani, Barnett Koven, Tim Luccaro, Noaman Al-Masoudi, Fiona Mangan, Christina Murtaugh, Maral Noori, Dan Serwer, Meredith Shea, Scott Smith, Kay Spencer, William Spencer, and Suzanne Wopperer.

Thank you to Deirdre Greene of Roaring Forties Press for believing in this book and making it a reality. It was a real pleasure to work with such a dedicated professional.

Thank you to the United States Institute of Peace and those who shared my belief in the promise of *Speaking Their Peace* and in the importance of never losing sight of the human dimension of peace and war. Those colleagues include Neil Kritz, who first approved the project; Dan Serwer, who saw its scope enlarge; Tara Sonenshine, who envisioned it reaching a general audience of youth and students; and David Smock, whose unwavering support and encouragement were utterly invaluable. Without David's leadership, this book would not have made it to the finish line.

Appreciation goes to Kay Hechler, who helped me navigate the details of getting the book into print. From the beginning of the project, Kay was a supporter and was always available to share her rich publishing expertise with me. Appreciation also goes to Virginia Bryant for her excitement about the book and her commitment to ensuring that the book's stories are shared with a large audience.

Finally, I want to say an enormous thank you to Patrick and Calvin, who lived with this project for six years and contributed to it, both directly and indirectly, in numerous ways. Without their support, patience, and encouragement, this book would not have been possible. ●

PART I

INTRODUCTION

INTRODUCTION

Leaving Las Vegas

I recall arriving home from the aftermath of genocide. I had been in Bosnia on behalf of the United States Department of Justice, helping put together a training program for the judges, prosecutors, defense attorneys, and police who were trying to bring some justice and security to their devastated land. I had traveled around the country with local officials, and had seen and heard the mental, physical, and social scars inflicted by the war. Now, as I walked into my comfortable townhouse in Las Vegas, I suddenly felt uncomfortable. I looked around at the stylish couches, the spotless bathrooms, the immaculate kitchen, and everything seemed hollow.

That night, in the first step toward a different life, I emptied my walk-in closet. Keeping only the bare essentials, I packed all the other clothes into boxes and addressed them to a friend in Bosnia, with a note asking him to distribute them to whoever needed them.

Las Vegas, with its glitzy casinos shaped like fairy-tale castles and ancient pyramids, with its million eyes focused on money and glamour, seemed too far removed from the human suffering that I had just witnessed. So, too, did my job as a federal prosecutor.

Before I had gone to Bosnia in 1998, I had devoted myself to my job, which meant building and trying cases against drug traffickers and bank robbers, as well as white-collar criminals who had bilked millions of dollars from their elderly victims. I had taken on Nevada's first church-arson case and had prosecuted the state's first case applying the federal Violence Against Women Act. It was interesting work and involving work. But now, as I packed my designer suits into cardboard boxes, I felt as though I had done everything I could as a prosecutor. Something was calling me to follow a different path.

Before I could lament my professional dilemma, I was offered a job in the Justice Department's overseas training office in Washington, D.C. The next thing I knew, I was on a plane to Kosovo, just weeks after NATO airplanes had stopped bombing the area to evict the Serbian forces who had been terrorizing the province. Some ten thousand people had been killed and hundreds of thousands had fled their homes during the fighting between the Serbs and the KLA, a Kosovo secessionist movement with its own record of human rights abuses. As I landed in Kosovo, NATO forces were moving into the province to provide security while various international and nongovernmental organizations (NGOs) set up operations to help the population start rebuilding their society.

After a few eye-opening weeks in Kosovo, I returned to Las Vegas with a new-felt sense of purpose, loaded all my belongings into a rental truck, and drove it to Washington, D.C., to work on international legal projects for the Department of Justice. I was soon seconded for a year to the Organization for Security and Co-operation in Europe (OSCE) and headed back to Kosovo to take charge of the OSCE's Rule of Law Unit and, subsequently, the Human Rights and Rule of Law Department. I helped develop new criminal laws, establish a system to monitor the work of judges, and build a more effective working relationship between NATO troops and civilians working for the OSCE and the United Nations.

After two years of witnessing the consequences of war firsthand—the human tragedies, the corrupt and often self-serving political factions, the well-intentioned but sometimes misguided efforts of the international community—I was ready to reflect on my experiences and work to find better ways to help countries and people emerging from conflict.

So when a colleague told me about a position opening at the United States Institute of Peace (USIP), I jumped at the chance. USIP is an independent institution created and funded by the US Congress and devoted to the nonviolent prevention and mitigation of deadly conflict abroad. From Bosnia to Libya, Afghanistan to Iraq, Liberia to Nepal, USIP has helped to strengthen justice and security through its work on constitutional reform, transitional justice, dialogue between civil society and the police, law reform, and other key initiatives. I was hired in 2001 to be part of its Rule of Law program. I discovered that I loved the work, and I gradually progressed from one position to another until I ended up as the director of USIP's Rule of Law Center and associate vice president for Governance, Law, and Society, working both in conflict zones and in Washington, D.C., on criminal justice and police reform.

Studs and Me

I recall opening a book in high school. It was called *American Dreams: Lost and Found* and it was written by Studs Terkel. Studs was a much-loved actor, writer, and broadcaster from Chicago whose weekly radio program ran for forty-five years, during which he chatted to thousands of Americans, both famous and unknown. *American Dreams* recounted the stories of regular folks, each with his or her own hopes and dreams, and many of whom had turned those dreams into reality through perseverance and hard work.

Studs' book spoke to me. It resonated with my family's own story. I grew up in Reno, Nevada. My mother worked in the laundry at the local hospital; my father worked as a musician and union leader. Like many of the people Studs met, my father had little formal education but a lot of wisdom. He was, indeed, the wisest man I have ever known. Born in 1912, he did not finish high school because he had to find a job to help support his family. He was one of eight children, grew up in Omaha, Nebraska, and drove from the cornfields of Iowa to the shores of California in an early Model T with his musician father, who carried a crate of sheet music from one silent movie theater to the next, playing whatever seemed to fit the pictures dancing silently on the screen. After serving in World War II, my father became a musician and business agent for the local Musician's Union.

He and my mother raised five children. Three were from his first marriage, and together they adopted two, including me. I was the youngest. He said that he knew when I was just four years old that I would become a lawyer. I would debate passionately with him, standing my ground and arguing my point whenever I thought something unfair had happened. I loved my family, but my childhood was not entirely lovable. For eight years, beginning when I was eight, my family went through rocky times, involving divorce, remarriages, stepfathers, alcohol abuse, and domestic violence.

At sixteen, I left home and went to college, and I became the first kid in our family to graduate. But I never left behind a belief in the wisdom inherent in all of us, whether educated or not.

I paid my way through college by taking a variety of jobs, working in a fast-food restaurant, a movie theater, a doctor's office, and a funeral home.

After college, I saved money for law school by dealing blackjack at a Reno casino. As soon as I had my law degree, I searched for my birth parents. My mother was living in Seattle; my father was in Germany. Getting to know both of them helped me fill in the gaps in my own story.

My career after law school took me from dealing with consumer fraud for the Nevada Attorney General's Office; to serving as a federal prosecutor; to Hungary, Bosnia, and Kosovo with the Justice Department; and then to USIP. Along the way, I wrote many reports and a handful of books intended to help lawyers, prosecutors, and peacemakers working in conflict-affected zones.

When I heard the news of Studs' death on October 31, 2008, I decided that I wanted to honor him by writing a different sort of book—his sort of book. This would be a book in which the voices of everyday people would be heard, in which they could speak their piece. These people, however, would not be Studs' peacetime heroes. These would be the people I have met amid the ruins of war. These would be people who have lived through war and now stand on the threshold of an uncertain peace. I would be a conduit for these people, giving them a chance to tell the world not only about the nightmares they had endured and that they could not easily forget, but also about their battered but dogged dreams for a better life in a country that one day would finally be at peace.

And that is why this book is called *Speaking Their Peace*.

Getting the Show on the Road

The people who work for USIP often find themselves in war-torn parts of the world. Wherever we go, we find ourselves talking with all sorts of people about all kinds of things.

One day we may meet with a general or a rebel commander, a prime minister, or a national religious figure. The next day we may sit down with farmers or shopkeepers, schoolteachers or junior police officers. Every day we also chat with clerks, security guards, waiters, and anyone else a visitor is likely to bump into. In most places we visit, we have local colleagues, many of whom become good friends, and we get to know not only these colleagues and friends but also their colleagues and friends, not to mention their families.

In short, when I decided to write this book, I realized I already had a vast but untapped resource close to hand. So I decided to tap it.

I recruited an informal team of colleagues, each of whom was well acquainted with a different part of the world—and several of whom were also fluent in the local language. (See the chapter entitled "The Team" in part III of this book for a profile of each team member.) The project was run on a shoestring. We would piggyback on other projects, conscripting anyone who might be able to help out: "You're going to Country X next week, right?" I would shamelessly ask. "Can you do an interview for me?"

Whenever I found myself in a country emerging from conflict, I would try to make room in my schedule for an interview or two. We would conduct interviews wherever we might be: a capital city, a provincial town, a remote village. Occasionally, when we had the luxury of time, we would take a road trip, taking our video cameras and audio recorders with us.

Over the course of six years, my colleagues and I at USIP's of Rule of Law Center interviewed people in Afghanistan, Myanmar (Burma), Iraq, Kosovo, Liberia, Libya, Nepal, Nicaragua, Peru, South Sudan, and Yemen. We spoke with everyone from taxi drivers to government ministers, grandmothers to guerrillas, artists to activists, veterans to widows. We also interviewed the "internationals," those men and women who are in these countries because they work for NGOs such as Amnesty International, intergovernmental organizations such as the United Nations, or government agencies such as the US State Department. We took their stories, their dreams, and their perspectives and wove them into this book.

That description, however, makes the process sound a lot simpler than it really was.

To begin with, we wanted to focus on countries that are moving from war to peace, but there's nothing simple about that movement. Professional peacebuilders describe such places as "countries emerging from conflict." The phrase is a good one because it underlines a key point about war and peace: there's no on/off switch. Wars don't suddenly end when a peace agreement is signed between the sides that have been fighting. Sometimes, in fact, violence can grow worse as soon as the ink on an agreement has dried. The road from war to peace is long, with many detours, roadblocks, and potholes along the way. Countries don't just hop out of the hot water of war onto the pleasant beachfront of peace; they emerge from conflict like a large rock emerges from a stormy ocean as the tide recedes, a little jagged piece at a time. But this tide can quickly reverse direction, abruptly swallowing up some or all of the exposed surface and plunging the rock back beneath the roiling waters.

We wanted to capture this uncomfortable reality, so we opted for countries at different points in the gradual, unpredictable transition from war to peace. In Afghanistan, for example, reformers are trying to tackle corrupt governing institutions while the government, with international support, continues to fight the Taliban. In Nepal, fighting between the government and rebel forces, which claimed fifteen thousand lives over ten bloody years, has largely died down since a peace agreement was reached in 2006, but the peace process remains very vulnerable, the new representative democracy totters from political crisis to political crisis, and large sections of the population continue to be excluded from power and prosperity. In Nicaragua, the last battles of the civil war were fought more than twenty years ago, but the psychological wounds still fester and political scars still disfigure the country.

We also chose the countries for *Speaking Their Peace* on the basis of geography. This book is not about a particular conflict or a particular peace, but about what people from around the globe make of the long journey from conflict to peace. We anticipated that there would be many shared perceptions and common experiences, but we also wanted to reflect the global diversity of the experience of warmaking and peacebuilding. By the time we were ready to put this book together, we had interviewed people in eleven countries scattered among very different regions of the world, from sub-Saharan Africa to the Middle East, South America to Southern Europe, South Asia to Central America.

In each country, we tried to interview people from different sides of the conflict. And for the most part, we succeeded. In some instances, however, practical reasons made it difficult or impossible to talk to people from a particular side. This uneven coverage in no way reflects any bias in favor of one or another side. The purpose of this book is not to point fingers at any particular person, group, or nation. To the contrary, the purpose of this book is to capture and embrace universal aspects and experiences of conflict and the transition to peace, but to see them within a local—indeed, within an individual—context. If there is any bias in this book, it is a bias in favor of people who have not before had the chance to be heard and who have something to say that will resonate with people across the world, no matter what their nationality, ethnicity, or religion.

Personal ties played their part in shaping the selection of countries. In each country we visited, we knew people who could guide us through the local history, culture, and geography and help us identity and introduce ourselves to potential interviewees. Thanks to the trust that existed between the local people we knew and those we wanted to interview, our interviewees generally felt at ease. At first, some might have been reluctant—naturally enough—to divulge sensitive memories, but we could usually develop a rapport quickly.

We also interviewed people we met by chance. In Nicaragua, for example, one member of our team became ill the day we planned to leave the city of León. We had to stay two days longer, and while my team huddled in our hotel's lobby to map out the rest of the trip and to find ways to recoup the lost time, Jim, the hotel's owner, visited USIP's website to learn more about this odd mix of personalities in his lobby. Moved by what he discovered about USIP's mission and work, Jim volunteered to arrange an interview for us with a former Sandinista fighter who had lost both hands during an ambush by government forces. Dexterous with his prosthetic hands, the former insurgent told us about his wartime experiences and how he now works with an NGO that provides services for disabled people.

What We Talked About

The interviews were conducted like conversations. We would sit down in the interviewee's home or office, or in a hotel or cafe, and chat for one to two hours, usually in the interviewee's own language. This informality encouraged people to tell their personal—and often painful—narratives of conflict, to comment on their country's current security situation, and to share their hopes for the future. One or two of us—or three, if we needed an interpreter, as we often did—would arrive at the interviewee's home equipped with a tape recorder or a video camera and a notepad.

We began each interview by explaining the nature and purpose of the *Speaking Their Peace* project. We let the person know that we wanted their personal reflections: their story, thoughts, views, and perceptions. After inquiring about their personal information (name, age, occupation, education, and so forth), with a few adaptations to fit the local context, we asked the same general series of questions in each interview.

The first question was about the conflict and the interviewee's personal experiences. We asked what motivated them to carry on during the conflict and the present. Each person had a different story to tell. There are so many stories in countries emerging from conflict; people have taken many different pathways into conflict, have left many people behind, and are now heading in many different directions for many different reasons.

We then asked broader questions. Some were quite abstract—such as "What does the rule of law mean to you?"—though many of the answers were very concrete and practical. This attention to the rule of law reflects the focus of my work at USIP. Like President Dwight Eisenhower, I believe that "only justice, fairness, consideration, and cooperation" can lead to "the dawn of earthly peace." At USIP, my colleagues and I in the Rule of Law program have worked with the people of war-torn countries as they build the kinds of legal systems that are essential to restoring peace. What kind of legal systems are those? Ones that can maintain law and order; are fair, impartial, and accessible; apply to everyone equally; and are respected both by their own people and by the international community. So, asking people in a country emerging from conflict about the rule of law makes perfect sense—to me at least! Indeed, the interviewees themselves were usually well aware of the extent to which peace and stability depend on the rule of law, and vice versa.

Other questions probed the interviewees' attitude toward the "internationals," the outsiders like us who are in the country supposedly to help put it back on its feet. Internationals, who are usually highly dedicated and hardworking individuals, often get the impression that they are making a real difference. Yet there is always a danger that they are cocooned in their offices and blinkered by their specific missions, and that they don't really see what is going on around them. What, we wondered, had been the interviewees' personal experiences of the internationals? What would they like outsiders to know about them and their country?

We also asked the internationals themselves about what motivated them to work in conflict-affected countries, and about their experiences with the local community and with other members of the international community.

We generally closed an interview by asking about the interviewee's hopes and dreams for the future. Some interviewees were firmly rooted in the trauma and planted in the past; it seemed, indeed, as if the past was right there with us in the room. It is easy to see how cycles of violence and revenge perpetuate themselves. Yet not everyone was mired in the past. Some focused on a simple desire to move on, reluctant to see themselves as either victims or perpetrators. They wanted to break with the old tradition of families and communities passing victimhood from one generation to the next. They wanted to start living a new story. We saw firsthand how someone can become empowered by changing their story.

The tapes of the interviewees (our trusty Marantz tape recorders can be spotted in several of the photos in the book!) were carefully transcribed and translated. Some ideas and expressions cannot be translated literally—their meaning would be hopelessly distorted or entirely lost in English—so when ever necessary we translated a phrase or a sentence so that the English-language version, although it might not mirror the interviewee's comments word for word, was faithful to the meaning and spirit of the interviewee's remarks. We also edited down the interviews to make them easier to read and to spotlight the main points. We haven't used ellipses to indicate where material has been left out ... but only because they would be distracting.

Most of the interviews begin with a few short sentences that capture the mood of the interview, its setting, the interviewee's body language, or some other important aspect of the interview that the text doesn't convey.

Some interviewees, concerned about their personal security in societies in which the divisions and scars of war have yet to heal fully, asked us not to use their names or photographs in this book. We have respected their wishes, of course, and given them pseudonyms. (The pseudonyms have quotation marks around them.)

I Learn to Walk the Line

Many internationals find it difficult not to become weighed down by the pain they see etched on the faces of those who have lived through violent conflict. They find it challenging to avoid taking on—and taking home—at least some of the emotional trauma they encounter. I speak from personal experience.

Having lived in Bosnia and Kosovo in the immediate aftermath of violent conflict, and having then spent more than a decade traveling to numerous other countries emerging from war, I have been affected by the stress that is part of working in the field. Seeing mass graves exhumed, treading carefully around landmines, waking to the sound of a bomb rattling my windows, trying to sleep to the sound of automatic gunfire, being shown the scars left by torture, meeting the families of the "disappeared": all these things have become part of the fabric of my life, of how I view things and who I am.

I find myself reacting physically and emotionally to the recollections and reflections of many of the people I meet in my work, as if I am absorbing their pain and experiences. Out of a primal desire to protect myself, sometimes I detached from or even physically exited a situation. I recall a meeting in 1998, where I was working with senior leaders of Bosnia's judicial system. After a workshop in Bosnia during the day, we gathered for dinner in the evening across the border in Croatia. As the wine flowed, the Bosnians began reminiscing with the Croatian innkeeper about the war. This was the first time I had heard them talk about the war. Perhaps it was the setting—being away from Bosnia and connecting together as a group—that unleashed such a torrent of memories. But as the conversation grew more explicit and the stories of horrors and tragedies accumulated, I found that I had to gracefully excuse myself and leave the room. I could not breathe amid the heaviness of their experiences.

I am not alone in trying to escape the vortex of such emotions. Many of us whose job it is to promote rule of law in countries ravaged by conflict focus tightly on the technical aspects of our work. We devote ourselves to finding out what laws are needed to defuse the explosion of criminality that often accompanies the signing of peace treaties. We preoccupy ourselves with determining what kind of training would best help the local police to be more responsive to the public, many members of which have come to regard the police as corrupt and thuggish agents of a repressive regime. When we focus on these technicalities, when we restrict our gaze to laws and institutions, we feel as if we have some control over the situation.

But this is an illusion. The technical approach is an attempt to keep at arm's length the reality of what goes on in a conflict-affected country: the trauma; fragmented communities; pervasive instability; and various kinds of violence—political and criminal, military and paramilitary, public and domestic. We avoid pulling back the curtain that people have drawn over traumatic events because we do not want to see what lies on the other side. We fear that the horror and the raw emotions, once exposed, will come flooding out and overwhelm us. So we focus on technicalities.

This is a mistake. The human element, full of emotional distress and psychological turmoil, is intertwined with the technical work we try to do in promoting rule of law. They cannot be separated, and if one wants to really understand and help the people in countries emerging from conflict, one should not try to separate them.

For my team and me, *Speaking Their Peace* brought us to the personal, to the human. It was an opportunity for us to connect with others. It gave us the opportunity to let go of the professional masks we often hide behind and to express compassion, for others and for ourselves. It also gave us a chance to acknowledge that we, too, carried all sorts of psychological, emotional, and physical baggage, even trauma, especially those team members who have themselves experienced violent conflict. And we found that conducting the interviews could help us heal.

I learned during the *Speaking Their Peace* project to walk the thin line between emotional engagement and professional detachment. At the beginning of the project, I would grow anxious before a trip, and when I returned home, I would spend days exhausted and jumpy until I could process what I had just experienced. I realized that I was taking on too much of the interviewees' emotional distress. I realized that if I was to continue with the project, I would have to work hard and use techniques that would enable me to be fully present, open, and accepting during the interviews but would also prevent me from absorbing and retaining the emotional energies. These energies would flow through me but would not take hold of me.

This, however, is often easier said than done! During many of the interviews, I was tossed about on a sea of roiling emotions and diverse realities and had to fight back tears with deep breaths and a determination to retain the interested but emotionally low-key manner of a newspaper reporter. At other times, I felt like a voyeur and have wondered whether I have a moral obligation to avert my gaze or to look unflinchingly at what the person in front of me wanted to show me.

Even seeing photographs of the interviewees and reading the transcripts of our conversations can transport me back to the interview. In chatting with other members of the *Speaking Their Peace* team, I have discovered that all of us have been indelibly affected by the project, by the process of being brought into the lives of the people we interviewed.

Bearing Witness

In every interview, I sensed a deep need by the person to be heard, to have their experiences recorded and thereby validated. Some interviewees wanted to be understood and not judged. Others hoped that by speaking to me, their voices would eventually reach the ears of people with the power to do something about the political and economic situation in their country. Still others hoped that their stories would be heard by, and would help, people in similar situations to themselves.

The interview process itself can be transformative, for both the interviewee and the interviewer. Each conversation was not just about getting a story to put in a book. It was a process of sharing between the interviewer and the person interviewed. In most interviews, we each took something away from the exchange. For some, it was the first time that anyone had come from the outside to hear their stories. We were able to be a witness to their experiences, a vehicle for processing what had happened in their lives, and a conduit for sharing their stories with others.

I recall an interview with a group of women in Huanta, in the mountainous, poverty-stricken Ayacucho region of Peru. The women were Quechuan, and the Quechuan-speaking people had suffered terribly at the hands of both the brutal Shining Path movement and the Peruvian counterinsurgency forces. As the other women told their stories, one woman stared at me suspiciously, sizing me up. At one point, she interrupted another woman and said to me, "I am sorry that you do not speak our language so you cannot understand what we are saying." Our eyes locked and I said, "I do not need to understand your language in order to understand your story. There are other ways to hear what you have been through." At that moment, everything changed. We instantly understood one another on a fundamental level. Thereafter, she grew more open and took every opportunity to look me directly in the eyes; despite my discomfort, I did not shy away from her gaze. After the interview, she grabbed my arm and resisted letting it go when it was time for me to leave. Several years later, I still feel that connection, and I doubt it is one that I will ever lose.

We were similar in age, but so different in what we had experienced in our lives. Yet, we connected. I could feel and honor what she had experienced, and she gave to me an acknowledgement of this: her smile. At that moment, I knew that we would both leave the interview changed, each forever carrying a piece of the other.

Listen

The international community pours billions of dollars into countries emerging from conflict while peacebuilding practitioners toil tirelessly to strengthen stability, good governance, and the rule of law. Unfortunately, the international community often fails to understand how the people in these countries actually view the concepts of justice, security, and good governance, and the international efforts intended to foster them. What outsiders believe is important to the people is often very different from what the people themselves deem important. A similar divide typically exists regarding the role the outsiders are playing. This perceptual disconnect is not merely unfortunate; it can seriously hamper peacebuilding efforts in conflict-affected countries.

There is almost no published material that documents this phenomenon. What does exist is fragmentary, dry, and usually buried in research or policy papers that focus on other subjects and are read by very few people. (I know—I've written some of them myself!) Insofar as they are presented at all, the views of international practitioners and the people in a country are often stripped both of their political and social context and of their personal and emotional resonance. If policymakers and practitioners are to design and implement programs that harmonize with local concerns and priorities, the international community needs to hear the real voices of the people in the field, locals and internationals alike, expressing their personal experiences, fears, and hopes.

These are the voices that can be heard in the pages of this volume. And I hope that they will be heard not just by policymakers and practitioners, but by anyone with an interest in today's turbulent world and an appreciation for the resilience of the human spirit.

How This Book Is Organized

That resilience is to be found throughout the chapters of part II, each of which weaves together interviews with members of a particular group of people.

We could have divided the interviews in any number of ways, because we set out to get a cross-section of opinion in a country, and thus ended up with a broad array of individuals, opinions, and experiences. In the end, however, we decided to categorize the interviewees according to their defining experience of the conflict or their job or role during the conflict and since. Apart from anything else, this structure bring outs some striking similarities within each group. One's role during a conflict evidently shapes one's experience of it.

For readers unfamiliar with the conflicts that have beset the countries featured in this book, the next chapter offers a series of succinct descriptions of the main protagonists, issues, and events involved in each conflict, as well as a summary of the evolving peace process.

Readers who want to know more about the *Speaking Their Peace* project will find the final part of this book interesting. They may also want to visit the website, www.speakingtheirpeace.org. ●

CONFLICT
PROFILES

Each of the following conflict profiles (presented in alphabetical order) provides a short account of recent conflict in one of the eleven countries we visited to conduct interviews. As the map below shows, we traveled widely. The countries are found on no fewer than five continents, in both the Eastern and Western Hemispheres, and both north and south of the equator.

Each conflict profile explains why and how war came to that particular country: the underlying issues, the main protagonists, and the nature and scale of the fighting. The profiles also describe how the violence gradually ended, or at least subsided, and how the country has since sought to rebuild, reconcile, and create a more secure and prosperous society. Few, if any, of these countries have put the past firmly behind them; peace is always a work in progress. And in several countries, violent conflict is not just a threat but a reality.

The profiles, which strive to be balanced and accurate, have been reviewed by experts. ●

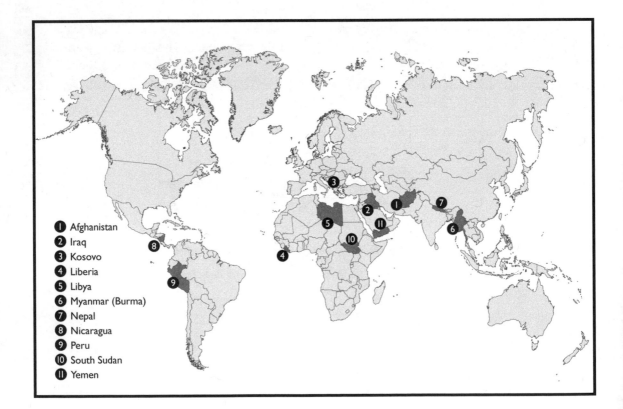

1. Afghanistan
2. Iraq
3. Kosovo
4. Liberia
5. Libya
6. Myanmar (Burma)
7. Nepal
8. Nicaragua
9. Peru
10. South Sudan
11. Yemen

Afghanistan

The modern state of Afghanistan first emerged in 1747, when Ahmad Shah Durrani established monarchical rule with the support of various Pashtun tribes. The state struggled from its inception to centralize and codify its authority over the country's many different ethnic groups, geographic spaces, and religious and social ideologies. The monarchy used state wealth and political patronage to reward its supporters while subjugating other groups. Ethnic minorities in the north, south, and west were treated as second-class citizens and given scant access to economic and educational opportunities. This legacy of ethnic division and often violent antagonism persists to this day.

Beginning in the 1800s, Afghanistan became the arena of the "Great Game," a geopolitical duel between Britain and Russia for strategic domination of the region. The Great Game involved periodic interference in enduring domestic rivalries between would-be Afghan rulers. Ultimately, the two empires decided to maintain Afghanistan as a buffer state between them, giving Afghanistan the borders that it has today.

For most of the twentieth century, Afghanistan enjoyed a slow and steady modernization process, remaining neutral in the two world wars and attempting a democratic opening in the 1960s. King Zahir Shah, who had reigned since 1933, turned out to be the last in line of the Afghan kings, being ousted from office in a nonviolent coup by his cousin Daud Khan, who became president. Five years later, Daud Khan himself was overthrown in a military coup led by the People's Democratic Party of Afghanistan (PDPA), which installed a communist regime.

Large landholders dispossessed of land through state redistribution policies joined with conservative religious leaders to organize violent resistance to the regime. In December 1979, the Soviet Union invaded Afghanistan to prop up the PDPA regime. With increasing financial and military support from the United States (funneled through Pakistan), resistance groups conducted a guerrilla insurgency that lasted nearly ten years. The PDPA's rule was marked by state-sponsored disappearances and torture, secret prisons, and targeted assassinations; the insurgency was marked by intense fighting within the multiple guerrilla factions known as mujahedin ("holy warriors") based in Pakistan. In 1989, the Soviet forces withdrew from Afghanistan; within three years, the PDPA was overrun by various mujahedin factions. In 1992, mujahedin fighters entered the capital, ending the communist government's rule. During the Soviet occupation, an estimated 1 million Afghans and fifteen thousand Soviet forces were killed.

The various anti-Soviet factions that had fought together in the 1980s proved incapable of governing in a coalition government after the PDPA's fall. The country descended into political chaos, with warlords assuming control of different sections of the country and carving up Kabul into a city divided by armed units. From 1992 to 1996, nearly one hundred thousand Afghans were killed, and a million others fled into refugee camps in neighboring states.

In response to the chaos, a group of young mujahedin fighters, led by a charismatic religious leader, Mullah Omar, emerged in the southwest of the country and promised to remove the warlords who had been responsible for so much death and destruction. This group, known as the Taliban, imposed law and order based on an ultraconservative interpretation of Islamic law. In 1996, the Taliban captured Kabul and forced the remaining faction of resistance fighters into increasingly small pockets of northern Afghanistan, where they formed the Northern Alliance. Most of the country succumbed to the draconian order of the Islamist Taliban state. Taliban police brutally enforced their vision of Islamic law, subjecting nonconformists to imprisonment, corporal punishment, including amputation of limbs, and execution for even minor crimes. The regime was particularly severe with women, preventing their employment and education and repressing their rights. Women were essentially barred from public life and confined to their homes.

In 1996, Osama bin Laden, a Saudi who had assisted the mujahedin during the resistance, returned to Afghanistan after being expelled by the Sudanese government and stripped of his citizenship by Saudi Arabia. Bin Laden, in the meantime, had created al-Qaeda, a terrorist group that during the 1990s carried out a number of attacks against US targets. After the terrorist attacks of September 11, 2001, the United States demanded that the Taliban hand over Bin Laden, who was believed to have masterminded the attacks. When the Taliban regime refused, the United States led a multinational invasion that drove the Taliban from power.

Following an international conference held at Bonn, Germany, the anti-Taliban factions agreed that Hamid Karzai, a former deputy minister of foreign affairs, would became the head of a power-sharing government. The international community agreed to provide financial and other support—including military support by the NATO-led International Security Assistance Force (ISAF)—to help Afghans build a new political order based on democracy and the rule of law within a constitutional framework.

The Taliban, which had received sanctuary in Pakistan, began to regroup and launched an increasingly formidable insurgency campaign, including suicide bombings of foreign and civilian targets. ISAF and Afghan troops were unable to decisively defeat the Taliban.

President Karzai stepped down in 2014 according to the constitution, and was replaced, after a contentious election, by Ashraf Ghani. In the same year, international forces ended combat operations, though the insurgency continued. The new Ghani government has pledged to end the fighting by seeking a political accommodation with the insurgents. So far, however, both sides remain far apart and the fighting continues. ●

Iraq

Iraq's modern-day struggle for stability and power is rooted in centuries of fighting for control of the country by contending empires, political systems, tribes, and ethnic and religious groups. Muslims conquered Iraq, formerly the heart of Mesopotamia, in the seventh century and established Baghdad as the capital. The city was a major cultural and intellectual metropolis for five centuries, until it was sacked by Mongols in the thirteenth century. Although it was part of the Ottoman Empire starting in the sixteenth century onward, Iraq saw little peace, with rival tribes and regional powers vying for control.

With the dissolution of the Ottoman Empire after World War I, Iraq briefly became a British-mandated territory before achieving independence in 1932. It was ruled under a constitutional monarchy by the Hashemites, the same family that ruled Jordan at the time.

A coup in 1958 brought General Abdul Karim Qasim to power. He introduced significant reforms, including the expansion of education and women's rights, and reduced ethnic and religious-based conflicts, but he was overthrown in a coup in 1963 and subsequently executed. Over the next twenty-one years, Iraq experienced no fewer than six changes of power, impeding the development of a cohesive national identity. The last of these changes, in 1979, was nonviolent—which was ironic, given that it brought to power Saddam Hussein, whose twenty-four-year rule was marked by savage repression internally and military confrontations with neighboring states.

The Iran-Iraq War (1980–88) established Iraq's military as the largest in the Gulf region, but it devastated Iraq's economy and widened cultural divides among the country's ethnic groups. The weary postwar society had to cope with the economic consequences of the government's massive accumulation of debt, as well as the instability generated by rebellions of the Kurds in the northern mountains. Saddam's government brutally repressed the latter, using chemical weapons against civilian targets.

In 1990, Iraq invaded Kuwait, drawing the attention of the international community and leading to Iraqi forces being expelled from Kuwait in February 1991 by a US-led coalition acting under the United Nations. After the war, the UN Security Council required the regime to surrender its weapons of mass destruction and to submit to UN inspections. But Saddam's Ba'ath regime refused to fully cooperate with the UN inspections, and for a dozen years it defied UN Security Council resolutions and coercive tactics, such as economic sanctions and regional no-fly zones. By the early 2000s, the United States and the United Kingdom, asserting that Iraq still possessed weapons of mass destruction, pressed the international community to authorize a military invasion of Iraq. Despite failing to secure explicit UN approval, and with uncertainty over whether or not Iraq was still trying to develop weapons of mass destruction, a US-led coalition invaded. After only a month of fighting,

Saddam was in hiding and his regime was in ruins. In December 2003, he was captured; he was executed three years later.

In the meantime, the coalition, international agencies, and nongovernmental organizations sought to prevent a general humanitarian crisis and help Iraqis create an effective administration and build a stable political future. A new constitution was approved, and parliamentary elections were held in 2005. The United Iraqi Alliance, a Shiite coalition, won nearly half the vote. The main Shiite and Kurdish coalitions agreed to form an alliance, which heightened hopes that the new government might win wide support among Iraqis from a range of ethnic and religious groups. A Sunni became the speaker of the parliament, a Kurd became president, and a Shiite became prime minister.

Unity and stability were to prove elusive, however. The decision by US policymakers to disband the Iraqi army and purge all members of the former ruling Baath Party from public life contributed to a security vacuum and exacerbated the sectarian and societal divides caused by the persecution of the Shiites under Saddam. As Iraq struggled to rise to the challenges faced by its new, inexperienced, and undeveloped democratic system, Sunni and Shiite militias targeted not only each other but also government and coalition forces and figures. Foreign Islamic militants continued to infiltrate Iraq and frustrate US attempts to eliminate insurgent strongholds. In the north, the Kurds continued to develop their own de facto administration, seeking to create a functioning society separate from the rest of Iraq (but in the process fueling political and social disputes across the country).

By late 2006, three thousand Iraqis were dying every month, and the fear of civil war took precedence over insurgent fears. Among the most divisive issues were doubt concerning the Maliki government's willingness to cope with the escalating violence, an evident strain on the relationship between the US and Iraqi governments, and Sunni-Shiite revenge attacks. Sunnis felt they were being marginalized politically by Malaki because he wanted to return the suffering on them that his Shiite people had suffered under Saddam. The first half of 2007 was tumultuous and violent, with suicide bombings, demonstrations against US occupation, and outbreaks of militia fighting. But thanks in part to cease-fires among militia groups and the deployment of a further thirty thousand US troops, violence began to decline. In 2008 the United States began a complicated and prolonged process of withdrawing from Iraq. US troops finally left the country in 2011.

Since then, Iraq's population of 30 million has continued to contend with severe security, social, and economic problems, and the state of Iraq faces existential threats from within and without. Although Iraq is an overwhelmingly Muslim country, it remains sharply conflicted by ethnicity and religion. In addition, a new threat has appeared in the form of the Islamic State, a ruthless and determined terrorist army seeking to establish a new transnational Islamic caliphate in the region. In 2014, the Islamic State took control of several key cities and areas in Iraq. The Iraqi Army, with help from the international community, was battling to liberate those areas and defeat the Islamic State. ●

Kosovo

At the heart of the Kosovo conflict that erupted into large-scale violence in the late 1990s was a struggle between two ethnic groups and their irreconcilable national agendas. On one side was an increasingly nationalist Serbian government in Belgrade and ethnic Serbs living in Kosovo who wanted to maintain Serbian control of what was then an "autonomous" province of Serbia. On the other side was the majority ethnic Albanian population of Kosovo, which at first rebelled against Serbian infringements on autonomy and then fought for an independent state.

Serbia lost control of its lands to the Ottoman Empire in 1389 after the Battle of Kosovo Polje. This battle acquired legendary significance for Serbian nationalists in the nineteenth century, when Kosovo became a symbol of Serbia's history and struggle for independence. In 1912, as the Ottoman Empire crumbled, Serbia began to reestablish control of Kosovo, where the Serbian Orthodox Church maintained many of its most important religious sites.

Ethnic Albanians claim to have inhabited the area long before the arrival of the first Slavic tribes. It is impossible to know if that claim is accurate, but it is certainly the case that Albanians have been increasing their share of the population of Kosovo for more than five hundred years. They became the single largest ethnic group by the nineteenth century, if not earlier, and their demographic dominance increased throughout the twentieth century. By the 1990s, Albanians made up more than 80 percent of Kosovo's population (today, they account for more than 90 percent of the 1.8 million who live there).

In 1946, in the wake of World War II, the Socialist Federal Republic of Yugoslavia (SFRY) was formed, comprising present-day Bosnia and Herzegovina, Croatia, Macedonia, Montenegro, Serbia, and Slovenia. The government was led by Josip Broz Tito, who controlled the one-party state and repressed anticommunist and associated ethnic nationalist sentiments. The SFRY established Kosovo as an autonomous province of the republic of Serbia. In 1974, constitutional changes enlarged Kosovo's autonomy, giving it a status nearly equivalent to one of Yugoslavia's republics.

Shortly after Tito's death in 1981, Albanian nationalists called for Kosovo to be granted the full status of a federal republic. Demonstrations by Kosovo Albanian students were repressed brutally, and Albanian nationalism came to be seen as a threat to the unity of Yugoslavia. Throughout the 1980s, ethnic tensions in Kosovo grew even as the economy stagnated. Some Serbs left the province. In the late 1980s, Slobodan Milošević became president of Serbia and established himself as champion of Serbian nationalism. In 1989, Serbia amended the 1974 constitution and revoked Kosovo's status as an autonomous province. Milošević dissolved the Kosovo Assembly and restricted the freedom of Kosovo Albanians in various ways.

In response, Kosovo Albanian representatives in the Kosovo Assembly declared Kosovo an independent republic within Yugoslavia, and in an unofficial referendum in 1991 a large majority of Kosovo Albanians voted for independence. But only Albania recognized the claim.

Meanwhile, other parts of Yugoslavia started to break away. First, Croatia and Slovenia and then Macedonia and Bosnia-Herzegovina declared independence. Fighting between the secessionist states and the federal army as well as Serbian paramilitary forces erupted. It was short-lived in the case of Slovenia, but far more protracted and bloody in the cases of Croatia and Bosnia-Herzegovina.

In Kosovo, Albanian nationalists staged a peaceful campaign for independence. Their lack of success, however, led to the growth of the Kosovo Liberation Army, which launched an armed struggle against Serbian control. The conflict escalated in 1998, when Milošević deployed Serbian military, police, and paramilitary forces in Kosovo. Serbia's counterinsurgency campaign resulted in the deaths of thousands and the displacement of approximately eight hundred thousand Kosovo Albanians, most of whom fled to Albania and Macedonia.

In response to the violence, in March 1999 the North Atlantic Treaty Organization (NATO) launched a bombing campaign to compel Serbian forces to withdraw from Kosovo. Within three months, the campaign succeeded in its goal. In June, the Federal Republic of Yugoslavia agreed to withdraw its security forces from Kosovo. The next day, the United Nations Security Council adopted Resolution 1244, which placed Kosovo under the administration of the United Nations Interim Mission in Kosovo (UNMIK) and authorized a NATO-led peace support operation. The resolution also authorized the United Nations to facilitate a political process that would determine Kosovo's final status. Despite international mediation, however, the governments in Serbia and Kosovo were unable to reach an agreement.

On February 17, 2008, Kosovo declared its independence from Serbia, having coordinated the action with both the United States and the major European powers. As of August 2014, Kosovo had been recognized by 108 member states and had become a member of the World Bank and the International Monetary Fund. The International Court of Justice has advised that the declaration of independence breached no international restrictions. Serbia has yet to recognize Kosovo as sovereign and independent. although the Serbian prime minister did visit Kosovo in January 2015, inspiring hopes that Serbia and Kosovo might eventually normalize their relations.

Kosovo faces several challenges. It was the poorest part of the SFRY, and the new state is striving to strengthen its economy. It has also been plagued by corruption and organized crime, and it needs to implement a system of accountable governance and to encourage adherence to rule of law. ●

Liberia

One cannot travel across Liberia today without confronting the scars and legacy of the country's two civil wars (1989–96 and 1999–2003). By the time the wars ended, nearly 6 percent of the population had been killed and 25 percent had been forced to flee their homes. The savagery of the conflict, with its dependence on child soldiers and fueled by trafficking in gems and precious stones, captured the world's attention, but only briefly. Far more enduring have been the conflict's effects on Liberia's long-suffering people.

Liberia was the first independent republic in Africa, founded in 1847 by freed slaves from the New World who were returned to the West African coast to create a new colony. The Americo-Liberians, as they came to be called, established a government and built an elite class that came to dominate the diverse, indigenous populations for the next 130 years. The tensions created by this distribution of power and the division of society into a powerful minority and a largely powerless majority set the foundation for the violent coup that, in 1980, finally overturned Americo-Liberian political dominance. Sparked by severe food shortages, the coup, led by Samuel Doe, was the outgrowth of lingering grievances among indigenous tribes about unequal uneconomic, educational, and political opportunities.

Doe ran an autocratic state fueled by paranoia and famed for intimidation. In 1989, antigovernment forces mobilized in neighboring countries; the most powerful groups were led by (future president) Charles Taylor and Prince Johnson (now a Liberian senator). Fighting escalated between an increasing number of factions, often built around tribal affiliations, in various parts of the country. Some factions saw themselves as self-defense forces; others were opportunists, looking for power or loot. The most notable image of the first civil war is perhaps the video of President Doe being tortured and eaten after being captured by Johnson and his forces in the capital of Monrovia in 1990. For the next six years, horrific violence gripped the country, forcing massive numbers of people to flee as various factions burned, looted, raped, and tortured their way across different parts of the country. The conflict gave rise to the most prolific use of child soldiers in history, with whole villages emptied of children, many of whom were forced to murder or rape family members. Over two hundred thousand Liberians were killed in the fighting before a tenuous peace accord was reached in 1996 between the major fighting factions.

In 1997, Taylor was elected president of Liberia, with the notorious campaign slogan, "He killed my ma, he killed my pa, but I'll vote for him." The rationale for many Liberians was that he was the only leader strong enough to ensure that the tenuous peace would hold. Taylor was accused of fomenting and backing violence in neighboring states, particularly Sierra Leone, where he was later indicted and found guilty of war crimes in the Special Court for Sierra Leone in 2012.

In 1999, rebel movements formed in neighboring countries yet again and besieged the Taylor government. Disenfranchised and victimized groups from the previous war recommitted themselves to overthrowing Taylor and began to slowly erode his military strength, laying siege to the capital and forcing the signing of the Comprehensive Peace Agreement in Accra in 2003. A transitional government took power until the election of Ellen Johnson-Sirleaf to her first term as Liberia's president in 2005.

In 2005, in response to the Comprehensive Peace Agreement, Liberia established the Truth and Reconciliation Commission (TRC), which was tasked with addressing the root causes of the conflicts dating back to before the Doe coup in 1980, and with recommending how to address victims' grievances and prevent future human rights abuses in the country. The TRC released its final report in 2009.

The Liberian conflict is infamous for the conscription of child soldiers, the use of rape as a weapon of war, the intensified tribal and political factionalization of the country, and mass forced displacement. Over the fifteen years of conflict, individuals moved between identities, often acting as both victims and perpetrators of violent atrocities. With 250,000 citizens killed in a population now estimated at 4 million, and an additional 1 million displaced, every family in Liberia has been affected in some way by the conflict. Their stories reflect both the harrowing tragedy of the conflict and the hopes for peace that have arisen since the conflict ended in 2003. For it was also amid the chaos and anarchy of the 1990s that a nascent peace movement arose from the multitude of ethnic and tribal groups to usher in the 2003 Comprehensive Peace Agreement. These peace activists helped the TRC set the foundation for a process of forgiveness and remembrance, and under the guidance of Johnson-Sirleaf, Liberia's economy has seen great gains since the war ended.

Johnson-Sirleaf was awarded the Nobel Peace Prize in October 2011, just before being reelected at president. Two years later, Taylor was taken to Great Britain to begin serving his fifty-year jail sentence for war crimes.

The wounds of Liberia's violent rifts still have not healed entirely, though, and many of the original causes of the conflict linger just beneath the surface. Liberia has also had to contend with a major outbreak of the Ebola virus, which killed more than three thousand Liberians in 2014 and has threatened the country's stability and economic progress. ●

Libya

Libya's history reflects a series of shifting alliances and conflicts, a product of its varied geography and cultural heritage, with its densely populated Mediterranean cities, mountain towns, and vast deserts. Today, it is an amalgam of three historically distinct regions: Tripolitania, Fezzan, and Cyrenaica.

The indigenous Berbers are said to be the first known inhabitants. Later, Phoenicians and Greeks settled, followed by Romans and then Arabs, who brought Islam and its culture with them. The influence of the Ottoman Empire can still be seen in architecture in parts of Tripoli. In the early 1900s, Italy took Libya from the Ottomans. Omar al-Mukhtar led a twenty-year insurgency against Italian rule, but he was eventually captured and executed, ending the resistance movement. Italy's plan to annex Libya was thwarted when, during World War II, Allied forces pushed the Italians out. Great Britain and France took control, dividing the country and each administering a part.

Libya gained independence in 1951 under the rule of King Idris I. In 1959, oil was discovered. The king had a pipeline built to export the lucrative commodity and opened Libya to foreign investment, including from American and British oil companies. The Western nations were permitted to maintain air bases in the country. In 1969, the king was toppled in a coup led by Colonel Muammar Qaddafi. Qaddafi, whose rule would last forty-two years, consolidated state control over the oil industry, closed the foreign air bases, and nationalized Italian-owned property. He used the country's oil wealth to fund a pan-Arab movement, of which he envisaged himself as leader.

In 1973, after Qaddafi claimed the majority of the Gulf of Sidra as Libyan territorial waters and declared it a "closed bay," tensions with the West increased dramatically. In 1981, the US Navy crossed the boundary Qaddafi had declared, and when Qaddafi ordered his forces to confront the US battle group, the resulting naval engagement ended with the sinking of two Libyan warships and the bombing of Qaddafi's compound in Tripoli.

In the wake of the sinking of his warships, Qaddafi allegedly ordered several terrorist attacks across Europe and the Middle East, including the bombing of a nightclub in Berlin, Germany, that killed two US servicemen and injured dozens, as well as the hijacking of TWA Flight 847 on June 14, 1985, and bombings of the Rome and Vienna airports on December 27 of that year. In 1984, the United Kingdom severed diplomatic ties with Libya after a British policewoman was killed, allegedly by pro-Qaddafi activists, during a protest in front of the Libyan Embassy in London.

After the Berlin bombing, the US Navy intensified its freedom of navigation exercises in the Gulf of Sidra. Once again, a military confrontation ensued, and the United States shot down two Libyan aircraft after they engaged US fighter planes. In response, Qaddafi ordered the downing of New York–bound Pan Am Flight 103 over Lockerbie, Scotland. The attack killed all 259 passengers on board the plane and 11 people on the ground.

Following the attack, the United Nations imposed sanctions on Libya. Tensions persisted until 1999, when Libya extradited two suspects to Scotland to stand trial for the downing of Flight 103. After a guilty verdict for one of the two accused, the United Kingdom reinstated diplomatic relations, and relations with the West began to improve.

During the early 2000s, Libya took steps to participate more actively in the larger international community and to mend relations with the West, including entering into talks with the United States. As part of this process, Libya agreed to take responsibility for and compensate the Lockerbie bombing victims, the families of victims of the bombing of an airplane carrying French passengers in 1989 over the Sahara Desert, and the families of victims of the Berlin disco bombing. Libya also agreed to abandon development of weapons of mass destruction, after which the United States restored diplomatic ties with Libya and US energy companies returned to the country. In 2008, a series of reconciliatory steps were taken by Libya, the United States, and Italy, including the provision of financial compensation to victims and visits by high-ranking officials.

In 2011, as the tide of popular unrest known as the "Arab Spring" surged through North Africa and the Middle East, Libya experienced a popular uprising that eventually swept away the Qaddafi regime. The uprising started in February in the eastern city of Benghazi and spread to other major cities, including Misurata, Zawiya, and Tripoli. In March, after attacks on Libya's civilian population by the Qaddafi regime, the United Nations authorized its members to enforce a no-fly zone for Qaddafi's aircraft. NATO took the lead, and began a campaign of aerial bombardments to push back Qaddafi's forces from population centers. Libyan revolutionary groups fought on the ground with Qaddafi's forces, which included many mercenaries. In August, Qaddafi went into hiding. In October, he was captured and killed, and his regime crumbled.

Over the next year, Libyans tried to establish a new post-Qaddafi Libya that would fulfill the ideals of those who had protested in the streets and took up arms to fight for his removal. The country has struggled with a legacy of weak state institutions and with clashes between militia groups unwilling to surrender their arms and control. Deep political and regional divisions have formed in the country, making it difficult to govern effectively and provide justice and security.

In September 2012, the US ambassador and three other Americans were killed in the consulate in Benghazi during an attack by Islamist extremists.

In the postrevolution environment, a security vacuum has allowed violent extremists and spoilers to take root in Libya. Assassinations of security personnel and civil society activists have increased. In July 2014, the United Nations withdrew its staff from Libya, and foreign embassies closed their doors. By August 2014, two separate parliaments had been set up, each with its own executive branch, each fighting for legitimacy and control. Efforts by the United Nations and other actors have yet to produce political consensus or reduce violence. ●

Myanmar (Burma)

Myanmar (Burma) has been fighting a civil war since its independence in 1948; indeed, Myanmar's is the longest-running civil war in the world today. At the heart of the conflict is the question of government legitimacy. Large portions of the country's population have refused to accept the legitimacy of the country's two postindependence governments: the democratically elected government, which took office shortly after independence, and the military government that ruled from 1962 to 2011. While both governments gave lip service to half-hearted peace efforts through the years, none of those efforts addressed the country's underlying political inequities and grievances, and each government continued to wage a brutal war against its opponents in various parts of the country. Not until a newly elected government took office in 2011 did a serious peace effort get under way that promised to deal with the difficult underlying issues.

Myanmar (as it was renamed by its military leaders in 1989; its name before then was Burma) is a multiethnic, multireligious state that developed from a series of smaller kingdoms and principalities over many centuries of warfare and domination by the ethnic majority that resides in the country's central regions. The country's modern geographic contours were consolidated and legalized by the British during a century of colonial occupation. When the country became independent, its many minority ethnic groups felt that they had lost the relative autonomy they had enjoyed under British rule and began to fight to regain that autonomy. They joined forces with an ethnic communist rebellion that had emerged from the original independence movement, but found the democratically elected government incompatible with their political ideology. During the 1960s, the armed ethnic and communist rebels, with strong material support from China, took control of most of the northeast quadrant of the country.

In fighting these rebellions, the army became very powerful politically and eventually took over the government in 1962. Once the communist rebellion had been suppressed, the army had to contend with armed ethnic militias, which controlled many areas along the country's borders with China and Thailand. During the 1980s and early 1990s, the government managed to conclude cease-fire agreements with most of these groups, bringing an end to the worst of the fighting. However, the cease-fires also allowed the government army to move into these minority areas and take control of resource-rich and strategic swaths of land that had previously been in contention.

The people living in these ethnic minority areas suffered decades of repression and brutality at the hands of both sides. Whole townships were razed and rendered uninhabitable, displacing hundreds of thousands of people, often across the border into Thailand. There was little semblance of order, let alone justice and security. When the army was not enforcing its own harsh form of justice, the rebel militias were meting out their primitive form of law and order. For many, the cease-fire agreements negotiated since 2011 by the democratic government have brought the first relative calm they have experienced in their lives. But the fighting has not ceased entirely, because much of it is locally generated between opposing forces battling for control of resource-rich territory. A wider political agreement may take years to negotiate.

Although the British introduced a common law system during the colonial years, it is practiced today primarily in urban areas and the ethnic regions in the middle of the country. Rule of law in the more remote ethnic minority areas is often determined by tribal customs; people do not trust the government legal system, which is perceived as unfair, corrupt, and expensive. The common law system was largely perverted during the years of military rule to control the regime's enemies, and judges became highly corrupt, often under pressure from their military masters.

The sweeping reforms introduced since 2011 have featured, among other things, a genuine peace process to conclude a nationwide cease-fire (to replace the multitude of bilateral cease-fires agreed upon in the past) and to negotiate a political solution to social and economic inequities; a serious assault on corruption in all areas of governance and economic life; and an effort to reform the judicial system. General elections are scheduled for 2015.

Reform will be a long-term task and can be expected to face many serious hurdles. The readiness of the military to permanently reduce its political role and the willingness of ethnic armed groups to join the political process are uncertain. However, the development of a proactive parliament prepared to challenge the executive branch, together with the emergence of a relatively free press, has created more space for questioning the system and debating alternatives. This may be the best guarantor of sustainable reform. ●

Nepal

Nepal has remained in many ways a feudal society, despite frequent changes in the political system over its 250 years of history. In 1996, with a democratic system barely functioning, the Communist Party of Nepal–Maoist (CPN-M) launched what it called a "people's war" against the government of Nepal, seeking to overthrow the Nepalese monarchy and establish a "people's republic." Over the next decade, fighting between the government's security forces and the CPN-M's People's Liberation Army (PLA) claimed more than thirteen thousand lives. The armed conflict was brought to a close in 2006 by a peace agreement that promised to usher in a stable multiparty democracy and lasting peace. As of early 2015, however, Nepal's political parties were still deadlocked on the country's constitutional future.

The roots of the conflict lie in centuries of rule by an absolutist monarchy and a repressive political elite, who kept the country isolated and its peasants impoverished. Hopes of a shift toward democracy blossomed briefly in the late 1950s and early 1960s, but political parties were soon outlawed and full monarchical control restored through military interference. A second wave of democratic pressure swept Nepal at the end of the Cold War, inspiring a fifty-day "people's movement" of mass protests that forced King Birendra to accept constitutional monarchy and to reinstitute multiparty democracy. A coalition of communist parties won the 1994 elections, leading to Nepal's first-ever communist government, but the government lasted only a year, and most Nepalese continued to be denied access to justice, political power, and economic opportunity, and to suffer from inequality and discrimination.

The CPN-M launched its people's war in 1996. The PLA attacked police stations, landlords, bureaucrats, capitalists, and anything that represented state repression and control. Almost all the rural areas of the country fell under the control of the Maoists, who established parallel judicial and governance structures. The insurgents enjoyed the support of many marginalized ethnic groups and untouchable castes, as well as backing from the poorest sectors of society. Even those Nepalese who did not agree with the Maoist political agenda and feared the PLA and its often brutal tactics were likely to be apprehensive of the security forces, particularly the army, which killed more civilians and committed more human rights abuses than the PLA.

In June 2001, a mysterious massacre of the king and many members of his family led to King Gyanendra ascending the throne. In July, his government declared a cease-fire and agreed to participate in peace negotiations. Those negotiations were short-lived, however, as was a PLA truce in 2003. Convinced that multiparty democracy could never defeat the insurgents, in February 2005 King Gyanendra declared a state of emergency, suspended civil and political rights, and reinstituted absolute rule. But rather than defeat the Maoists, Gyanendra unwittingly helped them into power. His totalitarian rule drove the seven largest legal political parties to join forces not only with one another but also with the CPN-M. Together, in late 2005, the eight-party alliance drew up a program aimed at restoring democracy. Just six months later, the second people's movement erupted. Nineteen days of strikes and mass protests forced the king to agree to reinstate the House of Representatives. An interim government was formed, and the CPN-M and the government signed the Comprehensive Peace Agreement in November 2006.

Hopes grew once again that Nepal would finally achieve a stable, accountable, peaceful political system concerned for the welfare of all citizens. The democratic momentum seemed unstoppable—at least for a while. In January 2007, Maoists entered the interim parliament, which had stripped the monarchy of its powers and adopted an interim constitution. Three months later, Maoist leaders joined the interim government. A Constituent Assembly (CA) that would draft a new constitution was elected in 2008.

But the impetus behind the peace process began to falter. A coalition government formed in 2008 and led by the CPN-M lasted only nine months. Political power struggles have produced deadlock in the constitution-making process, and even the election of a new CA in 2013 has not inspired concrete discussion of the content of the constitution. Issues such as the structure of a federal state and the governance and judicial systems remain divisive. In February 2014, Nepal Congress leader Sushil Koirala was elected prime minister, but his government has followed the same path as its predecessors.

Different governments have supported the establishment of a Truth and Reconciliation Commission (TRC) and a Disappearance Commission, but uncoditional support among many influential political figures for a blanket amnesty for serious human rights violations delayed the formation of those bodies. In 2013, the Nepal Supreme Court declared that no blanket amnesty could be given and that the government had to abide by international standards.

Outside parliament, mass demonstrations have repeatedly paralyzed the capital, Kathmandu, and other parts of the country. Every political party has formed its own youth wing, and these wings have often behaved more like militias than political institutions. General strikes and road blockades, many of which turn violent, have been common.

Outside the capital, a wave of crime and insecurity had threatened for several years to engulf the country, but then partly subsided. Even so, the border with India is still believed to be home to dozens of organized criminal groups engaged in cross-border smuggling, banditry, killings, extortion, abduction, and human trafficking. In the area north of the border—the lowlands known as the Terai—communal issues threaten to explode into violence. Many politicians have been exploiting and exacerbating disaffection among the country's ethnic minorities and poorest citizens.

Economic and social progress has been retarded by political stalemate and frequent changes of government, but popular frustration and political impasse have not led to widespread violence. The Nepalese people have so far shown remarkable patience. The key to a brighter future is bringing the peace process to a successful conclusion and promoting greater prosperity. ●

Nicaragua

Nicaragua's history seems to follow a cyclical pattern, with predatory statesmen, civil conflict, and natural disasters recurring and leaving the country one of the poorest in the Western Hemisphere. From 1979 to 1990, a civil war was fought between the Marxist Sandinista junta government and a coalition of resistance groups known as the Contras (an abbreviation of the Spanish word for "counterrevolutionaries," *contra-revolucionarios*). The fighting killed fifty thousand people, or one in every fifty people in the country. Since the end of the fighting, Nicaragua has continued to experience political turmoil, but has made some economic and social progress.

Nicaragua gained independence from Spain in 1838, and for the rest of the century the government was contested by Liberals and Conservatives from the country's elite. US Marines intermittently intervened in Nicaraguan conflicts and civil wars, on invitation, from 1909 until a peace was brokered by the US government in 1927. The United States extended its military presence and trained a "constabulary" that came to be known as the National Guard.

Opposed to the terms of the peace treaty and the US occupation, guerrillas led by Liberal general Augusto Cesar Sandino fought against the US presence from 1927 to 1933, when US troops were recalled, principally because of the Great Depression. Although Sandino achieved his goal, he was assassinated by a Nicaraguan National Guard commander, General Anastasio Somoza García. For the next forty-two years, Somoza and his sons ruled as dictators. They amassed a huge personal fortune, and the disparity between Nicaragua's poor and its elite widened significantly. The third Somoza in the dynasty notoriously enriched himself further by siphoning off international aid intended for disaster relief after the 1972 earthquake in Managua.

A clandestine, anti-Somoza insurgency was launched in the 1950s by students and peasants, led by Carlos Fonseca, a Marxist-Leninist. By the 1960s, "La Runga" (The Rumble) had taken on the name the Sandinista National Liberation Front (FSLN), having adapted Sandino's earlier anti-imperialist oratory to a popular revolution of self-determination. By the mid-1970s, the government had increased its tyranny, Fonseca was dead, and the FSLN was immensely popular. In 1978, violence escalated into civil war, which the Sandinistas and their allies quickly won.

Not long after the Sandinistas took power in 1979, however, many Nicaraguans began to suspect that the new government might be another variation on the country's authoritarian tradition.

The 1980s saw Nicaragua become a battlefield in the wider Cold War as East and West funded a war between the Sandinistas and the Contras. The Contras were made up of disenfranchised Sandinista veterans who had fought to overthrow the Somoza dictatorship, ex-National Guardsmen of the former regime, and others with no particular political affiliation who were disillusioned by the disintegrating junta's radical measures. The United States provided aid to the Contras, while the Soviet Union and Cuba supplied aid to the Sandinista government, which in turn funneled arms to a left-leaning insurrection in El Salvador.

The civil war was ended by a peace agreement signed in 1989. Elections the following year saw the defeat of the Sandinistas by a coalition of left and right parties. Violeta Chamorro, whose husband had been assassinated by the Somoza government in 1978, led a unification party and became president in 1990. Her platform emphasized the peace process, national dialogue, and reconciliation. Chamorro, the first female president in the Americas, introduced conservative politics that were supported by the United States. US-Nicaragua relations improved rapidly after her election, and the United States provided aid and support to the country. That aid, however, decreased shortly thereafter, once US policymakers concluded that the country was stable.

Many Nicaraguans consider Chamorro's presidency to be the turning point for postrevolution Nicaragua, which began to enjoy stability and prosperity, things the country had not experienced in a long time. Unfortunately, a variety of economic and political challenges impeded that progress. Natural disasters in the form of earthquakes, hurricanes, and volcanic eruptions have also bedeviled the country.

Politically, the country has yet to heal its divisions, and many Nicaraguans are increasingly skeptical of the integrity of political leaders. The election cycle continues to be contentious, with Daniel Ortega, the former Sandinista president, running each time. In 1996, Arnoldo Aleman was elected president, but in 2003 (after he had left the presidency) he was found guilty on corruption charges of stealing an estimated $100 million. In 2001, Ortega lost again, this time to the Liberal Party candidate Enrique Bolaños, who spent much of his time in office locked in a power struggle with the opposition alliance that controlled Congress. In 2006, the Sandinistas finally returned to power with the election, by a narrow majority, of Ortega.

Since then, allegations of electoral fraud and harassment of nongovernmental organizations and human rights activists have tarnished Ortega's democratic governance credentials, as have claims that he was behind a constitutional amendment allowing him to run for a third consecutive term in 2016. People inside and outside Nicaragua express concern that Ortega's rule is becoming increasingly dictatorial. To them, it seems a classic case of the oppressed becoming the oppressor. Meanwhile, in the past few years, Nicaragua's economy has been improving, raising the question of whether a combination of tighter political control and greater economic activity can endure for long. ●

(This conflict profile draws on an "In the Field" article published by the United States Institute of Peace, online at http://www.usip.org/publications/in-the-field-notes -nicaragua.)

Peru

Between 1980 and 1992, Peru confronted the Shining Path ("Sendero Luminoso" in Spanish), a Maoist insurgency. The conflict left an estimated seventy thousand dead and threatened to topple the state. In 2001, Peru convened a Truth and Reconciliation Commission (Comisión de la Verdad y Reconciliación, or CVR) to investigate and document the conflict. The final CVR report, released in 2003, determined that widespread human rights abuses—including torture, kidnappings, and assassinations—had been perpetrated by the Shining Path and by the Peruvian state. The report attributed 54 percent of the casualties to the Shining Path. and most of the rest to the state. (About 1.5 percent of the casualties were attributed to a second, relatively minor insurgent movement, the Túpac Amaru Revolutionary Movement.)

The Shining Path's origins lie in divisions within the Peruvian Communist Party. In 1964, it split into two factions: a pro-Soviet group advocated cooperation and co-optation leading to a peaceful transition to communism; a pro–People's Republic of China (PRC) faction sought the violent overthrow of the state. Three years later, the pro-PRC contingent split again after a disagreement over the speed of the revolutionary process. A final split in 1970 saw the expulsion of Abimael Guzmán. That year, Guzmán founded the Shining Path at the National University of San Cristóbal of Huamanga in Ayacucho in the southern highlands. Guzmán used his position as professor to promote the movement's ideology. In 1971, he became the university's personnel director, enabling him to hire ideologically compatible faculty and transform the university's curriculum. By 1981, some five thousand teachers had passed through the university, and many were spreading the Shining Path's ideology in remote indigenous communities where they taught.

After twelve years of military rule, violence broke out in 1980, on the eve of presidential elections that returned democracy to Peru. The insurgents, assassinating or intimidating government officials (and anyone else who opposed them), gained a foothold in the southern highlands, the most impoverished area of Peru, where people had always suffered from discrimination and little or no access to government services and economic opportunity. As poverty continued to worsen, the Shining Path's discipline and its targeting of corrupt local officials won it significant support. President Fernando Belaúnde Terry, who had been the victim of a military coup during his first term (1963–68), was reluctant to deploy the military to confront the insurgents.

By the mid-1980s, the Shining Path had expanded into the Upper Huallaga Valley (UHV), located between the Amazon and the Andes. A tactical alliance with UHV narcotraffickers involved the Shining Path protecting more than a hundred airstrips while raising millions of dollars yearly. At the same time, the Shining Path moved into the central highlands. By the late 1980s, when the guerrillas began attacks in Lima, the Shining Path had grown to about twenty-five thousand, including ten thousand full-time combatants, and controlled one in four of all Peruvian municipalities.

Despite its meteoric rise, the Shining Path alienated local *campesinos* (peasant farmers) by allowing them to grow only enough food to feed themselves, closing markets, replacing indigenous officials with Shining Path members, mandating the adoption of different religious and cultural practices, and using capital punishment, torture, and impressment. Recognizing discontent with the Shining Path, in 1989 the administration of Alan García (1985–90) began arming *rondas* (peasant self-defense patrols). The state also tried to curb government abuses against the *campesinos*, which were commonplace during García's initial, heavy-handed attempts to quash the insurgency.

The administration of Alberto Fujimori (1990–2000) used the threat posed by the insurgents and hyperinflation to justify a self-coup (*autogolpe*), during which Fujimori closed the Congress and Constitutional Court. In addition, Fujimori oversaw a campaign of repression that included targeted killings of leftist opposition leaders, the suspension of due process of law for suspected insurgents, and numerous massacres and other human rights abuses. However, Fujimori also continued many of García's reforms and boosted social and economic programs to win popular support. In September 1992, government forces raided a safe house at a Lima dance academy and captured Guzmán and several of his chief lieutenants. The raid recovered Guzmán's master files, and within a few months 90 percent of the leadership had been captured.

The insurgents did not disappear entirely, however. Two factions (one in the UHV and the other in the Apurímac, Ene, and Mantaro River Valleys, VRAEM) fought on, but they were largely confined to relatively small areas, where poverty persisted despite resounding economic growth elsewhere in the country. Both factions became enmeshed with the narcotics trade, and ideology became subordinated to greed. The UHV faction has now been decimated by arrests; the VRAEM contingent is also under increasing pressure.

In 2009, MOVADEF, a movement seeking amnesty for incarcerated insurgents, was founded. It applied to register as a political party but its application was denied. In April 2014, more than two dozen MOVADEF leaders were arrested and charged with terrorism, narcotrafficking, and money laundering.

Although Fujimori oversaw the drafting of a new constitution, which restored democracy to Peru, his administration was massively corrupt. In 2000, he was elected for a third term, illegal under the 1993 constitution. However, he served less than one year of this term before fleeing into exile to escape corruption charges. He was eventually extradited to Peru and convicted of human rights abuses and corruption among other charges in 2009.

Subsequent presidents have also been plagued by corruption scandals. Alejandro Toledo (2001–6) is being investigated for money laundering and conspiracy. García, who returned to the presidency from 2006 to 2011, has been accused of selling pardons to convicted narcotraffickers. President Ollanta Humala (elected in 2011) is accused of being linked to drug money.

Like corruption, inequality and social exclusion continue. Even though Peru has experienced impressive and sustained economic growth, these benefits have not accrued evenly across the country. Meanwhile, the political scene still features many individuals who were involved in the conflict. ●

South Sudan

Sudan has known precious little peace since it became a fully independent country in 1956. Even since 2011, when the people of South Sudan voted overwhelmingly in a referendum to form an independent country, their new state has been roiled by ethnic and political violence.

The First Sudanese Civil War (1955–72) arose directly out of the process of forming a government for the newly independent Sudan. That government was dominated by an elite class of northern Sudanese. The underrepresentation of the largely non-Muslim, black southern Sudanese, as well as other peripheral groups throughout the northern, eastern, and western parts of the country, became the motivation for an armed uprising. During the seventeen years of civil war, nearly half a million people died and hundreds of thousands more were forcefully displaced both internally and into neighboring countries. The Southern Sudan Liberation Movement (SSLM) and the Khartoum government led by Jafaar Numeiri signed the Addis Ababa Accord in 1972, formally ending the conflict and granting greater autonomy to the southern Sudanese.

In 1983, Numeiri tried to appeal to an increasingly powerful Islamist movement in the north by declaring sharia law to be the law of the land and reneging on many of the promises of autonomy for the south, further dividing the northern, predominantly Islamic population from moderate political groups in the north and from largely Christian and animist populations in the south. In 1983, a US-educated, military officer named John Garang formed the Sudan People's Liberation Army (SPLA) to take up arms on behalf of marginalized and disenfranchised groups throughout Sudan.

In 1985, a military coup overthrew Numeiri and led to an elected government headed by Prime Minister Sadiq al-Mahdi. In 1989, Mahdi was overthrown in another military coup, this one led by Omar al-Bashir. With the backing of hardline Islamists, al-Bashir rekindled the conflict with the south by further entrenching Islamic law throughout the country and ensuring Khartoum's power elite retained its tight grip on power.

From 1983 to 2005, the government and the SPLA fought the Second Sudanese Civil War, which claimed the lives of nearly 2.5 million people and displaced an additional 4 million. The conflict was characterized by the disproportionate use of force against civilian populations throughout the south. Revenge killings, forced displacement, slavery, massive starvation and famine, rampant sexual assault, and the use of child soldiers all characterized the atrocities committed against civilian populations by both sides. The divisions among the southerners were notable, and some observers believe that more people died in south-south fighting than in south-north fighting.

In 2005, European and American governments helped push the warring sides into signing the Comprehensive Peace Agreement (CPA). The agreement laid out a new path for peace in the country, including autonomy for the south and a decentralized system of governance throughout the country, a guarantee for national elections, and after six years a vote on independence by the south. Only a few months after the signing of the CPA, Garang was killed in a mysterious helicopter crash. His vision of democratic transformation throughout Sudan, with power divested to marginal areas and populations and with the role of Islamic law significantly reduced, died with him.

The Khartoum government proved unwilling to make the reforms needed to reduce tensions in the country or make unity attractive. It was, however, willing to let the south—despite its large oil reserves—secede in order to maintain a monopoly on political power in Khartoum.

In 2011, the people of South Sudan voted overwhelmingly for independence, and a new country was born. But outstanding issues persisted, including the demarcation of the border between Sudan and South Sudan, new barriers to the time-honored passage of nomadic pastoral groups, and the sudden isolation in the north of ethnic minorities and regional governments that had been integral parts of the SPLA and its political wing, the SPLM. SPLM leaders and civilian populations in various areas of the north—including the border states of Blue Nile and Southern Kordofan—soon bore the brunt of new aggressions from the government of Sudan. In 2008, President al-Bashir became the first sitting head of state to be indicted on war crimes charges by the International Criminal Court for the government's actions in Darfur. He has yet to be arrested or prosecuted.

Since its independence in 2011, South Sudan has struggled to form a new nation with sound governance and to meet its citizens' many demands and expectations in the wake of decades of war. Massive corruption, internecine fighting between armed guerrilla movements, and continued border disputes with Sudan have plagued the fledgling government. In 2013, President Salva Kiir (a member of the majority Dinka population) dissolved his cabinet and dismissed his first vice president, Riek Machar (an ethnic Nuer), claiming to be taking steps to improve governance and tackle corruption. Violent clashes erupted between Kiir's supporters and Machar's, and ethnic-based violence swept throughout South Sudan. Old guerrilla fighters who had become government officials fell back on what they knew best: armed violence. Peace talks have spluttered, and as of early 2015 ongoing efforts at mediation and temporary cease-fires have likewise failed to bring peace.

All told, the conflicts in the two Sudans have claimed more than 3 million lives and temporarily or permanently displaced more than 5 million others. Periods of acute and simmering conflicts have persisted for nearly sixty years. Sustainable peace does not appear to be on the horizon for either nation. Systemic failures to create inclusive and representative governments that recognize fundamental rights and freedoms of their populations have retarded nascent movements for sustainable peace and directly fuel the ongoing suffering and victimization of both Sudanese and South Sudanese civilian populations. ●

Yemen

Yemen has suffered from considerable turmoil and violent conflict over the past hundred years. In the early twentieth century, the Ottoman Empire, which had ruled Yemen since the sixteenth century, formally ceded control of southern Yemen to Britain. When the Ottoman Empire dissolved in 1918, northern Yemen came under the control of the Yahya family—members of the Zaidi sect of Shia Islam—which had held de facto power since 1904. Muhammad Hamid ed-Din Yahya became the first Imam of Yemen in 1918. Following a peace agreement after fighting with the neighboring Sunnis (who would found Saudi Arabia) in 1934, the Yahyas were able also to claim kingship over the nation. Southern Yemen remained a British protectorate.

When Muhammad Yahya's grandson was proclaimed imam and king in 1962, the military staged a coup and declared the creation of the Yemen Arab Republic (commonly known as North Yemen). Fighting between royalists and republicans continued until 1970, when the republicans finally won.

Three years earlier, the British had relinquished their protectorate in the south after several years of battling nationalist groups. The People's Republic of South Yemen (commonly known simply as South Yemen) declared its independence in 1967. A radical Marxist faction seized power in 1969 and turned the country into a one-party state, adding the word "Democratic" to the country's name.

In 1972, fighting broke out between the People's Democratic Republic of Southern Yemen and the Yemen Arab Republic. The conflict was short-lived, but relations between South and North remained tense. Fighting flared again in 1979, with the South supporting rebels battling the government in the North. In 1986, civil war broke out in the South.

Relations between the two states improved in the late 1980s, and in 1990, the North and South were unified, becoming the Republic of Yemen, with Ali Abdullah Saleh as president. But the relative harmony did not last long. A major civil war erupted in 1994, with the southerners threatening to secede. They lost, and Saleh retained power. but the state he ruled remained weak. In the absence of a state able to establish the rule of law, Yemen suffered, as it still suffers, from persistent low-level conflict.

The Houthis, a group that felt oppressed and marginalized by Saleh, began battling the government. Another focus of discontent was the Southern Movement, a grouping of southerners who wanted reparations for land taken by the state, as well as greater political rights. By 2009, some members of "al-Hiraak" (a collective name for the Southern Movement) began to demand an independent South Yemen, while others formed armed factions and clashed from time to time with government forces and other political groups.

Life in much of Yemen in recent decades has also been roiled by tribal blood feuds. With the state unable to establish the rule of law, minor disputes can quickly escalate into clashes between groups armed with AK-47s and even heavy artillery.

Criminal gangs, transnational terrorist organizations, and insurgent groups have found it easy to recruit members from among Yemen's youth, who face high unemployment. In the 1980s, thousands of Yemenis went to Afghanistan to fight as mujahedin against the Soviet occupation. When the Soviets withdrew, many of these fighters became affiliates of the new terrorist group al-Qaeda, which had been formed by Osama bin Laden, a Saudi of Yemeni origin. Al-Qaeda launched some of its most notable attacks, such as the bombing of the American warship the *USS Cole* in 2000, in and from Yemen. Al-Qaeda has since expanded its presence in Yemen, with most of its affiliates operating under the banner of al-Qaeda in the Arab Peninsula (AQAP).

When the Arab Spring surged across the Middle East and North Africa in 2011, Yemen was quickly swept up in the tide of popular protest and unrest. Angry over continuous high unemployment, rampant corruption, low levels of education and health, and the constant threat of food shortages, Yemenis (especially young Yemenis) took to the streets to call for change. Those demonstrations grew into a political crisis when the protesters were joined by major political figures and tribal leaders. Violence quickly escalated when the government deployed troops and even tanks against those calling for Saleh's ouster. Opposition groups also took up arms, resulting in numerous clashes in urban areas. With the government focusing most of its attention and resources on major cities, insurgents affiliated with AQAP were able to seize control of one governorate and to expand their operations elsewhere.

In November 2011, the country's main political parties finally came to an agreement that ended the crisis. Backed by the United Nations, the agreement initiated a two-year political transition during which Saleh left office (in return for immunity from prosecution) and a referendum confirmed a former vice president as interim president. Political and tribal leaders, together with women, youth, and other representatives of civil society, spent much of 2013 participating in a process of dialogue known as the National Dialogue Conference, the aim of which was to reach consensus on how to reshape the country's political system. The participants did reach agreement on some issues, but many of the most divisive issues and thorniest questions were left undecided, and the transition period was extended.

Peace and stability will remain elusive as long as the underlying causes of conflict are not dealt with. Indeed, Yemen could conceivably fragment under the continuing strains of the Southern Movement, the Houthi rebellion, and growing demands for independence in various parts of the country. State institutions remain weak and governments are vulnerable to intimidation. In January 2015, for instance, the president and his government resigned after a standoff with armed Houthi militias. Meanwhile, terrorist groups and criminal organizations have only grown stronger and more widespread. ●

Part II

The Interviews

WARFIGHTERS

For the warfighter, the drawing down of hostilities (violence never finishes neatly on a specified day) and the opening up of peace can mean dramatically different things and evoke a wide array of emotions. Some fighters greet peace with relief, some with regret, some with suspicion. The proud ones see themselves as having fought hard for a noble cause; the despondent ones believe that they have been put through hell for nothing.

In each country that we visited, we found a surprising degree of agreement among the former warfighters, whether government soldiers or rebels, about the merits of their country's recent war and the prospects for peace. That's not to say that different personalities didn't see the emerging peace differently; they did. But as a group, the fighters in a particular country tended to share a particular outlook. If the peace looked promising, the fighters looked back with pride and ahead with optimism. If the peace looked unstable and uncertain, they were wary and spoke of their readiness to return to the battlefield and finish the job they had started. If the peace was stable but dismal—with an elite fighting among themselves for the spoils of war—the fighters felt disillusioned; they might not have lost faith in the principles for which they had fought, but they felt betrayed by their leaders or by the political process.

We interviewed many different kinds of fighters: government soldiers and rebels; generals as well as the rank and file; eager recruits and reluctant conscripts; those who fought with a gun in their hand and those who staffed the political wings of military commands. But despite these differences, in each country similar themes and a similar tone colored the responses of most ex-combatants.

In Kosovo, those who had fought with the Kosovo Liberation Army to oust Serbian forces saw themselves as warriors for a just cause. Children of a society deeply divided along ethnic lines, they had no doubts that violence was the only means by which they could free their people and prevail against the Serbs. Now in charge of their own territory after seceding from Serbia, they also felt in charge of their own destiny. "War," remarked Nevruz Tola, whose brother was killed in the conflict, "the word itself sounds terrible. But it depends on how you look at it. . . . A war for liberation is something you can be proud of."

In Nicaragua, such confidence in a just cause has long since evaporated among some former fighters. Perhaps because more than twenty years stand between them and the last battles, perhaps because the country suffers from a government seen as corrupt and a stagnant economy, or perhaps because their conflict pitted brother and sister against brother and sister, a number of former fighters are weary and disillusioned. Some see the civil war as fundamentally useless. For them, their struggle for rights and equality was hijacked, and one form of oppression and inequality simply gave way to another. "The first thing I think of when I think of the war," reflected Claudia Pineda, who used to be a willing fighter for the Sandinistas, is what "a woman told me whose son was killed in the first wave of fighting. She said: 'For such a pitiful cause my son died.'"

In Nepal, those who had fought for the Maoist rebels saw themselves, as the Kosovo Albanian fighters did, as "fighters against injustice." But the Maoists were watchful rather than triumphalist, critical of a peace process that did not seem to be liberating an oppressed people from what they saw as a corrupt elite. Even the most optimistic anticipated a lifetime of struggle for social justice, and many hinted that they might have to return to the armed struggle and become "a martyr for the people."

Nepalese who had fought on the government side similarly saw their country fragmented by fault lines of mistrust. One conscript who had gone AWOL during the fighting felt that the fledgling peace would not last unless the political parties could come together. "Sushil," a general who had fought for the previous regime, also condemned political factions—the Maoists especially, but not only the Maoists—for putting party interest above the national interest. In Peru, another general, Daniel Mora, likewise pointed an accusing finger at political forces that foment war rather than work together to give the people a better life.

The wars in which the warfighters had fought were internal conflicts—insurgencies, revolutions, civil wars—that had broken out when one or more groups in a country had decided that change was needed and could be accomplished only through the use of violence. Some of the warfighters we interviewed were still confident in the wisdom of that decision. Carlos Fernando Chamorro, for instance, concluded that revolution was necessary in Nicaragua: "Somoza was not going to leave if not for a radical change." In contrast, Sushil contended that "an insurgency retards the growth of a nation. Change should come to a nation, but it should come as an evolutionary process, step by step, not a revolutionary process. The revolutionary process creates such great change that a nation cannot sustain that change, and then you have problems."

Whether they see war as necessary or not, none of the warfighters romanticized the fighting they experienced. In Liberia, former rebels Morlee Gugu Zawoo Sr. and K. Johnson Borh recalled how they were drugged and then ordered to do "wicked" things, how they were indoctrinated to believe that "the gun was our father and our mother." "Suicida," a former Contra commander, felt betrayed by peace agreements that weren't properly implemented, but he was adamant that he didn't want Nicaragua to return to violence. "The war, any war, is not a thing of good angels, I tell you. A lot of suffering on both sides. Healthy brothers killing other Nicaraguans. . . . Combat is horrible; you can't imagine."

While some former fighters tended to look back, be it nostalgically, critically, or cynically, others were determined to look ahead and to help their country overcome the divisions and violence of the recent past. "Ahmed" from Libya wanted to move forward. "Whether we were supporters or opponents [of the former regime], we should try to flip that page and not dwell on the past. If we do [focus on the past], we will get nowhere, and that would be in the interest of those who benefit from continued chaos." ●

F. Henry "Baquilita" Ubeda Zeledon *(Nicaragua)*

"We were allergic to war."

We interviewed "Baquilita" (a nickname he picked up when he was a soldier) on his coffee farm in San Rafael del Norte, Nicaragua, in 2009. Baquilita didn't want to fight for either side in the civil war, but ended up fighting for both. He saw combat more than sixty times, but he deserted more than once and went back to farming. He now grows organic coffee.

◄◄ In 1985, the war was going strong. I was a student at school, and I worked, too. I'd already begun to avoid military service, because I was [draft] age. Although we went to class, we were always alert for the trucks that went around picking up people for military service. We were allergic to war. So, we were on the run from the army. And there were already armed Contra groups, so we had to be on the alert for them, too, because they also said, "Come with us."

We'd be working on farmland and shooting would start, and we *campesinos* [farmworkers] would be in the line of fire. So, I'd look for somewhere to run to. The guerrillas would say, "Get over here, they're going to kill you," But the soldiers would say, "You're with them [the guerrillas], so you're a collaborator." If you wanted to avoid both, you had to lie low like crazy, hiding out and fleeing, avoiding both. That was the best thing [laughs], getting away from both of them.

For a time, we were hiding and living a life completely like pigs—just eating, sleeping, and waiting for the day you'd be killed.

The Contras would come to me and tell me to give them something to eat, and me having food, I had to give them something to eat. Then the Sandinista Army would come and tell me to sell them food or give it to them.

[Eventually, the Contras made me fight for them.] I was in combat three times for the Contras. The time that I was with the Contras was brief, maybe four, five months. My brother also was in the Contras. He stayed in until the demobilization.

WAS HE IDEOLOGICALLY COMMITTED TO THE CAUSE?

Yes, yes. His ideology is more focused. But me, I didn't want anything to do with either side.

[Once, when I was en route to visit my mother], the army captured me at a checkpoint. They grabbed me and the people I was with and recruited us. We were put in a truck, and they took us [to various military camps]. We spent forty-five days in training. Then they sent us to fight, in the mountains, all kinds of battles. Braaap-braaap-braaap—two dead, three dead, so-and-so deserted, and so on. A little later, braaap-braaap, and more of us were killed. It went like that for a while. They would kill one of ours, a little later we'd kill one of theirs. Sometimes wounded, yes, there'd be wounded.

I was meant to do twenty-four months of military service, but I took off after fourteen months. I went to Honduras . . . I have been slippery. But [at some point] the army grabbed me again, put me in jail, and I was in for a bit more. So I kept going back and forth [laughs].

I must have been in combat some sixty times, more or less, during my time in the Sandinista Army.

DID YOU FIGHT ALONGSIDE WOMEN?

There were women. We'd use them for recruiting: "Look how lovely this woman is. Come on, you can have one, two. Man, there are lots." Pah-pah, like a magnet.

But the women also fought. A woman is brave, braver than a man when dealing with confrontation. When I was in the war, women were in the line of combat, always. They let bullets fly, and they cooked for the soldiers when not in the field. And they stuck around those who had the most power. For example, the commander had one, the platoon chief had one, the chief of the detachment had one. But [women] were always in the line of combat.

There are people who say, "I'm [made to be in the] military." And they enter an academy, train, gain rank, and become good military men. But me? Me, I'm allergic. It is not for me.

WHAT WOULD YOU TELL FOREIGNERS ABOUT NICARAGUA?

I'd say that it is a lovely country. And that now we are at peace. Yes, that is the most wonderful, to have peace. What the heck: we have education, we have health, we have it all! But in war everything gets complicated for us [laughs]. So there is nothing like being at peace.

WHAT DOES "RULE OF LAW" MEAN TO YOU?

For me, it means that all citizens are permitted to express themselves freely, period. All their thoughts can be expressed. That's all, I guess. **>>**

Rosa Maria Toruño Montenegro *(Nicaragua)*

"There was no difference, my being a woman."

We interviewed Rosa Maria in a hotel in León, a former stronghold of the Sandinistas in the northwest of Nicaragua. She was tough and combative; she had lost a leg in the war but she did not want pity. Although she had a vague sense of sadness, she was animated and had few regrets about fighting for the revolution.

◄◄ When the war started here in Nicaragua I was sixteen years old. My house was a safe house of the Front [the Sandinista Front for National Liberation], because my brother Luis Manuel Toruño Charrasco, known as Charraka, was one of the main leaders who rallied high school and university students against the Somoza dictatorship. We couldn't stand the murders [committed by the regime] any longer, and so in one way or another we gradually got involved. For example, in 1977, I served as a courier, because as a woman, I didn't attract as much attention as men. I began delivering mail, communications.

In 1979, the Front was more organized than before and launched its "final offensive." I was married to Commander Abel—it was he who commanded here in the Rigoberto López Pérez Western Command—and my house was a Sandinista militant command. There we prepared ourselves politically, ideologically, and militarily for the offensive. On June 3, we left in single file to attack a National Guard command post. My husband died on June 20. Afterward, we liberated León and then advanced on Managua, where we arrived on July 19.

I lost my leg in combat in La Ceiba in 1979. The same year, since now the Sandinista Front was in power, we the disabled had many benefits and underwent rehabilitation. They sent us out of the country because there were social programs that covered us, for prostheses, to treat us psychologically, for psycho-traumatic problems.

There was no difference, my being a woman. No. We belonged to the squads, same as men, and they trained us ideologically, same as men. They prepared us politically the same too, because the truth of the matter is that it was in fashion at that time for us to fight to find women's emancipation, women's liberation. I wanted to be a Sandinista militant, which was very difficult because you had to go through a process, through different stages of training. You had to be ready to answer the call and, if it was necessary, grab a gun. And when you were in combat against Somoza's National Guard, you were given more power and had more desire to keep fighting. When you saw that a friend had fallen, you were more determined to continue the fight.

In 1990, Commander Daniel [Ortega, leader of the Sandinistas and president of Nicaragua], called for elections, and Violeta Barrios de Chamorro [the head of an anti-Sandinista alliance] wins. When she wins, he hands over power, a power won through arms, to find peace in Nicaragua and so that the [US-funded] Contras, who were in the mountains, would disarm.

For the next sixteen years, the government freezes our [veterans'] pensions. When the Front wins elections again in 2006, they don't give us a dignified pension, but they do increase the amount we get. The Front may have political power, but it has to share economic power. And the economy is bad not only here in Nicaragua but on an international level. They have said that for that reason we don't have all the benefits that we had initially. But we hope that one day it will change; for that reason we don't want the Front to leave government.

WHAT DO YOU ASSOCIATE WITH THE WORDS "RULE OF LAW"?

When I entered the Sandinista Front, rule of law was always spoken of. We were going to have total liberation, we were going to be emancipated, we were going to be given rights. And the Front has given a woman the right to register her children even if she is not married. Another of the rights that was won here in Nicaragua is the right to express whatever political ideology we have.

But the laws are not always implemented. For example, there is a law that says for every ten employees of the state, you have to have one employee who is disabled, like me. But the law is not being carried out. **>>**

"Sudhil" (Nepal)

"I had joined the army as a last resort."

"Sudhil" sat very straight in his chair, as if he were being interrogated, and gave short, terse answers. His face betrayed both the trauma of his military experience and his unease about discussing his desertion.

<< I grew up in a good family. But my father and mother are poor. They farm a small plot of land, but, when I was growing up, we also worked as laborers, loading gravel on trucks or working on other people's farms.

When my schooling ended, I came to Kathmandu and worked at restaurants and bars. But I didn't like the job, so I joined the Nepal Army, to the displeasure of my family. After I enlisted, a state of emergency was imposed on the country, and the conflict worsened. I encountered rebels three times during the war. The third time, I was caught in our own ambush and barely survived. Two of my friends died there.

I had joined the army as a last resort. I felt that I was always under surveillance: not allowed to call home for months and not allowed to go outside [the barracks]. The army thought that because I am a Tharu from [a district that supplied a lot of Maoist fighters], I wouldn't return to the barracks if I went home. They used to punish me because they thought that I was a Maoist too.

I decided to leave the army. I just walked out without asking anybody. I took all my personal belongings, but didn't take any things issued by the army—just took my own stuff and fled.

When you left the army, didn't they prosecute you or take action against you?

They sent five or six of my friends to visit me. I used to live near Pashupatinath Temple, and a friend of mine had seen my room. I told them that I didn't want to serve in the Army anymore. They didn't try to threaten me; they wanted to persuade me. When I told them what I wanted, they didn't try to do anything more.

Did your family suffer because you were in the army?

There was trouble at home. The Maoists were constantly threatening my family: "Bring your son back home, or else face the consequences." My family was often terrified and harassed. Before the Maoist conflict, it was very peaceful in the villages. There was not any fighting. During the conflict, the Maoists used to abduct people from the villages [to fight] for their cause. We lived in panic during wartime. The Maoists used to take our friends and make them fight and beat others.

Did the peace agreement bring about any changes in the villages?

No. It is the same as usual. Nothing has happened. But I think mutual trust and consensus would bring peace. The political parties are often at loggerheads. If they work together, then there will be peace. **>>**

Morlee Gugu Zawoo Sr.
and K. Johnson Borh (Liberia)

*"She asked me where I had been. I said, 'Mama, I have been
in this fight, and when killing people, I was afraid.'"*

*Morlee Gugu Zawoo Sr. and K. Johnson Borh run an organization called
the National Ex-combatants Peacebuilding Initiative (NEPI). It seeks to
reintegrate former child soldiers—as both men had been—into society.*

*We interviewed them at their office, which was stifling but well
equipped by Liberian standards. They were very eager to talk. They
were among the few people we talked to in Liberia who volunteered
to talk about their wartime experiences, although they did not go
into much detail about what they had done. Both had been through
a reconciliation program provided by the Lutheran Church, and their
comments revealed their familiarity with the conflict resolution field.*

<< MGZ: I am one of the founding members and an executive director
of NEPI. It is a local organization that works with former child soldiers on
reconciliation, trauma healing, and rehabilitation and reintegration of ex-
combatants in the community. We had many years of civil crisis, and now we
have to work on psychosocial reintegration.

KJB: Before the war, society was integrated. Then the society was disintegrated.

Many different factors led people to war. Ignorance, hardship, revenge, hunger. Some people fought to protect their family. And some people were forcibly recruited. People were dehumanized and given a false perception. Like a lot of us who took part in the war, they made us believe that the guns were fathers and mothers, that anyone who stood before us was an obstacle. Norms and cultures were broken down. Children were no longer respecting their parents. Communities were being destabilized. A lot of us who were children at the time did not understand what society was like. We took what we wanted, forcefully. That became a way of life, which is not normal in a normal community.

MGZ: We didn't know what we were doing. We were given drugs, we were given alcohol, and we were given African charms. So we felt that we were heroes. In our ignorance, we began to do what we did.

Such people now need to be made to understand that that way of life, which they followed for fifteen years of war, was not proper.

The community also needs to understand that these very sons and daughters are yours. They need to understand that they came from within those communities, and if you don't accept them, it will impose more burdens on the community, because they will remain in their own clique of society and their ways will always be full of violence. Where there is no reconciliation, there is the potential for the reoccurrence of violence. No matter our hurts, our pain, we must reconcile. So there is a need for people to understand what went wrong, how it went wrong.

When the ex-combatant goes back to the community and asks for forgiveness, he will feel free and know within himself, "I know what I did. I know that I was wrong. I did this and I did that. But I feel sorry for what I have done." The people will not forgive him if he doesn't go back to ask for forgiveness.

HOW DID YOU PERSONALLY GET INVOLVED IN THE CONFLICT?

MGZ: I remember in 1990, when the war started, my family was in Monrovia. I was in school. When the war started, we went to Tubmanburg to wait for the war to finish. Monrovia was the target of the rebels [the National Patriotic Front of Liberia, which came to be led by Charles Taylor, who was trying to overthrow the government of Samuel Doe]. In our ignorance we were rejoicing, "Let the rebels come and get rid of this government." We had been suffering for too long.

Later, the town where we were started to get fighters. In August of 1990 it was captured by rebels. That whole night up to the morning, there were grenades and bullets, so we were on the floor. Some of us were lying under the bed in fear. What happened in the morning is we heard this noise: "Everybody come out! If you remain inside you are the enemy. If you remain inside, you will be killed." Everybody came out. And they moved us to this other area. But there we hear people crying, and their parents are killed, their brothers are killed, their sisters raped, and these kinds of things, so at the end our parents said we should move.

We moved to a village, but then these guys would come and beat up people and sometimes kill people, so we had to go back to the town.

While we were in town, things started getting very tough; we really needed food. Some parents started encouraging their children to go on the rebel base. The rebel base had food. We used to go around and sometimes wash their dishes, and at the end of the day bring home something like two or three cups of soup.

At one point in time we were in their base at the battlefront. Some of their commanders and fighters had been killed, and there was this rush. People who were standing in the soup lines started running. A vehicle came, soldiers were jumping down. They started grabbing people forcibly, throwing them into the truck. That was how I was caught. They threw me in the truck. I started yelling, and they said, "Shut up little child!" And they were beating people with the gun butt. At the time, I was like fifteen years old. In the truck, there was this intense fear. We were shivering. Then they drove us from the base right away to Brewersville.

They dropped us just a few miles from the battlefront. You could actually hear this intense battlefront sound. The RPGs launching. Sometimes when you hear the sound you want to run. They say, "You guys haven't reached the main battle line yet, don't be afraid." They gave us guns, showed us how to open the gun and put the hand on the trigger and fire. And sometimes we even experimented and would shoot a bullet in the air. Then they say, "My man, you're good. You can make it." They say we can make it and things like that. So we got in line and started marching to the battlefront.

In battle, fighters started moving here and there. I just drew back a little, but I didn't know what to do. I just fired and fired. In the evening, our guys started retreating. I was taking cover, and they told me I was a foolish soldier. A commander took my gun from me and took my magazine. It still had bullets.

They sent us to a training base for a month. They asked me which class I was in. At that time, I was in the ninth grade, which was very surprising information for them, because most of the others were like in the fifth, sixth, and eighth grades. They say, "This guy, he knows how to read and write, and so what we want you to do now is list all of the guns, the type of weapon, the serial numbers, and then you lead the squad. If anything goes wrong with their weapon, you will be held accountable." I said, "Yes sir, chief." And from that day, I entered the battlefront.

The battlefront line was a terrible life. Every day you are in fear, every day you are thinking whether you will survive that day or not. So I was in that activity for two, three years, moving from one zone to another, from this battlefront to that battlefront, until they flushed us out of Tubmanburg.

When ULIMO [a force formed by supporters of President Doe, who had been killed in September 1990] captured Tubmanburg, we left and started coming toward Monrovia. Some of the guys hid, but I surrendered my weapon to the peacekeepers [deployed by neighboring West African nations]. But we had to regroup later, under the administration of a new commander. He brought some rice from Charles Taylor, and brought us some cash, and he brought us gifts and some marijuana at the time. Those who could smoke dope smoked, those who could drink, drank, and we were organized. The next morning we opened fire, and that was how [Operation] Octopus started [a very bloody attempt by Taylor to gain complete control of Monrovia; it began on October 20, 1992, and lasted 120 days].

I got wounded when I fell into an ambush. A rocket hit me and blew up my arm. Some of my guys got killed, and some started retreating. I was lying in cold blood until the evening. After I started retreating, I met some friends. They put me in a pickup and took me to a hospital in Kakata. I didn't get treated there and went to three more hospitals. At the last one, in Yekepa, I got good treatment. I was there for more than a year, but at the end my hand could not move; I was crippled.

After more military engagements, a lady who is now my wife came to Yekepa and told me my mother was very ill and if I didn't go she would end up dying. With many roadblocks, this was risky, so I went to Guinea, a short distance from Yekepa, and was able to obtain a refugee card that said I was a Liberian refugee. In fact, I bought the card.

The next morning, my wife and my daughter packed our things, and we got in a UN truck. We were examined at many checkpoints. I was pretending like I was very sick and I should not get close to anyone. I never wanted anybody to identify me and say, "Oh, this is Zawoo, we know this guy. This guy has been fighting here."

After we got to Monrovia, I went to the displacement camp, where my mother, father, and sister were. When I got to the camp, even my father was afraid of me, but my mother actually took to me. My mother was concerned and said, "You have to be careful. Do not get involved in problems or into fights, because once somebody identifies you as a rebel they will kill you."

So every day I was home. Lonely, living in kind of a nightmare. Terrible dreams. Confused. I found myself in this little island just all by myself. My mother kept asking me, "What do you want to do?" I said I wanted to go back to school. I want to be in the church. She asked me where I had been. I said, "Mama, I have been in this fight, and when killing people, I was afraid."

We went to this medicine man, and he gave us this charm for protection. We went to the pastor, who started giving me some counseling on spiritual ceremony and things like that so at least my mind can be settled. I joined the Lutheran Church in 1997. Then the Lutheran trauma healing came about, and the peacebuilding and reconciliation work, and this was how I came to awareness training. Then I went on to TOT [Training of Teachers] and met this guy [K. Johnson Borh].

KJB: I was in Kakata when I was "collected" with others and taken to training. After a couple of years of training and fighting, I was wounded and taken to Yekepa Hospital.

My case was different because I never fought in my own community. It made my reintegration process easier. When the war was over, I got involved with NGO [nongovernmental organization] training. I received awareness training, went to counseling, and finally to TOT. As a result, I was able to engage people, even though it took time for many to trust me because I was an ex-combatant.

SO YOU SET AN EXAMPLE, SHOWING THAT EX-COMBATANTS CAN BE ACCEPTED BACK INTO THEIR COMMUNITIES?

KJB: If there has been no transformation in my life, community members will not sit in a workshop that I am going to teach. They will not listen to the very first thing. I will be stigmatized. Though all ex-combatants are stigmatized in general, how much stigmatization depends on your own interaction with people in the community, how they come to perceive you. So, in my introduction [to a workshop], I will start by telling people what I have done and the bad world I have come from, how I have come to be where I am, and why I think that I need to work with the community. **>>**

Claudia Pineda *(Nicaragua)*

"Never again; it was too much, too much blood, too much pain."

Claudia Pineda grew up in a family committed to the Sandinista
cause, and she volunteered to fight
for the Sandinista government in
the early years of the Nicaraguan
civil war. But she was depressed by
the deaths of many of her friends,
and she became disillusioned as
the Sandinistas grew corrupt. We
interviewed her in her office in
Managua, where she works for a
research organization, the Institute of Strategic Studies and Public
Policy (IEEPP), She was somewhat
standoffish and wary at the start
of the interview, but she relaxed
a little as the conversation progressed.

◀◀ I'm forty-three years old and a sociologist. I was born in Matagalpa [a
city in the middle of Nicaragua] but now live in the capital, Managua.

I was born into a Sandinista family. My mother's brothers were guerrillas
as early as the 1960s. My grandmother on my mother's side was a courier for
Sandino [who led a rebellion against the US occupation in the late 1920s
and early 1930s, and whose name and legacy inspired the Sandinista National Liberation Front], and she took care of the guerrillas in the house on
her farm in El Cuá, an area that in that era was absolutely remote.

From 1974, I visited the Modelo Prison, where my uncles were in jail for
being guerrillas. My oldest brother went off to war in '78. I clearly remember
when, in April 1978, we high school students were occupying the school
where I studied, the Mistral Gabriel Institute, and the National Guard entered to dislodge us and we had to run. I was twelve years old at the time. My
mother and my grandmother were always on top of the conflict, listening
to Radio Sandino at night. So we always prepared ourselves for the war, at
school, in the house. Maybe you didn't feel the shot in the head every single
day, but every day you felt as if the National Guard could show up at any moment and pull you out of your house and kill you. I had to change schools,

too, because they expelled me for the same reasons. When the war erupted in 1979, we fled. I was thirteen then.

When I was seventeen, I entered the army. For me it was a foregone conclusion to go into military service and stay for as long as necessary, because for me the conflict [against the US-backed Contras] had to be resolved. I was in the air force for four years. It was a difficult time because I had to go to the war zone and stay there. Initially, before entering the army, while in a reserve battalion in 1983, a lot of my friends and classmates were killed in the fighting.

It fell to me to do the terrible work of burying a lot of people: I worked in the political section of the air force, and every time that pilots died, every time a helicopter was shot down by the Contras, we had to go and pick up the dead and go and explain to the mothers that we'd brought a cadaver. That era was hard, really hard. I had to spend some time medicated. I spent one month asleep, I'd gone to a psychiatrist because I couldn't sleep. It was a terrible thing. I think the schools of war are a dreadful thing.

When, more or less, I managed to stabilize myself emotionally, I went to Germany to study for one year. It did me a lot of good, distancing myself from the war, the horror of the war, the death, the blood. When I came back at the end of '89, the Sandinista Front lost the elections. I had already made the decision to leave the military. I retired totally from the army and went to study sociology. After I hung up the uniform, I retired the weapon and never again in my life have I touched one. Never again; it was too much, too much blood, too much pain.

For most of the 1980s, I had been totally convinced that what we were doing was right and that the war was necessary. But at the same time, I didn't want my friends to die. I didn't want my brother who'd gotten out alive from the War of Liberation to die in another war, but off to that war he went. I didn't want my classmates to die. Yankee imperialism was the easiest thing to blame, and the US did give the Contras support over so many years. But what kind of stubbornness and arrogance was shown by the Sandinista government, which sent us to war to honorably oppose North American imperialism? It was a war of geopolitical egos that sent us to die. The ego of the US government that was trying to keep control of Nicaragua, and the ego of the Sandinista government that challenged American imperialism so arrogantly.

When Doña Violeta [Chamorro] won and the Sandinista Front lost the elections [in 1989], that whole mess started what we call the *piñata*—that horrible plundering of state property by both sides. When that started, the mother of one of my best friends, who died in '84 in the first contingent of military service, told me something that went to my soul, and even today it is the first thing I think of when I think of the war. She said, "For such a pitiful cause my son died."

He was a kid of seventeen, a poet, a dancer, a happy, healthy kid, and he died. He died, and that's all there is to it. There are really paltry reasons for which no youngster deserves to die.

There are two roles that it plays: the political role and the funding role. I think in both roles we have had bad and good experiences with the international community. I have had more experience with the Europeans than with the United States. My experience with the Europeans has been that there is a sort of double dimension with the cooperation. On the one hand, they demand a lot of the government. They demand things that they have in their own country, for example, transparency in the political and legal systems. They opine about our laws and policies. They say, "If you don't agree to do it in this manner, I won't give you any resources." On the other hand, when something turns out bad, they tell you, "I am only an observer, I have nothing to do with this decision; it is a sovereign decision of the Nicaraguan government." In that respect, I have been quite in agreement with this government, that cooperation has to be much more respectful. But I am not in agreement with the way the government wants to negotiate that respect, to demand respect. The government thinks that the donors are like a money box from which the government can withdraw and withdraw without offering any accountability!

WHAT WOULD YOU LIKE FOREIGNERS TO KNOW ABOUT NICARAGUA TODAY?

I would like to tell foreigners that Nicaragua is a lovely country, a comfortable country, a country of lovely people, people in solidarity, kind people—a country that unfortunately has a disgusting political class. But the people, no. The country is more than its politicians. **>>**

Emanuel Alonso Alonso Garcia *(Nicaragua)*

"I said to myself, 'I don't want to die here. I want to die outside.'"

Emanuel was very reserved, slightly awkward, and seemed uncomfortable talking about his wartime experiences. He preferred to focus on the future. He was proud of his work helping other disabled people, and he was determined to give his son a better life.

◄◄ In 1978, I was fifteen and living in León. My mother was a very hard working lady, but things could be difficult sometimes. I was living in different neighborhoods because we didn't have a proper house. Sometimes we didn't have anything to eat, we went to bed early because we didn't have dinner—that's normal, almost normal here. And sometimes I didn't go to school because I didn't have money, my mother didn't have money to buy me a pair of shoes. My family was not an exception. It can happen. It was normal in those days.

I was going to study my ninth grade, and I remember that I had a normal life: classmates, girlfriend, neighbors, friends, relatives, cousins. But once the war began, everything was totally different. In September of 1978, the [Sandinista] rebels attacked León. I didn't have anything to do with them, but the army was drafting all the youngsters, and I was fifteen or sixteen years old, so [to avoid being drafted] I spent days in the mountains without my parents, without any contact with my family. I was with three of my cousins. When the fighting finished, we came back to León and then I continued studying in the same school, but the problems were increasing. Some of my classmates left the school, and then the school shut down for our year, because it was impossible to be a student walking down the street going to school, because the army was putting students in jail. So my relatives left the country. My mother didn't have the opportunity to send me away, and one night the army came and took all the youngsters from our neighborhood. It was a miracle that they didn't take me.

So I had to decide: am I going to be taken by the army or join the rebels? It was easier to be a rebel than going to the army, no? So I joined the rebels. Those were very hard days and nights. We were sleeping in different places, fighting with the army, and lots of times we were being shot at. It is a miracle that I survived.

The night when I lost my hands, I was with a group of rebels, and we were walking down the street. The army ambushed us, and they began to kill my friends. I had four grenades in my hands and then I threw two. That stopped the army convoy. But they began to shoot me with a machine gun, thank you. I was interested in watching how many bullets were coming very close to my body. I stumbled, and the grenades exploded. I knew that I didn't have my hands anymore. I was bleeding a lot, and I survived because I fell down a hole—they were digging a well, and I fell down it. It was completely dark, and I was bleeding a lot. My jeans were wet, because of the blood. I said to myself, "I don't want to die here, I want to die outside. I don't want them to find my body here." So I began to pull out my body with the backs of my feet. I got out and walked a few blocks, where a man found me and helped me. He drove me to the old hospital here in León. I spent more than one hour bleeding inside. I don't know why I didn't die.

I woke up after the surgery, and some of the nurses told me that the army had come to the hospital and found me and wanted to kill me in the operating room, but the doctors refused to let them do that. So they put me in the janitor's closet, among the buckets and brooms, for a week. Then I left the hospital because the army wanted to see my body. The hospital had told them that I had died, but they wanted to see the body.

So they went to my house, and they destroyed everything. But my mother and my father, they were not living in that place. It was a miracle. That's why my mother decided to take me to [the capital] Managua, to ask for exile, political asylum. So that's when I flew to Mexico.

I stayed there almost a year. I came back as soon as the dictatorship was overthrown.

It was hard. My classmates and eight of my cousins had died. My girlfriend. Even her. So it was very sad, it was unstable. I began to study, but I had to figure out how to write with my prosthesis, because I hadn't had any training. I hadn't been a good student before I lost my hands, but afterwards I studied hard. Now I love to read anything.

Now I work for myself as a translator. I have taught secondary school. I have volunteered for an NGO that helps people with disabilities. I am working with a rural school that gets support from people in Massachusetts. We are advancing because we are receiving help from abroad.

If a person were to ask me what do I want to change in my life, I would say that I don't want to change anything. You know? Here I am happy. I think that I am a mature person. I have my goals, my life, my son, I am the head of my family. I live with my son and my mother.

Nowadays I am not thinking only in my present. I am trying to build a legacy to give to my son, and the best thing that I can leave him is a land in which he can work or study without going away, without leaving the country, without killing a person, without living in danger.

There are different kinds of feelings of peace: our peace inside, that is for me one of the most important; and the peace that we have to preserve at any cost in any place, it's that peace that is going to guarantee us a better future, to be a family together. With peace in our environment and our souls, we can do anything. **>>**

Three Maoists *(Nepal)*

In Banepa, a city about fifteen miles east of Kathmandu, we met with four ex-Maoist fighters and interviewed three of them, who went by the noms de guerre "U.D.J. Proletariat" (above left), "Shital" (above right), and "Bibek" (top of next page). They had dissociated themselves from Nepal's main Maoist party but were affiliated with an underground armed movement called "Revolutionary Left Wing." We met them on the third floor of a small guesthouse, which had sentries posted at every entry point. Other ex-Maoist cadres kept coming in and going out of the room, and everyone in the house seemed fearful of being attacked by security forces. They viewed us with some suspicion but appeared to relish the opportunity to talk about themselves and their political agenda.

U.D.J., the smallest of the group, had belonged to the party's political wing and was extremely talkative, gesturing with his hands as he fired off communist rhetoric, quizzed us about the interview process, and criticized our "bourgeois" backgrounds. He declared that the party's leadership had "misled" the fighters into laying down their arms: "Now we are re-forming our army again and re-establishing the people's court and returning to war." When we asked him what "rule of law" meant, he replied: "Laws are made in accordance with the interest of the ruler and the system. If the state authority is under capitalism, the law serves the interest of capitalists; if under socialism, the law serves the proletariat. Yesterday, the law was in the hands of the royal courtiers. Now the law is in the hands of political parties and their organizations. The 'rule of law' depends on which political party I belong to."

Shital, a former commander in the Maoist People's Liberation Army, fit the stereotype of "strong and silent." He was very controlled in his movements, very polite, and very careful in his responses. He seemed a lot older than the others in the room even though they were all in the same age range. He dismissed the idea that a parliamentary system could help the poor: "The goal of revolution can be achieved only by war. . . . War cannot be won by making an agreement with those whom the war is waged against. The revolution was waged against the parliamentary system; and the revolution shall not be completed by making an agreement with this system."

Bibek was a restless and imposing presence in the room. He was short and stocky with a wild look in his eyes. Throughout the interview, he paced back and forth, checked his phone, and locked and unlocked the door. Finally, he took off his shirt and sat on the bed in a casually defiant manner. Clearly, he was conscious of the fact that two of his interviewers were female, and he was deliberately trying to make us uncomfortable. He said that he was sad about the loss of life in the conflict, but that sadness wasn't to be heard in his voice. Every time he described a skirmish, he would get excited and speak loudly and proudly.

◀◀ To talk about the conflict is to feel more sorrow than happiness. Some fifteen thousand comrades have been killed, and some eight hundred have been forcefully disappeared.

I fought more than eight encounters, and so I am a wounded warrior. However, we were mentally prepared for the conflict. Getting wounded, getting arrested, meeting death: these are secondary things. The primary thing is our dedication to the goal for which we have been fighting: the victory of the working classes. We were prepared for war, so we fought the war readily. We fought promptly and joyfully.

How did you feel when the peace agreement was announced?

We had been fighting for ten years, and fifteen thousand people had been killed in the cause of establishing a proletarian state. But the agreement was concluded without achieving that goal. The conditions of the mass of the Nepalese people remain no better than before the conflict. No transformation has been made in their livelihood at all.

To me, the peace agreement is a matter of sorrow rather than a matter of happiness for the Nepalese people. All aspire to peace, prosperity, and progress, but will the agreement bring them? No, scattered fighting is still continuing. And the Nepalese leaders are carrying out the state affairs of Nepal under the guidance of foreign "courtiers." Foreign powers have used Nepal for their self-interest. They tried to make Nepal a failed state. The imperialist America has played tricks against us. The colonialist and expansionist India has always intended to colonize Nepal.

The ICRC [International Committee of the Red Cross] and the United Nations have played good roles, however. During the conflict, when we sent back police or army personnel whom we had captured, we used to send them back under the protection of the ICRC. The UN was also helpful at times.

HOW DO YOU INTERPRET THE "RULE OF LAW"?

Under the rule of law, the law is enforced by a supreme body. But, in Nepal, everything is concerned with politics. Wherever we go, we are touched by politics. Nepal has no rule of law. The laws have been a toy of the rich. The laws have been a jail to entrap the poor.

HOW DO YOU DESCRIBE YOURSELF?

In the days to come, I would like to describe myself as a combatant. I am ready to fight for the freedom as well as for the justice of the people, if needed in the future. If the party needed me as an organizer of the party, then I must be ready even for that. Until a radical change is established, I shall be fighting: now, tomorrow, and the day after tomorrow.

If I am killed in the course of fighting, I shall be a martyr for the people. If I am not killed, I shall see the success of our politics for empowering the people. We see our future bright. Whether we die or live, we dream of a bright future. **>>**

"Ahmed" (Libya)

"We collected 350 bodies.
They had been tied up and shot, and then burned."

*We interviewed "Ahmed" in a little town outside Zawiya. We talked at
a cultural center that had been looted by Qaddafi supporters. Inside,
the center was bare, so we sat outside in the hot afternoon on fold-
ing chairs. The Mediterranean Sea shimmered in the distance. He was
dressed like a businessman and spoke in a matter-of-fact manner.*

<< I was born and raised in Zawiya [a city on the Mediterranean Sea in the
northwest of Libya]. All my education, elementary, high school, and university, was in Zawiya, and my job is also in Zawiya.

Before the revolution, I was a full-time student. I studied in Egypt for six
months before I got fired because I was not a follower of the Qaddafi regime.
In the last coup d'état, in 1992, a member of my family was one of those who
tried to overthrow Qaddafi. My relative was killed by the regime, and after
that the regime closely watched anyone with our surname.

I also had graduate brothers. One of them is a martyr; he was killed at
the beginning of [the revolt against the regime]. He had a law degree and
was unemployed for five years before I managed to get him a job, but he was
fired the next day because of his last name; he served only one day in that
job. After that, he worked as a lawyer at several courts, but again he was fired
because of his last name.

I got involved in the revolution [early on]. In Zawiya, eleven people were
killed by government forces even though they were only participating in a
peaceful strike. I also had a cousin who was captured by the security forces
because of his religious orientation; he used to pray in the mosque. Things
started building up. Confrontations with the supporters of Qaddafi started.
My uncle died on the first day of the fighting, followed by my brother on the
third day. [In early March] Zawiya fell to Qaddafi supporters.

After that, they began intimidating us. I had to send my wife to stay with
her family. My father insisted that I stay in the family house and never leave
it. I stayed home with my mother, my married sisters, and their children. I
was the only one who could not leave. My father told me that if I left, the
Qaddafi supporters would take over the house and they would leave my family homeless, so I had to stay and be patient. I was beaten once, twice; they
came to my house once or twice.

If I turned on a light in the house, I wouldn't be able to turn it off because if they noticed any movement inside the house, they would raid the
house again. They searched the cars of the families that visited our house
to offer condolences. Anyone who visited us would be searched and ques-
tioned, "What are you doing here?" "What do you want?" "Do you have a
gun?" and so on.

I was helped by a Chinese person who stood by me during the events because I had helped him get 150 Chinese out to Tunisia. We managed to bring them micro buses and buses and drove them to Tunisia.

There was also a small group of twelve people—doctors, engineers, head of companies—whom we transported to the port. A person from one company, a Muslim from Egypt, handed over all the company's assets to us and told us that if the company could restart its normal business, we would hand the assets back, but if not, the company would claim on its insurance for the loss of the equipment and we could keep it.

We tried to protect the company's equipment and machinery from looting by building a fence around them with the help of the tribe and local people. Squads of Qaddafi supporters came and opened the fence, because they wanted to use it to transport ammunition. When I refused, they pointed guns at me and threatened to hand me over to Abdullah Al Sunessi [widely believed to have ordered a massacre of two hundred prisoners in Bouslem jail]. They said, "You are either a traitor or we should thank you for your deeds." I said, "No need to thank me, it is a national duty to preserve the state assets, I don't need thanks or money." I finally had to give them the machinery after they had promised not to turn me in to Abdullah Al Sunessi.

[In the spring, I was part of a small group that carried out attacks] against the squads. We hadn't had any military training. We knew only how to load and fire the weapons. We had to move quickly. If we missed our target, the squads would be on us in no time. We used silencers.

The squads captured most of us in June. We were having lunch on the farm [where we were hiding]. They raided us, and I hid in the bushes for four hours in the middle of the day. They did not capture me, but they took five of us, four brothers and their cousin. One of them managed to get away. One of the [captured] brothers was on the "wanted" list. They took those brothers and transferred them to a camp and then to Brigade 32 [also known as the Khamis Brigade, a security force under the command Qaddafi's son Khamis], and then to the Yarmouk military base [south of Tripoli]. We did not hear from them until the day Tripoli was liberated on August 23.

[I was with the rebel forces when we] entered Tripoli on August 23. We besieged the Yarmouk detention camp for two days. When we finally entered, we found 150 prisoners locked in a fifty-square-meter barn. [Members of the Khamis Brigade] had thrown eight grenades at them, and they all died. It took us four hours to remove the bodies.

We found a person who had lost his leg and gave him first aid. There was someone with him, maybe his older brother, who had been tortured for sixty days. He had sat for three days with nothing to drink; he had to drink his own urine. They all were very young, born in 1994 and 1995. We collected 350 bodies. They had been tied up and shot, then burned. When I got to the camp, I found 70 bodies that had been hidden. We documented it. After that, we collected bodies, bones, and skulls in bags and moved them to the al-Zawiya Street hospital in Tripoli. We collected 350 bodies in bags, we prayed over them. That was our life with Muammar [Qaddafi].

WHAT DO YOU DO TODAY?

After the revolution, I left the labs where I had been working. I left the academy as well. Now, I am a member of al-Shura [the local advisory council]. I am also a member of the Tribal Accord Council, and the Warriors Organization. We communicate with revolutionaries and we supervise military and local activities.

We reached an agreement that all revolutionaries, brigades, military, and local councils should be removed from the refinery [in Zawiya] and that it should return to its normal operations. There were two people, my coworker and I, who managed to remove the brigades from the refinery. We honored and thanked them for their efforts, but we wanted to operate the refinery to its full capacity and have all brigades return home or join the Ministry of Interior or Ministry of Defense. That applied to the revolutionary union as well. Also, the internal and external security services are not to be activated under any title whatsoever so as not to cause any disturbance or unrest in any way. We have given a bonus to people who work at the refinery—the bonus has one condition, though: regime followers who carried weapons or committed slander that led to death, torture, or arrest are excluded.

Thank God, people now are aware of human rights. We live in an international environment and are not secluded anymore; we are communicating with the outside world. Our stability matters to the world because we are part of it; we are not living on Mars, doing whatever we feel like doing. The stability of Libya is in our interest, to preserve human rights is in our interest. Whether we were supporters or opponents [of Qaddafi], we should try to flip that page and not dwell on the past. If we do [focus on the past], we will get nowhere, and that would be in the interest of those who benefit from continued chaos.

WHAT DO YOU WANT THE INTERNATIONAL COMMUNITY TO KNOW ABOUT YOUR COUNTRY?

The Libyan people are good and yet naive. All they need is acceptance and respect from others. I hope that the international community will support and encourage them, and support civil society institutions and workshops. We can reform Zawiya, but without imposing our ideas on more than one side; the prime minister could have an opinion, but we, as a popular base governed by our traditions and customs, could have another opinion. God willing, we will extend a helping hand to the international community in Libya—unconditional, clear, and transparent support based on equity.

WHAT DOES THE RULE OF LAW MEAN TO YOU?

The rule of law should be applied in general and in particular. It should be applied to all levels of authority, accountable and nonaccountable, without favoritism and nepotism and with justice and transparency.

WHAT DO YOU WANT FOR THE FUTURE?

I hope that the future will be better than before, that justice, equity, peace, and prosperity will prevail. **>>**

Nevruz Tola *(Kosovo)*

"The title of his diary was 'From the Departure until the Return.'"

We met Nevruz at his kiosk where he sells cigarettes and candy, and then walked to a cafe. His brother's fate still weighed heavily on him. He spoke softly and had a gentle manner.

❮❮ War—nobody likes it. But in our case, the war was imposed on us by the Serbian regime, which intensified its repression of us.

In the '90s, [Serbian president] Miloševic brought in the military and police to rule Kosovo. All Albanians working in the public sector were dismissed from their workplaces. I was dismissed, too, and I left Kosovo and went to Germany and stayed there until January 1998, when I returned to Kosovo voluntarily and joined the KLA [Kosovo Liberation Army] to defend my people and my country. My brother had already joined the KLA.

War brings only bad experiences, never good ones. I will share one of these experiences with you. Before my brother and I joined the KLA, before the war, I was driving to a village to buy vegetables for my household. My brother was traveling by bus to another village, where he used to work. As I drove through that village, I saw that the Serbian forces had stopped the bus, and they were beating my brother Aziz very badly. I can never forget those moments. The Serbian military and police continuously provoked, beat, and ill-treated the Albanian population.

When the war started, my brother fought with the KLA. My family and I were forced to flee to Albania. We walked throughout one night from Prizren to Kukes [in Albania, near the border with Kosovo], about eight hours' walk. We found hundreds and thousands of other refugees in Kukes. We then moved to Tirana [the Albanian capital]. Families in Tirana opened their doors to us and welcomed us. I rented a house for my family. Tirana Military Hospital was nearby, and I spent my spare time in that hospital helping the wounded soldiers from Kosovo. I got a letter from my brother who had found out that we were in Tirana, and in that letter he asked me to go to the military hospital and help people in need there.

The peace agreement of Kumanovo was very good news for our people. War came to an end, and everybody was happy. However, the joy of our family didn't last long. The next day we received a message that my brother had been killed, on the 10th of June, 1999. In his diary, he wrote: "We heard about the Kumanovo agreement, but I am somewhat skeptical about its implementation in practice. They might do harm to us in their last minutes while withdrawing forces from Kosovo." Unfortunately, he was killed during the last days of the withdrawal of Serbian forces from Kosovo.

We returned home. Fortunately our house had not been burned down. We started our life again from the beginning, as all other Kosovans did. Following our traditions, we opened the doors for people to come and express condolences. After two weeks, I went to Junik village to check with the brigade with which my brother had served. I met the commander; he expressed his condolences and gave me some things that belonged to my brother: his uniform, some personal belongings, and also his diary. The title of his diary was "From the Departure until the Return." The diary contains stories of the heroism of soldiers, meeting other brigades, and so on.

My brother was very close to his family, very pleasant and lovely. He was passionate about freedom. He had two daughters and a son. Whenever he used to hear about a KLA soldier killed in the fighting, he used to tell his little son that they both should stand up and pay tribute to the fallen soldier. One time, my mother told my brother: "Aziz, I see that you are planning to go to war. I am concerned about you." Aziz replied: "Mother, even if I get killed, my children will tomorrow go to school and learn our language and history and they will be free."

After the war ended, a new life began. It was a great feeling. Our long-awaited dream came true. A new life began; people came back to their houses, reconstruction started. People were motivated. International organizations were helping with humanitarian aid and reconstruction. I started to work. I worked for three and a half years with the German section of KFOR [the UN peacekeeping force] as a translator. My experiences were very good; KFOR soldiers were very hard-working and wanted to help the population.

During 2002 and 2003, the hope for a better life started to fade a little. The people had high expectations, which were not being met. Our development pace was slower than we had hoped.

How do you feel today?

A lot has been done. We have declared independence. Our infrastructure is not so bad. But the international community should allow us to manage our own affairs.

WHAT ARE YOUR FEELINGS ABOUT THE WAR?

War . . . the word itself sounds terrible. It depends on how you look at it. We didn't want war to happen; it was imposed on us. And a war for liberation is something you can be proud of, whereas a war for conquering territories has a completely different meaning.

WHAT DOES THE TERM "RULE OF LAW" MEAN TO YOU?

This is a very commonly used phrase these days. Laws are rules of the game. If you follow them, they can be of benefit to you. Rule of law in Kosovo is in its infancy. There is still a long way to go. In Kosovo, there was no rule of law for more than a century. Law should function in all areas of life. We need to understand better the meaning of the rule of law and to start to respect the law and values of humanity.

WHAT WOULD YOU LIKE TO TELL THE INTERNATIONAL COMMUNITY?

The international community should adapt to the reality of the host country. They should not give favors to a small percentage of the population [the Serbs still living in Kosovo] and not offer those favors to the rest of the population.

WHAT MOTIVATED YOU DURING THE WAR AND TODAY?

Every person needs to have a reason to move forward. Before and during the war, we were motivated by the strong desire to be free and to have an independent country. Today, my wish would be that war never happens again. I also wish that our children could be educated in Western universities. One "hidden" personal wish of mine is for all Albanians to be united. **>>**

Nait Hasani *(Kosovo)*

"They lined up six hundred prisoners in a field and opened fire on us."

Driven by his past and his ambitions for Kosovo, Nait was fast-talking and fiery.

◄◄ I am forty-four years old. I studied German and Albanian language and literature, and I have a master's in political science. I am a member of the Kosovo Parliament, for the second term.

I was imprisoned [by the Serbian authorities] for the first time when I was in secondary school. This was in 1983. I was sentenced to three and a half years in prison for writing that Kosovo should become a republic. And I spent all three and a half years in jail. I was released from prison in June 1987.

A year later, I was arrested again for "hostile activity against Federative Republic of Yugoslavia" and sentenced to six years' imprisonment. I was released in 1990 as a part of an amnesty. In 1993, together with some friends, we established the Kosovo Liberation Army. I was the main person responsible for coordinating the KLA from 1993 until 1997, when I was arrested and imprisoned.

When the war started in Kosovo, I was in prison. I was released at the request of the international community after the war ended. One hundred and fifty million euros were given to the Serbian authorities for our release.

My family was affected by the war. Our house was burned down. Forty civilians were killed in my village.

WHAT ARE YOUR FEELINGS ABOUT THE WAR IN GENERAL?

Wars have always been horrifying. They are never good. War is a terrible thing, but war for freedom and liberation should by all means be fought.

Our mission was to liberate our country from Serbia and to live in freedom. War came when all other diplomatic and nonforceful means of conflict resolution had failed. Our war was a war to liberate our country and protect our people; it was a holy war.

WHAT IS YOUR STRONGEST WARTIME MEMORY?

While I was in prison, a terrible thing happened that I will remember forever. This was the massacre at the Dubrava prison, where there were about one thousand prisoners. I was one of them. Because NATO was bombing Serbian military targets, the Serbian prison authorities were angry and took revenge on Albanian prisoners. The police and guards, who by law were supposed to take care of us, lined up some six hundred prisoners in a sports field and opened fire on us. This field was called the "field of vengeance," and it was full of blood and dead prisoners. Three hundred prisoners were wounded and 170 were killed. This massacre happened on May 22, 1999. I was wounded in my back. No one was ever sent to court or held responsible for this horror. Serbia should be held responsible. Dubrava is the Auschwitz or the Matthausen of the twenty-first century.

WHAT DOES "RULE OF LAW" MEAN TO YOU?

Rule of law to me is state building. It means lawfulness, freedom, and equality for all citizens. **>>**

"Sushil" (Nepal)
"If you win the war, everything is justified."

We spoke to "Sushil," a high-ranking member of the Nepalese security forces, in his well-guarded house in a wealthy area of Nepal's capital, Kathmandu. The walls of the sitting room where we spoke were adorned with art. A servant who served coffee during the interview treated Sushil with great deference.

◄◄ The Maoist insurgent leadership wanted power. They didn't want to address the grievances of the people they said they were fighting for. They wanted power. It's ultimate, absolute power they want, and they still want it.

An insurgency retards the growth of a nation. Change should come to a nation, but it should come as an evolutionary process, step by step, not a revolutionary process. The revolutionary process creates such great change that the nation cannot sustain that change, and then you have problems.

WHAT WERE YOUR EXPERIENCES DURING THE INSURGENCY? WHAT KEPT YOU GOING WHEN THINGS WERE DIFFICULT?

Three things. One, it was my career. Second, it was my duty. Three, you are fighting for your life.

After the war starts, no matter who says what or talks about "rule of law," when you see your subordinates being killed and wounded, you have to show some concern and you've got to tell the rest of the soldiers, "Look, here is the situation, we have to be in the proper frame of mind to fight, now you are fighting for your life."

Whatever happens in war, it is success that justifies whatever you have done. If you don't succeed, then it will be difficult for you to justify what you have done. If you succeed, success is what justifies it. Forget the rule of law; you know tomorrow your nation will support you.

I mean, a person is there shooting at you and your soldiers. Ultimately, he finishes you or you finish him. So, there are laws and rules of engagement [intended to govern how troops should behave in a given situation], but when you go into fighting, you fight, you cannot think about these one hundred things. Rules of war are good things. But the end justifies the means. If you lose the war, you've had it. If you win the war, everything is justified.

Situations in peacetime are completely at odds with the situations in wartime, or when you face a bullet. "Use of excessive firepower": how can you define that? I don't know. I still feel that use of excessive firepower is justified if your mission is successful. If your mission is not successful, you've had it. Simple as that.

WHAT ABOUT RAPE OR TORTURE OR RAZING VILLAGES?

Now those are crimes, those are crimes. It's nothing to do with warfighting, it's crime. And crime must be stopped, and prosecuted. You cannot commit actions that would get innocent civilians motivated against you and create recruits for the opposition.

WHAT LED YOU TO JOIN THE ARMY?

My whole family have all joined the army [laughter]. My uncles, my cousins, they either joined this army or that army, a foreign army, the Nepalese Army—but we've all joined the army [laughter]. It was expected that I would join the army.

The army looks at itself as a protector of the nation and the Constitution. The nation, if it is a sovereign and independent nation, should have at its discretion this instrument of power and have the ability to use it whenever it wants; there should be no rules [governing when to use it] because you are preserving the nation and protecting the people.

WHAT DO YOU WANT FOR YOUR FUTURE AND NEPAL'S FUTURE?

I am now sixty [years old] almost. I do not have any ambitions. I just want Nepal to remain a sovereign, independent, and united nation. All that Nepal wants and seeks is dignified treatment from its neighbors—from all of the international community. Dignity is sovereignty, it's independence, it's national unity.

HOW DID THE CONFLICT AFFECT YOUR FAMILY?

I was a general. I had security for myself, security for my family. It did not affect me, except that I was out in the war, and my family worried about my safety and security. My family did not suffer. But the people suffered, and part of the blame for that goes to me, because I, as an army commander, could not protect the people.

Pacifist thinking will not provide good governance. "Peace" is such a relative matter. A dead body is absolutely peaceful. That's not what we want. It is security we need. And through security you get peace. The pacifist way of thinking will not bring you governance, and without good governance you will not get development, and without development, you will not have prosperity and the people will be deprived of their opportunities. You need not peace, per se. Security gives you everything. **>>**

Carlos Fernando Chamorro (Nicaragua)

"When they killed my father, that changed many things in my life."

Carlos seemed to carry a burden of repsonsibility for his country. We interviewed him in his office, which was more modest than one might have expected for the office of the son of one of Nicaragua's former presidents. He was very open, thoughtful, and matter-of-fact.

◀◀ I was born in Managua in 1956. All my life, for some thirty years, I have worked as a journalist. I have done a lot of work on the political beat.

My perception of the problem in Nicaragua is formed quite directly by my father's and my family's influence, and obviously by my own generational experience. In truth, when I was born my father [Pedro Joaquin Chamorro Cardenal, editor of *La Prensa*, the main opposition newspaper] was in and between jails. He was a democrat, a person who since his youth participated in different political initiatives in the struggle against the Somoza dictatorship, the dynastic dictatorship that stayed in power through a combination of repression and co-opting. Some Nicaraguans were allowed to develop businesses, and there was a period in which the economy prospered. But those who engaged in politics to oppose Somoza were harshly punished, and my father was reprimanded, imprisoned, tortured, and exiled. My father's example had a great deal of influence on me.

In high school, I was part of a Christian student political movement. In my generation, there was a question we asked ourselves, "If I wanted to change this country, what is the way to do so?" Peacefully, or by fighting?

I wanted to understand how things worked. And I wanted to understand how things could change. I had an anxiety, an intellectual need to understand what was happening and how to change it. I was not an impulsive person or someone spoiling for a fight, but a person who wanted to understand and reflect. And so it was that I came to be familiar with Marxist literature, leftist literature. When I went to university [in Canada], my goal was to develop and prepare myself to return to Nicaragua to work and get involved. I didn't know exactly how or in what area.

I started to collaborate in '77 with the Sandinista Front in a, let's call it, semi-clandestine way, but it was collaboration. When it comes to revolutionary organizations, there are different types of collaboration. There is militancy, but mine was a more intellectual collaboration, like creating a magazine called *Critical Thinking* that offered socioeconomic and political analyses that would form the basis for explaining the revolution's necessity in Nicaragua. It was principally directed to university students and intellectuals.

I was engaged in this when they killed my father in January 1978, and that changed many things in my life, because from that day on—which signified a change or parting of waters in the history of Nicaragua, because it produced a huge, popular, and spontaneous rebellion within both popular and moderate sectors, as well as the business sector—it was the breaking point, because it established in this society that the possibility for peaceful or gradual change did not exist. And one had to seek some form of involvement, of radical change via radical methods, because via other means it would not be possible to overthrow the Somoza dictatorship and his repressive system.

I put aside my plans to return to the university for my master's and continue my education. I joined the Sandinista Front, no longer as a collaborator but as a militant. I plunged into journalism and started working for *La Prensa*.

LOOKING BACK, HOW DO YOU FEEL ABOUT THE REVOLUTION?

You can't change history. What happened, happened. I think that the decisions that I made over the course of my life in one way or another were bound to be made. I don't regret anything. It is certain that a radical change was necessary in Nicaragua. [But] now I believe that the vision my father had was more appropriate for [Nicaragua's] reality.

Profound but lasting change was necessary, change that could take root in society. Sudden, dramatic changes are what we sought, what we fought for, and they were epic, producing great moments of euphoria, but their roots, in my opinion, were not very deep. I think that to a great extent that has to do with a certain lack of democratic culture. We didn't have a democratic culture. It was also somewhat due to the influence of the times, the vision that the Left had at the time about how to adapt itself to leadership and how to exercise power. The process that we lived in the '80s was a revolution with a great democratic dimension, but also an authoritarian dimension. That wasn't seen in the moment. Only after the revolution lost power were we able, some of us because others never acknowledged it, [to see] that here was not just a matter of external aggression, that what happened in Nicaragua wasn't only the responsibility of Reagan's dirty war, and the covert operations and Contra financing, but also that here we'd had a civil war. That is, we lived a combination of civil war and a war of aggression. In the 1980s, we acknowledged only the war of aggression. Only after the Frente lost power, when 54 percent voted against the Sandinista project in 1990, did we reckon with what had happened.

When I look at the past, I see that today the changes that Nicaragua needs in terms of democracy and social justice are much more in tune with the manner in which my father saw the process. But sure, the revolution was necessary. Somoza was not going to leave if not for a radical change. My father's death demonstrates this: someone who wanted another type of change was killed. As were many others.

WHAT IS YOUR VISION OF THE RULE OF LAW?

In the '80s, I didn't think about such things. I thought about a society where [harmony] would exist, a society led by a single party. And that party was not very democratic. We believed that the centralization of power, with the support of the population, would bring about social change. Social change before democracy. Social justice was more important.

It was only when the Frente lost power that the Left started to develop a vision that the rule of law was not necessarily an invention of the bourgeoisie or of a middle-class democracy. That the rule of law protects universal rights, which is good for the Left as well as the Right. For me, accountability is one of the fundamental issues of democracy and the rule of law, and there are many institutional ways to establish it. But for me it is fundamental. That is to say, if there were electoral democracy, the election would be the method for resolving political difference, and not war and arms. For me, the concept of rule of law has a lot to do with counterweights, with more decentralized power, and rendering of accounts.

In the late 1970s and the 1980s, we embraced the idea that arms were lawful to change or to intervene in politics. After '90, that vision began to change, and I had a severe break with the Frente Sandinista over that. A group on the left called Punitive Forces of the Left drew up a list of people they were going to kill because they were on the right. And they killed one called Arges Sequeira. That for me was the moment of rupture with the Frente Sandinista. I wrote an article saying that we could not accept that there are left-wing death squads, that somehow the [right-wing] death squads in El Salvador and Guatemala are bad, and ours are somehow good.

WHAT DO YOU THINK OF THE ROLE THE INTERNATIONAL COMMUNITY HAS HAD HERE?

There is a sector in Nicaragua society that would like the international community to resolve its problems, resolve its political problems and its institutional problems and its economic problems. I think the international community can't resolve problems that Nicaraguans themselves cannot resolve.

I have the impression that there is a certain fatigue on the part of the international community with regard to its relationship with Nicaragua. The international community has invested a lot in Nicaragua, a lot of resources, but the external aid has not had an impact in terms of helping build strong institutions. In some cases that is because the international community has tried to transplant formulas, laws, that won't take root here. But there is a very high level of dependency in this country on the international community. We need to acknowledge that external aid is a complement, and not the base of the state.

WHAT MOTIVATES YOU TODAY?

I think that journalism can be an agent of change in a society like this one, where there are many institutions that don't function, there are no sources of trustworthy information with which people can make decisions. The press can give voice to people who don't have means to communicate or express themselves. In a society that continues to be very elitist, that continues to have a monopoly on a block of public opinion, journalism contributes.

Before, I believed more in the power of the press. Now, I think the power of the press is relative. I think the power of the press lies in knowing that we are unable to substitute for what justice needs to do, what the political parties need to do, what the social movements need to do, and the police.

I want a country with less poverty, but with freedom, with democracy, with transparency. I can't accept a political model that proposes a society where we only see democracy and we forget about inequity, or where they say they will fight to eradicate poverty and to create equity while sacrificing liberty, sacrificing democracy, sacrificing the right of the people to act in complete freedom. I believe that there is a false dichotomy between social justice and democracy, freedom and socialism, the state and the market. In Nicaragua, we need more market and more state. And we need more democracy and we need more social justice.

I can't live peacefully in this society if I don't dedicate my energy and my passion and my work to try to make Nicaragua a better country. The people deserve it. In Nicaragua, there is a tendency to blame just one group for the pain and death of the '80s. They say, "No, all the blame is on the gringos," on the Contras, the mercenaries, Reagan. Or they say, "No, the Sandinistas are to blame; they destroyed the country, the revolution." I think not. I believe that the last fifteen years have achieved something of that vision to establish shared responsibility. I think that what has happened in nearly three years of the Daniel Ortega government [he was elected president in 2006] is a serious movement backward, because there is a polarizing rhetoric, a discussion charged with hate, charged with a simplistic vision, one that uses poverty as a tool of politics. And that is a grave step backward in Nicaragua. I could say a bunch of things that I think about this government, but it seems to me a crime to the memory of this country that it is once again constructing a rhetoric of polarization, of hate, of cults of personality.

I don't see an easy solution to the problem in Nicaragua. At times, I see things with pessimism because I don't see a solution around the corner. I am a long-term optimist, but in the short term, no. **>>**

Daniel Mora *(Peru)*

"The people don't let anybody fool them anymore."

Very likeable and keen to speak to us to make sure we understood the complexity of Peru's situation, Daniel had a professorial air.

◀◀ I am a general of the Brigades Army. I went to the military academy, and also studied in France, the US, and Italy. I have studied engineering and construction. I have a diploma in science and technology. I also studied international humanitarian law and the law of war. I have been a university professor for the past twenty years in Lima. Right now, I am the president of the National Intelligence Council.

[In the fight against the Shining Path terrorist movement in the 1980s and early 1990s,] our intelligence service was a great success. But [in 2000, after the ouster of the corrupt government of Alberto Fujimori], the transition government of Valentin Paniagua disarmed the whole apparatus of intelligence that the state had. He destroyed it completely, which was a huge mistake. It was an intelligence service that was considered one of the best in the world at one time. Many intelligence units were dismantled, and some agents ended up unemployed and then working in different parts of Latin America.

There were extreme measures taken. Many people went to jail because they had violated human rights, which was also a mistake. The armed forces went out to combat terrorism under the rule of law. We were in an emergency situation, which was what the Constitution mandates as a prerequisite for armed forces to be able to intervene. In reality, it was a problem for the police. The armed forces went out to combat [the Shining Path] because of a democratic decision. We are not in a tyranny or dictatorship.

Today, there are between twelve and fourteen hundred military [personnel] being processed by the justice sector. And with the theory of collective responsibility, we have a whole army infantry being processed as well. Because one army official killed a citizen, now even the cook is being processed as well! That is an extreme. It is true that this has also helped build more institutions in the country today.

IN WHICH WAY?

The country has strong institutions. Unfortunately, the armed forces are one of the less able institutions we have in the country, but the armed forces have been strengthened over the years, and the level of trust people have in them is increasing. And they are part of Peruvians. The soldiers [who fought the Shining Path] came from the people's strength; in many regions that were at the heart of terrorist activity, it was the people who asked for them to stay. They said they would even feed the soldiers themselves if they had to.

In such a diverse country like ours, where its geography is so difficult and complex, sometimes the only way to secure the state's presence is through the armed forces. Peasants would consult with the armed forces about their everyday problems, because there were no other state officials around.

I think Peruvians have begun to better appreciate democracy and to want more democracy. Today, we have a country that does not think in terms of the Left or the Right. It is a country that wants someone to solve their problems. Its problems are education, health, housing, and so on. They don't care about the rest. Right now, Peru is asking for what is just. To ask the private sector to pay income taxes is not to be a communist.

Peruvian society has matured. The people don't let anybody fool them anymore; they know how to evaluate what is just. That is why I think that the population has matured and we have to continue to build our institutions. Peru must go on independently from the government.

WHAT DOES THE "RULE OF LAW" MEAN TO YOU?

The rule of law is a nation of citizens. When the country has matured, then it demands from its elected institutions and the people running them that they enforce the law, fulfill their duties, and respect the rights of citizens. That is fundamental. A place where my rights are respected but where I also have obligations.

Before, many Peruvians wanted to leave. Today, more than 95 percent are proud of being Peruvian because we have built the country ourselves. After we [rescued the hostages and killed the terrorists at] the Japanese ambassador's residence [in Lima in 1997], many Peruvians thought that the operation was conducted by foreign commandos. It was Peruvians who did that! They would not believe that Peruvians could do such a thing. Imagine the level of our self-esteem. Even the media, they all said we looked foreign when in fact we were all Peruvians running that operation. Peru is a millennium country. If you go to Ankas, you will find a culture that is more than five thousand years old. Even our food and cuisine that are blossoming now are extremely old, like the *tiradito*, which is a pre-Incan food. It is only now that people are beginning to feel proud of what they have.

We need more education, a better quality of education. Education is the one vehicle that can lead someone to development. The only thing that can get you out of the blindness and teach you what democracy is all about is education.

WHAT DO YOU THINK IS THE ROLE OF THE ARMED FORCES AND INTELLIGENCE SERVICES WITHIN THE RULE OF LAW?

The armed forces have their role under the Constitution: they have to protect the independence, sovereignty, and territorial integrity of the country. The intelligence supports the role of the armed forces under the Constitution. They should not get involved in the internal part of affairs. The armed forces are subordinate to the civil authorities and respond directly to the president of the country. The armed forces should not intervene in political affairs or even offer their opinions or even applaud acts of government. The armed forces should remain completely neutral. **>>**

F. Javier "Suicida" Rendero Ortiz (Nicaragua)

"The war, any war, is not a thing of good angels."

We interviewed Javier, a former Contra commander, at his house in San Rafael del Norte, in the highlands of Nicaragua. The roof was made of metal, the floor was cracked, and the walls were painted a drab mustard color. He showed us several family photographs on the wall, including one of him as a baby, one of a woman in an elegant wedding dress, and one of his father surrounded by books and looking like a well-groomed intellectual. Five diplomas also hung on the wall. Javier was very reserved.

<< I am forty years old. I'm a cabinetmaker, the trade my dad always had.

I joined the Nicaraguan Resistance [the Contras] when I was thirteen. And I was in for six years. They call me "Suicida" because I was a child when I joined the Resistance. I was based in Honduras, at a base that the gringos had. They trained us hard over there in Honduras. Yeah, and it's good because, look, good training is important. I became a commander.

I was wounded three times. When we were wounded we were taken to a clinic [in Honduras], an excellent hospital. And from there we left healed. If we wanted, we could come back to Nicaragua; it wasn't demanded.

Today, I ask God to give me strength and to let us live in peace in this country, because there are rumors, especially with the reelection of the president [the former Sandinista leader], which is illegal, of a commotion. Many ex-commanders have come here, and the first thing they tell me is, "Look, Suicida, be ready," [for] whatever. And that hurts because the war, any war, is not a thing of good angels, I tell you. A lot of suffering on both sides. Healthy brothers killing other Nicaraguans. And simply because a president thinks the way he does, or allows himself to be manipulated by other countries, like we were in that time, as the president let Cuba manipulate him.

In the night, I'd get up and my father would say to me, "What's wrong?" I'd tell him, "We heard shots, right?" A little crazy! Combat is horrible; you can't imagine. Sometimes we fought forty-eight hours without letting up. The peace treaties said they'd give us psychological help and three thousand dollars. They didn't. Look, I'm renting, I don't have anything. Nothing. **>>**

MOTHERS, WIVES, AND WIDOWS

By turns harrowing and inspiring, the interviews in this chapter testify to the persistence of horror and the resilience of hope. The women we interviewed are as varied in backgrounds and personalities as the countries from which they come. But they are united in their revulsion at the physical and the emotional carnage of war—at the opportunities war presents not just to kill and destroy but also to humiliate, terrorize, and traumatize. These women are also united by their determination to carry on, to remember but also to rebuild, and to build for their children a future that is better and brighter than the dark past they have endured.

Almost all the voices we hear in this chapter have lost a husband or a son—and in some cases both a husband and a son—to war. Some of these men and boys were ripped from their families and brutally murdered; others went willingly to fight and died fighting. Some, in other words, had some choice in the matter. None of the women they left behind had a choice. Circumstances far beyond their control dictated their destinies, and their destiny was to be a casualty of war, a victim. Not the kind of victim tossed in a mass grave, but a victim nonetheless.

But if fate decreed their shared victimhood, they decided for themselves that they would not be passive victims. Confronted by adversity, they responded with indomitability. Hounded by horrific memories, they chose remembrance. Their homes and families demolished by conflict, they elected to rebuild.

Those who are mothers explain that they have no choice. There are no options for them but to carry on. "If they see me sad," says one widow of her children, "they get sad, too. That's why I try to hide the sadness and to look strong and move forward with life." The determination to look ahead, and to see something better there, if not for themselves, then for their children, is wonderfully strong. It is also very pragmatic, with good schooling and good jobs at the top of the mothers' agendas. Alice Sackey lives in poverty in Liberia and worries constantly about finding enough money to buy food and medicine for her children, but she remains determined to somehow give them what she never had herself: education. "If I can get education for my children," she says, "I know that they will do something for themselves."

Um Ahmed's husband was killed in Baghdad by terrorists who turned out to be her neighbors. Then her house was set on fire. At first, she wondered how she would survive, how she would make a living. But she refused to be beaten or to focus on revenge. Instead, she has maintained her pride, getting by on a modest widow's salary and selling syrup that she presses herself from the dates she harvests from her small orchard.

The tragedies these women have suffered can be hidden but not erased. The memories won't go away, even when one wishes that they would. "Sometimes," admits Herminia Orea Aquilar, a Peruvian woman whose husband was tortured to death by soldiers and whose baby was horribly burned, "I just don't want to remember any of that anymore."

The pain may dull a little, but it does not disappear and can reappear with searing intensity. For some of the women we interviewed, ten or even twenty years had passed since the terrifying events they described to us. Some of those women said little, but their body language spoke volumes. It was as if time had stood still; the past was fully present. In the village of Junik in Kosovo, the women at times seemed embarrassed by the emotions that still overwhelmed them. As an interviewer, I found the experience intensely moving. As a mother, I found the women's stories almost unbearable. They blessed the photo of my young son that I showed them. They showed me the graves of their own sons, whose remains had only recently been unearthed from mass graves in Serbia and shipped back home.

If memories are a scar, that scar can at least be worn with pride, as a testament to the sacrifices made for the cause of political struggle or national liberation. But what happens when one's own people seem indifferent to one's suffering? The sense of abandonment is all too common. In Kosovo, for instance, most women had been wives and mothers before the war; the family income had been earned by husbands and sons. Those who were widowed in the war were thus left without a provider. And when, after the war, returning combatants and their families received government help, civilian widows received nothing.

Even moral support can be scarce. Shemsie Hoxha, who lost her husband and two sons in the fight to oust Serbian forces, recalls the day that the new country declared independence. "That particular day I expected people to come and visit me, to ask me how I was feeling, or maybe to wish good luck to my daughter. That day my daughter asked me, 'Mom, who are you waiting for?' And I said to her, 'Maybe today someone will knock on our door.' That day I felt very disappointed because no one came to see us."

The women in Peru and Kosovo were grateful that we had come to meet them and hear their stories (many of them previously untold). They need to be heard; they deserve to be acknowledged.

And they are hungry for meaning—for a sense of purpose that may or may not alleviate the pain of the past but that will make the present more bearable and the future more promising. Whether because they have to look after themselves or because they have chosen to look after themselves, the women we met have discovered or created this sense of purpose themselves. Some have found meaning through a community of women that supports one another and lets them realize their potential. Others have found it in their work outside the home and their vocations as journalists or lawyers. But many have a similar mission: to push for social justice and prevent injustice and violence in the future,

Rosa Villarán, a Peruvian whose rebel husband was killed by soldiers, explains that "the loss I had to deal with also made me understand the loss of those relatives who lost their family members fighting on the other side." So Rosa organized a get-together with the widows of policemen and soldiers. And they have continued to "engage in dialogue, solidarity, tears, silence, enjoyment." "In a way, we were all victims," notes Rosa. But "more than being a victim, you should be a citizen." ●

The Widows of Huanta *(Peru)*

"Sometimes, I just don't want to remember."

Huanta is a small town in the central highlands of Peru. Women in brightly colored traditional skirts sell all kinds of fruits and vegetables from market stalls. Palm trees dot the central plaza in front of the small cathedral. The Andes rise above the town. Despite its poverty, it is very picturesque. But in the conflict between the terrorists of the Shining Path and the troops of the Peruvian government, the people of Huanta suffered terribly.

We interviewed five women on the patio of a pink house in Huanta: Andrea Horagua Castillo, René (Andrea's daughter), Felicitas Jorge Agala, Asunta Anao Pacruz, and Herminia Orea Aquilar, (right to left in the above photo). As we talked, guinea pigs, which appear on local menus, ran across the concrete floor. The women were very reserved at first, their arms crossed, protective. Rene was shy and often averted her eyes. The older women were clearly still affected by the trauma they had endured; their pain seemed so fresh, as though everything had happened yesterday, not twenty years ago. Yet they were grateful that we had come all the way to Huanta to hear their stories.

For our part, we felt honored to be trusted with those stories, but awkward, even guilty, to hear them. As I explain in the introduction to this book, one of the women, Asunta, interrupted the interview at one point to express concern that I did not know enough of the local language to understand everything that was being said. I responded that I could understand in ways other than words. Asunta fixed me with her unflinching gaze and decided that I meant what I said. For the rest of the interview, we both felt a powerful bond between us. I still carry that sense of connection with me.

Felicitas Jorge Agala

<< In 1983, thirty-five military guys, marines, entered my home, took my documents, and beat me up. They put my two boys in a room, and then they continued beating me up. And then I was raped by six of them. Ten years later, in 1993, the Shining Path killed my husband. **>>**

Herminia Orea Aquilar

<< The marines came to Huanta in February 1983 [the marines were part of a government effort to combat the Shining Path, which was active in the region], and committed atrocities for two years. It was very dangerous and sad because you would see bodies in the parks and on the sidewalks. The marines would enter all the houses and take people out of their beds. They took my husband. Once, when they searched my house, they found medical instruments and anesthesia, and they thought that I performed operations there for the terrorists. So they took me away, together with so many neighbors.

After four days of being there, they let me go because one of my daughters was badly burned in a fire caused by a candle (we had to use candles during the electricity blackouts). I had three small daughters of three, five, and nine years old and a nine-month-old baby. My daughter was severely burned all over her body. Today, she still has scars on her face and arms. That is why they let me go, but they took my husband all the way to Ayacucho [the provincial capital]. A local person helped me try to find my husband and gave money to one of the army officials, which is how we ended up locating my husband. He had been abused and was completely destroyed.

Sometimes I just don't want to remember any of that anymore.

Today, I am president of the Association of the Families of the Disappeared and Tortured from the Province of Huanta. There are six of us on the board of the association, which has four hundred members. We founded it four years ago. We have heard on the radio that when you are organized, you can do anything! That when you walk together you can do it. We support each other and fight for reparations for each family that suffered from atrocities [whether committed by the Shining Path or by government forces].

I hope we will get reparation for all the suffering our members have experienced after losing their loved ones. That loss has no price. But the dead will not come back to life, and those who have suffered abuses are incapacitated, disabled, uneducated. That is why we are after the government for reparations. We must receive something, not only for us but for our families.

The association has been great help, and we have been able to achieve a lot through a lot of sacrifice from all of us. When we submitted our papers [for reparations] to the prosecutor's office, that documentation helped us get health coverage that is different from the health insurance for the poor, which does not help at all. Eight of us are studying free of charge in some institutes and universities.

But we have no support coming from the state. There is no political will on the part of the government to help us. We have submitted claims against the perpetrators, and they have been investigated, but no judgments have come out of that yet. The cases are stuck with the prosecutor's office and nothing has happened yet. Two of our members have died waiting for justice. I could give you a copy of the documents we have submitted to the government, the Ministry of Justice, and Congress. They are testimonials, very sad and true testimonials of the people who suffered during those years.

The marines who killed all these people today are free. That is the reality. The marine commander, for example, is free today, and he has his own business in Venezuela, Costa Rica, and even in Lima. They did what they wanted, but we do not find justice because they keep being defended by the state. The state gives them lawyers, while a huge number of people who were victims cannot afford a lawyer. The association does not have a lawyer. I am its lawyer.

Sometimes, you just get tired of asking so often and getting nothing. And if the victims are not part of the association, we cannot help them at all.

HOW CAN YOU REACH OUT TO THOSE VICTIMS WHO ARE NOT PART OF THE ASSOCIATION?

We need the help of other countries. We have the labor, but we lack financial support. We need some so that the association can do many more productive programs.

I truly thank you for your presence here. Getting your story out gives you freedom. That's what we do here: when someone wants to share her story, we let her do it. The same thing happens when they report their cases to the authorities. At first they say, "I don't want to remember, I don't want to talk about it." But I try to help them tell their stories, and when they do, they feel relieved and say that much of the heaviness they had inside has gone. **>>**

Asunta Anao Pacruz

<< My husband was murdered by the Shining Path. I have four kids. After the killings, we were displaced. One is in Lima, and he has mental problems. Two kids live with me at the farm; they don't have professions. I cannot work much because of the physical pain caused by all the suffering I have endured. I have sent my papers to the prosecutor's office, but nothing has happened yet. I haven't received anything, not even psychological attention. **>>**

Andrea Horagua Castillo and her daughter, René

◀◀ ANDREA: In '83, they killed my mother. Then in '85 they went and beat up my father, and we were sent to the marines with my daughters, one aged eleven and the other two and a half. They took all our belongings, animals, everything.

Later, we went to Lima. And there we lost my daughter. She was eleven. Lima is big, and I would be told that it would be very difficult to find her. We found her there only three years ago. Today, she is thirty-six and lives with me.

RENE: I got lost when my mother took me to Lima. My brothers found me there three years ago.

I did not speak Spanish. Nobody could understand me and that is how all these years went by. I worked as a maid to survive and eat and have a place to sleep. Sometimes, I would have to sleep on the streets. Up until they found me. And now I am back here.

I have a daughter; she will be twenty years old soon. She is in Lima; she does not want to be here because she does not like the farm life. She works and studies in Lima. She wants to become an accountant, but I don't have the money to support her at college. In Lima, sometimes you just work for the food because things are very expensive, unlike here. I don't have the means to support her, so she will have to make her own money to pay for it. ▶▶

Sabitra Adhikari *(Nepal)*

"We survived by hiding under the bed."

With her husband, Sabitra runs a little tea stand in a small village in the green hills of central Nepal. She never went to school, married young, and has three children. When we interviewed her, we sat next to her on a wooden bench in the dimly lit shop. Her toddler kept peeking in through the door distracting her until she finally put him on her lap. She has a very high, soft voice, and she seemed to be a very gentle person. But when she began to describe being caught in the middle of an attack by Maoist rebels on the nearby police station, her entire body stiffened, her face turned red, and her voice began to shake. Clearly, the trauma still haunted her.

◄◄ Before the fighting started, when I was a teenager, we used to have fun without any kind of fear. I am the second daughter of my parents. They never used to send me out, because I was the younger one. I had to do the household chores. I was married at the age of seventeen. It was only after I was married and started to go out that I came to know about a lot of things, including politics.

When the Maoists started fighting the government [in 1996], we were very much afraid. We were scared even to go out, thinking of what would happen if the Maoists came. We were in fear of the Maoists and the army in those days.

I started running this tea shop ten years ago [in 1997], and it was during that time that the police post was attacked by the Maoists. My shop and the police post share a door. The police always used to eat in my shop. I was inside the police post when it was attacked. Fourteen policemen were killed.

I was shocked. I had lost my hope of survival. After the incident, we closed the door and stayed inside. The curfew was declared early in the morning at 4 o'clock, so we couldn't go out.

I stayed here even after such an incident because at that time I had my small son with me, and maybe I survived because of the blessings of God and my parents. We survived by hiding under the bed. We survived even after seven bullets went through our door and into our room. I survived because of good fate. My son survived.

WHAT DID THE VILLAGERS THINK OF THE MAOISTS?

Whenever there was any kind of dispute in the village, some people used to call the Maoists in [to adjudicate the disputes]. Everyone was scared of them. But nowadays, since the peace agreement [signed in 2006], we have started understanding who the Maoists are. I find them very good.

HOW DO YOU FEEL ABOUT THE CURRENT SITUATION?

I felt very relieved when the peace agreement was announced. I think things will get better. I don't like to go on the rallies [which the Maoists organize, and which often involve bussing locals into Nepal's capital city, Kathmandu]. I am always tense whenever anything happens. My husband never used to go out in the earlier days. Last time, though, he went to Kathmandu, and I started worrying as it started getting darker. On the third day of this month, Sunday, the Maoists collected people from various places and took them in a vehicle. Then I started wondering when he would come back. I like to go to places where they talk about security issues; otherwise, I don't like to go at all.

DO YOU KNOW ANYTHING ABOUT THE RULE OF LAW?

No. I am not literate, so I don't know. But I know that male and female should be treated equally. We should not discriminate between son and daughter. They should be treated equally, that's it.

IN RECENT YEARS, A LOT OF FOREIGNERS HAVE COME TO NEPAL. WHAT WOULD YOU LIKE THEM TO DO?

Provide drinking-water facilities in places where it is not available. Help the needy people and children and help those impoverished farmers by providing food, income-generating jobs for the marginalized people. I am quite hopeful.

WHAT DO YOU THINK WILL BE THE FUTURE OF YOUR CHILD?

I will provide education to my children as long as they want to study, even if I have to live on morsels or do without food. As long as I live, I will not let my children suffer because of poverty. After they are educated, I will help them find some good jobs so that they can survive on their own. **>>**

The Widows and Mothers of Junik *(Kosovo)*

We spent a day in the village of Junik, near Kosovo's mountainous border with Albania, talking to four women who had all been part of the same convoy fleeing Serbian forces. All had lost a son or a husband or both. We met them in the living room of a house that had been destroyed during the war but had since been rebuilt. We sat in the living room, sipping soft drinks and making polite conversation as the atmosphere grew heavier and heavier. We talked of my family, and I passed around a photograph of my son, which brought some smiles. One of the widows said, "Thank you for coming to hear us. Your visit lightens the pain in our heart."

The women decided that the interviews would be done separately, because they did not want to cry in front of each other. So we took each woman into one of the bedrooms and sat on the floor on top of a shredded wool rug. Each woman held photos of her loved ones. During one of the interviews, one widow said, "You have a son. I know you feel me. You can feel what I am going through." Her daughter wears a photo of her father and brother around her neck. Another widow said, "I won't cry. I told my children I won't cry." She gave me a big hug.

We had lunch together, and then we went with one of the widows to the graveyard where the remains of some of their loved ones were buried. It was a fairly recently made graveyard, because the remains were not returned from Serbia (where they had been transported so as to leave no evidence behind in Kosovo) until several years after the end of the conflict.

One of my colleagues, Teuta, was familiar with Junik before the war, because her aunt lived there. At the outset of the war, when Teuta was working for the international Kosovo Verification Mission, she had gone to Junik to warn everyone to leave before Serbian troops and paramilitary forces reached the village. She remembered speaking to the husband of one of the women we had just interviewed. It was only during that interview that Teuta discovered that he had been murdered.

Faze Miroci
"That's why I try to hide the sadness."

<< Before the war, I lived a very good life. My husband was employed in a textile factory here in Junik. I had three children, a daughter and two sons. When the war started, most of the inhabitants had left the village; only some elderly stayed. My husband, together with some other villagers, stayed here to take care of the elderly who could not leave the village. The day they took him, he was driving one of the tractors in the convoy of civilians who were forced to leave the village. Around fifty people were in that convoy.

The first man that the Serbs stopped was my husband. Then they took other men, too, tied their hands and lined them up in a field just across the road. My uncle's son and my sister's son were in the group that was told to step down from tractors. Then they took my son, too. When he saw his father, he stood up, and they took him. He went to his father in the field. My husband told the Serbs that our son was young, so why were they taking him. He was beaten by one of the paramilitary soldiers.

We were telling them that we would not go anywhere without our men. They wanted to shoot us, too, and forced us to move on. One of our cousin's sons was told to drive the tractor. He was only fourteen years old. We were stopped several times during our journey to Albania by the paramilitary forces and were forced to give them money and whatever valuables we had with us.

We crossed the border and went to Kukes [a town across the border that took in 450,000 refugees and became the first town ever to be nominated for a Nobel Peace Prize]. Three nights we slept in the fields. Then we went to Tirana [the Albanian capital] and were put up at a house, all fifty of us in one house. We stayed there for two months and then came back here to Junik. Our houses were all burned down.

Four years passed after the war. We were constantly going to Pristina and trying to find out what had happened to our family members. Some said they were still alive. Some prisoners were released at that time from Serbian prisons. I was the first one to go and meet them and ask whether they knew anything about the men from Meha [the village where the paramilitary had taken the men from the convoy]. We also went on hunger strike to protest that very little was being done to find information about missing persons.

After four years, the remains of my son were found. It was very difficult to hear the news. Two policemen and a person from the Red Cross came to my house to give me the message that my son's remains had been found, along with the remains of four other men from Junik. They asked me whether I wanted to bury the remains, and I said of course I did. I wouldn't find relief if I did not bury him. The remains of my husband were found six months later. Another cousin was found a year later.

Throughout this time, I was strong enough and didn't cry in front of my son and daughter. If they see me sad, they get very sad, too. That's why I try to hide the sadness and to look strong and move forward with life. I suppressed my emotions, but that's worse than expressing them. I was very strong until now. Now I take a lot of sedatives. Now, I cannot sleep at all.

WHAT MOTIVATED YOU DURING THOSE DIFFICULT TIMES?

Hope in God kept me alive, and also my family and my husband's family helped me a lot, supported me morally and made me stronger. Today, I want my son to finish his studies and my daughter to get married to a good person in a good family. My children are very nice, they love me a lot, they are very caring, very humane, just as their father used to be.

WHAT DO YOU UNDERSTAND BY THE TERM "RULE OF LAW"?

Law is good for everyone and should be respected and applied equally. But the rule of law is not functioning as it should. If you don't have money, no one helps you.

DID THE INTERNATIONAL COMMUNITY HELP YOU?

The international organizations have done a great job, but there has been injustice among ourselves. Aid coordinators did not distribute aid equally. I lost two family members, yet I received only a very small amount.

Things have changed a lot after the war. There is no solidarity among people as it was before. They all have jealousies against each other. For example, many people are unhappy because my son has been accepted at the university. My husband helped everyone as if he were helping his own children. We expected that after the end of the war, people would like each other more than before. But this didn't happen. **>>**

Shemsie Hoxha

"They took my husband and my two sons."

<< I grew up in Junik. I was married and I had three children. The war brought a tragedy to my family. It was April 27, 1999.

When the NATO bombing started, we were forced by Serbs to leave our village. The entire village was told to leave their houses and to go to Albania. Our convoy of tractors took a route that passed through a village called Meha. Serbian paramilitary forces stopped the convoy and told all men to step out of the vehicles and told the women to continue their journey. They took my husband and my two sons. My older son was eighteen, my younger son was sixteen years old. When they took my older son, he turned to me saying, "Help me." I couldn't do anything. I hugged my younger son and held him in my arms, telling the military that he was so young, just a child. But, they took him from my hands and beat me because I was refusing to hand them over. I was left in the tractor with my daughter only. She was eight years old at that time.

I refused to let my sons join the group of men that was set aside. I argued with the Serbs, and they took me with the group of men. My daughter screamed from the tractor, and they let me get back on the tractor.

Did you see what happened to the men?

No. They tied their hands and lined them up in a field just across the road and told us to continue our way to Albania.

For the next four years, we heard different rumors. But then it was confirmed that they were killed in that field. Their remains were found, four years after the war. I buried my husband and sons on June 18, 2005. No matter how difficult it was, when their remains were found and buried, I felt a sense of relaxation and spiritual relief, and the hope to find them alive one day was buried together with their bones, forever.

Since then, I have been living in a house in Junik with my daughter and my mother-in-law. I have been living with God's mercy. I received a modest social assistance until my daughter turned eighteen, and then the government stopped the assistance. I had no other support from the government or from the municipality or any other authorities. No one ever knocked on my door to come and ask me how I was doing, whether I needed anything or not.

NOBODY TOOK CARE OF THE WIDOWS?

Absolutely not. Nobody did anything for us, no one supported us, and I'm talking not only about economic support but also about moral support, which is very important. When Kosovo declared independence, that was a day we had all dreamed about. That particular day I expected people to come and visit me, to ask me how I was feeling, or maybe to wish good luck to my daughter. That day my daughter asked me, "Mom, who are you waiting for?"

And I said to her, "Maybe today someone will knock on our door." That day I felt very disappointed because no one came to see us.

WAS IT HARD FOR YOUR DAUGHTER GROWING UP?

I had problems with her. I took her to psychologists and to therapists. I have to thank her teacher who helped her a lot. Sometimes she came back from school crying, and maybe it was my fault because she had seen me crying so many times. But I really did everything to be a good parent, to give her hope and everything for her to be happy.

Today, my daughter is grown up. She is studying at the university, and I hope that she will be successful in life. I want her to live a good life and not to think of what happened to her father and her brothers. I have never stopped her from doing anything. I have given her complete freedom, to go out with friends and do whatever she thinks she should, so that she doesn't have time to think of the past. She often talks to me about it, cries, and we often visit the graves. The meaning of my life is my daughter. She means everything to me.

WHAT DOES "RULE OF LAW" MEAN TO YOU?

In Kosovo, rule of law has a long way to go, or it doesn't exist at all. **>>**

Faze Idrizi
"My heart is dark."

<< My husband, me, and our three sons aged fifteen, thirteen, and ten were in the convoy of tractors and vehicles that was traveling to the Albanian border. We were stopped by the Serbian military, who took the men and boys aside. My husband was among them. We never saw him again. It was a horrible feeling. I never thought that I could live without him.

When they took Isuf's son, I was terrified and thought that they were going to take my eldest son, too. And then I saw him with the group of other boys and the men who were told to step down from the tractors. I was so upset that I passed out. When I came round later, I discovered that the Serbs had changed their minds and told my son to get back on one of the tractors and drive it, because they were holding all the men who had been driving.

HOW DID YOU AND YOUR CHILDREN COPE AFTER THAT?

With many difficulties. Since we found the body of my husband, five years ago in September, it was so hard, it was so difficult, I couldn't stop my tears every day, and then my children were sad even more when they saw me crying. I cannot sleep, I cannot eat properly, I always think of him. Someone asked me, why are you still dressed in black. I told her I will never dress in other colors. My heart is dark. Until I join my husband, I will be thinking about him.

WHAT COULD THE INTERNATIONALS DO TO HELP YOUR FAMILY?

I would like them to help my sons find jobs. It is hard to find jobs, and no one cares about us. All three of them are grown up and need to work. I don't think about myself and my life. I live only for my children. **>>**

Hyre Miroci

"After all that we have witnessed, I wonder how we have survived."

<< Before the war, we lived a decent life. I had seven children: four daughters, three sons. My husband worked at a factory. Then the war started. Serbs expelled us from the village. We moved from one village to another, and then on April 27, in Meha, they stopped the convoy and told all the men to step out of the vehicles. My sister's husband, my uncle's son, my son, and my sister's son were among them. They were telling us that if you don't move on, we will kill you all.

When we came to another checkpoint, the Serbian police and military took the little money we had and collected whatever they could find on the convoy. They were heavily armed and were pointing their weapons toward us. The children were scared to death. We moved on to the Albanian border. When we got there, they took all our IDs and told us to cross.

After two months we came back. Our house was completely burned down and destroyed. We stayed at a neighbor's house that had survived intact. Then they built containers for us, and we stayed in those containers for two years. We were very sad. My husband suffered from heart problems as a result of the sadness for the loss of our son, who had just completed secondary school. Since the end of the war, I have been taking medicines, as I have problems with high blood pressure. All from sadness.

For four years we heard nothing about our son and the others who were taken. Some said they were still alive. Then, after four years, they identified the remains and brought them to us.

[When they took my son,] my eldest son had already left to walk to Albania, and the youngest one was visiting his uncles. I had no idea whether he was alive or not. I cried every day. He came to Tirana later on and found us there. He didn't know that Serbs had taken his brother. It was very difficult. After all that we have witnessed, I wonder how we have survived.

I try to be strong [for my children] and not to show my sadness and devastation, although it is very difficult to hide it. **>>**

Izeta Karanxha *(Kosovo)*

"We were no longer afraid to go out."

<< I was born in Bosnia and Herzegovina, but I moved here to Prizren [in Kosovo] when I was fifteen, in 1963.

During the war we stayed here in our house. We were seventeen people altogether in my house, including friends and sisters-in-law with their families. We were scared all the time during these days. We all slept in one room, stayed dressed all the time, because we never knew when the Serbian military would come to take us.

We were afraid that the military would come to our house. Boys were hiding all the time, and crossed the walls of neighbors' yards every time they heard the police coming. One day, the military came and took notes on who was in town and who had left the town. We hid the boys on the roof. The municipal building [town hall] was just across from our house, and the Serbian police were located there. They could see our yard from the windows of that building.

When the war ended, on the first day of liberation, we went to Gjakova to visit our family members who lived there. When we went there, we saw a ghost town. Houses were burned down, and lots of people were missing. This was a horrifying experience for us. One of our extended family members who was missing was later found dead.

How did you feel in the first months after the war?

We were thrilled the night that we heard that NATO troops would enter Prizren. We went outside in the streets and waited for hours for NATO to come. All the people were out, happy and excited that NATO would come to rescue us. When they finally came, the Serbs were leaving the town. We thought that this was the end of our suffering. Emotions were so high, happiness was so great, especially for those who had not lost any family members during the war.

In the first few months, people were running around to find any job to work and to restore their normal lives. International organizations came. People were trying to get employed in these organizations. Those who had left Kosovo gradually returned to their homes. We were happy because we were secure. We were no longer afraid to go out. NATO troops were everywhere. Both of my daughters found jobs.

Today, in our new state, we feel more secure, we feel much better. But here law doesn't function as it should. I have my own experiences to support this opinion. I have had a case in the courts for nine years now that hasn't been resolved. And this is because of corruption. The people I am bringing my case against have friends in the system who can stop my case from moving forward. Corruption is very widespread. We trust the law, but it is not functioning properly. **>>**

Doma Sherpa *(Nepal)*

"The poor cannot speak."

We met Doma in the Buddha Stupa area of Kathmandu, where she is a street vendor. She grew up in the mountains and still wears the traditional Sherpa dress. She is a jolly, chatty person, very positive about life. Our conversation paused every time a customer stopped at her stall; she would smile and ask us to wait a minute while she bargained. Her remarks were also punctuated by the bells of the Buddhist temples, which rang sporadically.

<< In the village [in northern Nepal] where I grew up, we did not have to study. In those days, daughters were not allowed to go to school. To earn money, I would work as a porter, carrying loads for twelve or thirteen days up to Namche Bazaar [the gateway to the high Himalayas].

When I was about sixteen, I came to Kathmandu. First, I stayed at others' houses by washing dishes for some eight or nine years, and then I got married. My husband was a police officer and is now retired.

During the Maoist conflict, everybody was afraid of everyone. My husband was posted to different parts of Nepal, and his life was often in danger. I missed him very much. What a dreadful situation! Always anxious! No hope for life at all. My older daughter went to school, but the school would often close. Now, since the peace agreement, we are feeling a little tranquility of mind. But I am not confident; there is no guarantee of peace.

WHAT DO YOU THINK ABOUT THE FOREIGN ORGANIZATIONS THAT ARE NOW IN NEPAL?

We are not directly involved with them, and I am not interested in politics. But I hear that they have been spending money on schools meant for poor children, here in Kathmandu and in remote places. In general, the children of the rich receive a good education at good schools while the poor do not. Those who are bold enough to speak out and are powerful have opportunities at school. The poor cannot speak and do not know where, when, and how to speak, so they are deprived of opportunities.

The Nepalese do not like to obey the rule of law. We often tend to violate it. If you give someone 100 rupees, he or she will be bought. **>>**

Babita *(Nepal)*

"It was hard to be the wife of a member of the army."

Babita, an office cleaner, was not only very shy but also very nervous about being interviewed. She was worried that her husband, who serves in the Nepal Army, might get into trouble because the Army was wary of publicity. Her eyes filled with tears when she spoke of her hardships.

<< I was married in 1996, when I was sixteen, and my husband joined the Nepal Army in 1997, three months after the birth of our daughter.

During the conflict, it was hard to be the wife of a member of the army. It was very difficult to stay in a rented room. The house owners used to say that bombs might be exploded at houses where army men were staying. They gave us an ultimatum to leave the house.

If we had gone to our home villages, they [the Maoist rebels] would certainly have killed us. My parents were abducted because their son-in-law was in the army. They were released after the ransom was paid: 50,000 rupees and some dishes and bowls.

My husband is in a musical band in the army, so he did not have to go to the battlefield. But I was always anxious over whether he would come back or not. And I often heard that soldiers' children were kidnapped from schools. Every day I used to worry that my children and husband might not come home.

When the peace agreement was signed I was quite excited. I thought that now there would be no more killing among Nepalese brothers and sisters. But after a few months I felt a mixture of happiness and dismay, because people were still killing and being killed.

Today, it is neither good nor bad. Many people are unemployed. Many have gone to foreign lands to make their livelihood. Political leaders and government ministers are all seeking power. Rule of law is very deplorable. For many, justice is not available. Whatever we ordinary persons say, it does not matter. **>>**

Um Ahmed (Iraq)

"I lived with pride when he was alive, and I want to keep doing so."

One might have expected Um Ahmed to describe an endless river of sadness, given how her life had changed since her husband was killed by the people who are still her neighbors. But she displayed remarkable strength and self-control and was focused on creating hope rather than pursuing revenge.

<< I live in the outskirts of Baghdad, in a house with three of my children. Only one is in school. My fourth child, my son, is fourteen but quit school after his father died.

My life has changed since the death of my husband. He was killed in 2004, along with my niece's brother-in-law. It was terrorism, and the terrorists themselves work with the government, in Baghdad Governorate. Those who killed him are my neighbors; they live opposite my house; I recognized them when I heard his killers talking about it on a TV program. They mentioned his full name and how much money they received—500,000 [Iraqi dinars] for each person they killed.

Later, they were asked, "Do you mean he was innocent?" and they said, "Yes, innocent." They were asked, "Then why did you kill him?" They answered, "We made a mistake, we were there to kill someone else and we mistook him for that person." He used to cover his face and wear the *shemagh* [traditional Arab headdress] when he went to visit the tribes to solve their problems. Sometimes he dressed like a city man and sometimes he wore the traditional village costume.

A year after his death, my house was set on fire. I lost everything. Even my shoes and socks. It happened when I was asleep on the roof of the house with my children. The asphalt of the roof, as it had no tiles, began to boil. I called the police, and they said that it was arson.

After he died, I asked myself, how would I make a living? But some of my friends visited me and prayed for God to grant me patience. I always pray to God and read the Qur'an. I see many people, some with problems, some who weep over their grief. But I lay my small rug in my orchard, and I read the Qur'an or some other books about Zainab al-Hawraa [the granddaughter of the Prophet Muhammad]. If the mother weeps all the time, this will affect her children. Actually, they would have lost their minds if I had not helped them to forget and told them to let God, not them, seek revenge.

So I tried to be strong and to accept that what has gone will never come back. I take Zainab as my role model. I don't want others to laugh at me or feel happy for my suffering and say, "Look at Um Ahmed, how broken she feels now. Her arrogance is gone." But I have never been arrogant or conceited. The closest people to me used to think that. One of them is my sister; she loves me but she used to tell my husband, "Your wife looks like Sajida" [Saddam Hussein's wife], and I tell her that she is mistaken. I have always been elegant. I used to wear a skirt and boots. But after the death of my husband, I put on the *abaya* [a long, black, robe-like dress].

He was the candle that lit my life, my husband, but now I have only his pictures. He was very ethical and decent. I can show you his pictures on my cell phone. I will never forget him.

After the death of my husband, I suffered a lot—hunger, oppression, and gossip—but I cared nothing for that. I do not want to ask for charity. I always say that I am doing well even when I am starving. I tell others that I am the one who gives to others. I lived with pride when he was alive, and I want to keep doing so.

With the help of the Women for Peace organization I started going out of the house. I started to act with no fear. I go to the Governorate [offices] with no fear, to the police station with no fear. I go to ask about compensation for my husband. The police officer in charge of the police station shows respect by standing up when I enter the police station. The police officer tells my stepbrother: "Um Ahmed is brave like a man, you should not be worried about her, and she is like my sister." However, I bring presents to the employees here. I always take presents with me; it is in my nature. We are a well-known family. My father is head of the tribe.

I have a small widow's salary. And I have a small orchard. When it is time to harvest the dates, I make date syrup with the help of my daughter-in-law and daughter. We squeeze the dates and then put the syrup in bottles. I do not sell it myself as I feel shy. I do that with the help of my cousin and her husband.

Do you think that law prevails in the country?

Where is the law? What did it help me with? There is absolutely no law, and if you want to hire a lawyer, you will need a lot of money. Where can a widow find such money? What has the law done for us? Did the law protect our men? Can the law protect our children now? When my son leaves the house, I die of worry.

My son told me this story; he said it happened in front of him. A car pulled up, two men stepped out and two remained in the car. They took one of the passengers, who was an old man, and he cried "What did I do?" But they shot him in the forehead and drove away. The National Guard was there and did nothing. No one moved or did anything to help the old man. Later it turned out that this old man was a translator who worked with the Americans.

What do you wish for the future?

I want to receive compensation so that I can complete [building] the house; my husband died before completing it. I also wish for good health and good reputation, which is the most important thing. I also wish for safety, stability, and prosperity for the Iraqi people. I want Iraq to be like other countries. **>>**

Nekibe Kelmendi *(Kosovo)*

"They gave their lives for today's freedom."

I had known Nekibe for a decade before she was interviewed. We had first met when I was in Kosovo working for the US Department of Justice and she was a lawyer and human rights activist. She was one of the signatories of the constitution of the independent state of Kosovo (a copy of which she proudly displayed in her home) and became its minister of justice. She had a richly deserved reputation for the strength and passion of her commitment to build a new Kosovo. Some internationals found her rigid and uncooperative, but she was not about to let foreigners who had not been part of the struggle for human rights in Kosovo dictate what Kosovans should do.

This interview was important to her, because she wanted her story to be heard in her own voice. She died in June 2011.

◄◄ I was born on May 11, 1944, in Peja, a city that is the "capital" of that region of Kosovo. My family never accepted and never adopted the communist ideology [of the post–World War II regime in Yugoslavia] and was a patriotic and nationalist family. This was why my uncle Ramiz Kolica was murdered, on December 13, 1945. They took him from his house and executed him. He was twenty-eight years old. From that time, our family was proclaimed an enemy of the state and was constantly persecuted until the liberation of Kosovo.

On March 24, 1999, NATO made the decision to stop the humanitarian catastrophe in Kosovo and attacked Serbian military targets in Serbia and Kosovo. That night, Serbian military, paramilitary, and the special federal police broke into our house and took my husband and my sons from their bedrooms. They hit my husband, Bajram, in both kidneys with their weapons, whereas I was forced to lie face down on the floor and put my hands behind my neck. They kept us for an hour or so in that way. They searched the entire house thoroughly, made a real mess, and started to sing nationalist songs. They told us, "You asked for NATO help, you will see now what you will get." Then they ordered us to stand up. My husband stood up and so did my sons, Kastriot and Kushtrim. Kastriot was thirty years old; Kushtrim was sixteen years old. When they stood up, I wanted to stand up as well, but I was ordered not to move. However, I stood up anyway.

They ordered them to move down the stairs and to leave the house. Bajram was hit by the butt of a rifle, and he fell down the stairs. I thought he either had had a heart attack or had died. Then two policemen, pointing their guns toward Bajram and toward my sons and me, talked to their superior. They said, "We are taking your son with us and your wife." Bajram said, "No, leave my wife here." They took our son and went downstairs.

Kushtrim was confused, frightened. On both sides there were policemen and military with their automatic guns pointed at us. I stood up and cried, "Don't take my son, he is a child, he is only sixteen. Please." But they took him.

They put them in vehicles and sent them to Hotel Herzegovina in Fushe Kosove [a town near Pristina]. Then they called the executioners.

According to an eyewitness. . . . Excuse me, please, this is very emotionally straining for me. . . . First, they ordered Kastriot to shoot his father; they gave him the gun. Kastriot said, "No, I cannot do that." Then they turned to Kushtrim: "Here is the gun, kill your father." He said, "No, I can't." Then they gave the gun to Bajram and told him to kill his sons. Bajram said he could not do that. Then they told him: "Now you'll see that we can do that."

They shot my older son, Kastriot, with one bullet in the heart. Then they shot my younger son, also with a shot in the heart. They both fell down in blood. Bajram then held his head with both hands and screamed with all the voice he had. As it is not easy to see his sons being killed. Then they asked him, "Why are you screaming"? And came closer and shot him with two bullets in the forehead [indicating exactly where he was shot]. Then they shot the three of them as much as they could.

I had no idea that they had been executed. The next morning, I was talking with my daughter Kosovare, who was married and lived in Peja at that time. I told her: "Kosovare, the Serbs took your brothers and your father. I don't know where they are. They took them from the house and I am afraid that they will take you, too. So, don't stay here." It was 7 a.m. She left the house and went to her uncle's in the village of Lutogllava.

I started to search for my family members in police stations, being almost sure that they had not been killed, but imprisoned. Wherever I went, whatever police station I visited, the police threw me out forcefully and told me: "Go ask UCK [the Kosovo rebels' force]. They will find them because they killed your family." But I told them, "No, they wouldn't kill my family, because my husband defended them in politically motivated trials."

Later on it turned out that the execution was ordered by [Serbian president] Milošević. When President Rugova went to The Hague to be a witness in Milošević's trial [for war crimes], the prosecutor asked him: "Mr. Rugova, when you were forcefully sent to Belgrade to meet Milošević, did Milošević know about Bajram Kelmendi's execution without a trial"? Rugova replied "Yes, he did." Apparently, they had talked about that.

After the execution of my family members, a brand-new life started. I became the head of the family, taking care of orphaned nephews and nieces. Kastriot's daughter was six and a half years old when her father was executed. Her name is Elena. She will be eighteen years old this autumn. Kastriot's son, Sokol, was only two years and three months old; now he is thirteen years old.

During the bombardments I was here in Pristina [the capital of Kosovo], hiding in a cellar for eighty-three days. I didn't dare go out until the police and military left. I was afraid that they would execute me. When I came back, I found the house had been plundered. Everything was stolen except for these pieces of furniture that you can see.

WHAT MOTIVATED YOU DURING THAT TIME, WHAT KEPT YOU ALIVE, AND WHAT MOTIVATES YOU TODAY IN SPITE OF ALL THESE HARDSHIPS THAT YOU ARE DESCRIBING?

I was motivated by the cause of my nation, to be liberated once and for all from Serbian occupation and colonization that had lasted some 150 years. I wanted to work for the good of my people. For all to live in peace, welfare, and freedom, and to use the fruits of democracy as other nations do. I wanted to use my professional experience to help rebuild the judicial system of Kosovo. I had never been involved in corruption, I had never made any distinction between people—Albanians, Serbs, Roma, or others. I was committed to provide justice to all. I fought all the time to have equality among people, and I continue to do so today.

UNTIL VERY RECENTLY YOU WERE MINISTER OF JUSTICE. TO WHAT EXTENT IS THERE RULE OF LAW IN KOSOVO TODAY?

The rule of law does not function properly yet. We must work hard to strengthen the rule of law, so that everyone and all institutions will be equal before the law.

In the beginning, when the UN mission came, they did not know which laws and regulations were in force, which areas were covered by which laws, and which laws were made by the Serbs and which by the people of Kosovo. I became, in a way, their trainer.

Overall, however, we were helped by UNMIK [the United Nations Interim Mission in Kosovo] and especially by the United States government in building institutions and strengthening democracy in Kosovo, in particular in the domain of the rule of law. But unfortunately the job is not finished. It is a process and continues to be a process, but I am confident that it will not be long until the rule of law will govern fully in Kosovo.

I am extremely happy that I have put my signature on two very important documents for the Republic of Kosovo: the Declaration of Independence and the original document of the Constitution of the Republic of Kosovo. I have joked that if the United States had fathers of its constitution, Kosovo has also mothers of its constitution, because females were involved in the drafting process.

* * *

I put these photos here [on the table] on the day I got back to my house after Serbian forces left Kosovo. This is the photo of Bajram, my husband, who was the most famous Albanian lawyer. This is Kastriot. He was my eldest son, and he continues to be my eldest son, because I do not accept that they are dead, because they left great deeds behind, they gave their lives for today's freedom. This is Kushtrim. He was then a student at secondary school.

I also have a watch. The Serbs broke the glass of the watch, and the hands of the watch have remained in this position. They show the time of my husband's and my sons' execution: 1:55 a.m. **>>**

Alice Sackey *(Liberia)*

"That's all I am fighting for, to educate my children."

Alice lives in a tiny ram-shackle house. We sat on her front steps to interview her, and she showed us photographs of her husband, who had died. To judge from her appearance and that of her daughter, infant grand-son, and son-in-law, her family is one of the poorest in Montserrado County in the northwest of conflict-ravaged Liberia. Alice seems to have given up hope for something better from life for herself. She has not, however, given up hope for a better life for her children.

◄◄ In 1997, I was living in Monrovia [the capital of Liberia] with my hus-band, who was working for a radio station. He and another man were work-ing on the radio tower—I mean the long antenna. The antenna broke, and both of them died. We had eight children, and I was pregnant when he died. I received his salary for two months, but in the third month the managers of the radio station cut it off.

I had to do something to support my children, so I went to learn tailor-ing. Then the Red Cross opened a nursing school. The people asked me, "Why are you going to do nursing?" I said, "I went for nursing because I have many children. And as a widow, if I learn it, I will be able to do first aid for my children." I studied first aid and midwifery. When I graduated, I came here to Careysburg for an internship in the clinic. I am still working in the clinic, as a volunteer.

It has been a struggle to bring my children up. Sometimes, I don't have any money. One of my sons got seriously sick. He was going to die. One of my friends gave me money. I went to the drugstore. I bought Dexorange [a medicine that treats anemia], an injection, and they treated my son. You see, I have gone through so many trials.

Many days I cried, and on the worst one, my mother just passed away, and she was by my side. She used to make business. You know old people are strong in business. So sometimes she could help me. Her children in the

United States of America would send money for her, and from this money she could sometimes give me fifty US dollars to help me buy food. But since the death of our mother, I have had no communication with my family members in the United States. Even though they promised that they would do some things, nothing has been done. I don't even hear from them.

Anywhere you go in Careysburg, people will tell you that Alice Sackey is a midwife. Even the police people, they know me. Sometimes, in the night, when they are passing in their cars [the police station is a block and half away from the house], the dogs bark and I get up and I look around, so that any person can come to me here for treatment. The police can drop them off and I am willing to treat them.

Sometimes, some of the pregnant women I help to deliver pay me four hundred Liberian dollars [about five US dollars]. Sometimes, if they develop other problems, I charge more—five hundred [Liberian] dollars or fifteen hundred dollars. They say it is too much, but I have to buy gloves and other things.

Many people in this town owe me, and if they hear me talking, they will say, "Yes, it is true." Some of them owe me fifteen hundred Liberian dollars. I can't sue them. But I have my children. I need food to work. I've got to wash clothes.

What does "rule of law" mean to you?

Good rule of law, oh, that is what we need. Yes, that is what we need because even though I have nothing as a poor person, armed robbers do not think whether one is poor or not. They will not know if you are poor or not as long as they see that I can put my pot outside and see it is boiling every day.

What do you want for your children and for yourself in the future?

Education. I want education for my children. I never went far in education myself. I can't read and I can't write—that is where my disadvantage is. I want to push my children. If I can get education for my children, I know that they will do something for themselves. That's all I am fighting for, to educate my children.

I do not have the money to send them all to school. When they do go to school, they come home and are hungry, and cannot study seriously. I try to lie down at night, but I can't sleep. I worry a lot. When day breaks and some of them come with money business from the school, I worry. For example, one was just telling me that one of her friends is sick, and the school asked everyone to bring fifty Liberian dollars. When she said this, I started thinking, because if I don't give it to her, she will worry, and when she worries, that's my worry.

But I tell God thank you for what he is doing for me. He is using me, to help deliver babies and in the nursing field. When people see the treatment I can give, and when others tell them, "This woman did not go far in school," they can be surprised. >>

Rosa Villarán *(Peru)*

"The first thing we had to do was to open up and trust."

We interviewed Rosa in a hotel conference room in downtown Lima. Despite all that had happened to her, she was very bright-eyed, outgoing, and talkative, and had the energy of someone twenty years' younger. Her passionate commitment to her work was unmistakable.

◄◄ I am a widowed mother of two children. I am twice a widow. This has marked my life. I have worked for many years as a journalist. In recent years, I have been working to promote communication for memory and remembrance. I am executive secretary of the Citizens Movement for Never Again [Movimiento ciudadano para que no se repita], which is a network of networks in Peru. It brings together around seven hundred institutions from all over the country.

I was affected by the conflict in Peru in a brutal way. My husband was assassinated in Ayacucho at the beginning of the conflict. I was twenty-two years old and was pregnant. He was twenty-six.

How do you process death? How do you deal with the desire of revenge that is so natural? What helped me the most was my baby daughter, because she was the triumph of life over death.

The loss I had to deal with also made me understand the loss of those relatives who lost their family members fighting on the other side. Many years later, when I had the opportunity to work in the [Citizens] Movement, I suggested the importance of understanding the pain and suffering of the widows who were on the other side—the widows of policemen, soldiers. We were divided by the conflict. But today, we should never be divided into two sides.

One of the things we were able to achieve was that the two sides got together in a very human and very simple way. We approached the widows and the disabled from the armed forces and the national police and shared our common condition of being abandoned by everyone. The first thing we had to do was to open up and trust. That is the first step—maybe the most difficult one. That step that will get you closer to the other's suffering, the opportunity to engage in dialogue, solidarity, tears, silence, enjoyment.

I remembered that once we were asked [by Peru's Truth Commission, which investigates atrocities committed during the conflict] to provide pictures of the victims. So I called my colleagues among the widows of police officers and soldiers and told them that we also wanted pictures of their relatives and husbands. In a way, we were all victims. There was a lot of resistance to providing the pictures of their husbands. They did not want their husbands appearing right next to the "terrorists." I told them, at the end of the day, they had all been killed! The moment when I presented my husband's picture led the other widows to release their husband's pictures.

Some months ago, I had the opportunity to meet with Mario Vargas Llosa [the Peruvian novelist and journalist who won the Nobel Prize in Literature in 2010], and he could not believe that it was possible to put the two different sides in the same room! We need to tell each other our common stories, to explain that we are victims of different conditions and backgrounds—but without victimizing ourselves, because that is the big risk. More than being a victim, you should be a citizen. That is one of the main challenges for societies in conflict or coming out of conflict.

When I was young, I would go out to the streets to fight for freedom. I was not the only one. I went to fight together with youth from Argentina, Chile, Paraguay, and Uruguay; I thought I had a moral duty to protest and fight. We did not think twice about whether to join the Left or not.

The problem arose when things got complicated and violence became an option. It is true that many of us got it wrong. We thought that using arms and guns was the right way to achieve social equality. Then we learned quite fast that that was not the right way. It is very important to acknowledge if you made mistakes and tell it like it is.

We all have the right to make mistakes. But we also have the obligation to rectify ourselves. Doing it publicly is difficult but gives you legitimacy to keep on walking. We should not lie or be silent. And we have to promote that.

WHAT DOES "RULE OF LAW" MEAN TO YOU?

To me, it means equality and no discrimination in public life. As simple as the breath we take. The perception we have in Peru is that the rule of law is a lie. There is rule of law for some but not for everyone. You have justice when you have money; if you have no money, then you have no justice.

Today, there are many Peruvians who are not registered and don't even have an identity card, which means that they don't exist as far as the state is concerned. The day that the state goes to every single part of the country to register everybody, then trust will begin to emerge again. And when other state agencies begin doing their part, they will also begin to have the trust of the rest of the citizens. When nothing gets delivered, then the rule of law is meaningless. The rule of law needs to be institutionalized, to become a reality with a face and be real.

The rule of law has to be built every single day to make it a reality. Each one of us has a role to play in doing this, whether as a teacher, a parent, a journalist.

WHAT CAN THE INTERNATIONAL COMMUNITY DO TO HELP?

The role of guardianship of international agreements [regarding, for example, human rights] is very important. The international community can also play a very important role in channeling our voices when our own country does not listen to us. The Internet has become very valuable as well, because it can connect us immediately and you can interact at many levels with different parts of the world. Today, we as individuals are also part of the international community.

International organizations that work in countries like mine should know that they must not only stay and invest in the capital of the country but also be neutral and work across party lines. Otherwise, they end up helping only the political parties or people in power. They need to expand the networks and opportunities for all.

WHAT KEEPS YOU GOING TODAY?

My family and doing the things that I like doing the most. I have made my choices in life, and I am happy about them. I like the idea of contributing to make things a little bit better than how I found them. **>>**

CHILDREN
AND YOUTH

Children can seem very vulnerable at the best of times. In times of war, they are exposed to terrors and horrors that seem certain to crush their spirits, destroy their hopes, and inspire only constant fear and a paralyzing sense of helplessness. The young people we spoke to, however, were anything but defeated. Unlike some of their elders, for whom the trauma of conflict was still inescapable, these young people were determined to build better lives, both for themselves and for their societies.

That determination is all the more remarkable given the devastating losses and disorienting experiences they suffered as children and teenagers in wartime. "Haseena" left behind her house, friends, and dog in Afghanistan when she fled with her family to Pakistan. In Pakistan, she longed "to live life like a regular . . . kid" but was always forced to hide her identity. Raúl Arotoma Oré was eleven when the Peruvian military showed up at his house and took his parents away for questioning. He never saw them again. "M.T." was a student in Baghdad when a close friend was gunned down on M.T.'s doorstep. Five other college friends were kidnapped while driving to classes; all of them were raped or killed. "We were haunted by fear," he says. Too scared to leave the house, "we became hysterical."

Yet our young interviewees also described how they quickly adapted to the dramatic and dangerous changes in their lives. At the age of eleven, Miloš Tomić, along with his two brothers, was sent by his parents to live in Serbia, away from the violence that was engulfing Kosovo. The boys looked after themselves for three years, "preparing food, washing our clothes, and everything." "I had a childhood," Miloš remembers, "until I was eleven."

Liridon Shurdhani lived on the other side of the ethnic divide in Kosovo from Milos, growing up as relations between Serbs and Albanians went from bad to worse. Serbian youngsters with whom he had once played basketball returned to town armed to the teeth and intent on intimidating the Albanian community. Rumors of mass graves circulated as Serbian militiamen cruised the streets. Although I was young," remembers Liridon, "I was all the time thinking, 'Oh, today we are still alive just because they want it.'" It was, he says with remarkable understatement, "difficult to live in that time, but I imagine that for our parents it was even more difficult," because they understood exactly what might happen.

Some of the young people we spoke with were too young to remember the conflict but have adopted the memories and legacies of their parents. One young woman from Nicaragua, Nohelia Mendiola, recounted the story of her mother, who had left her two toddlers at home while she went to forage for food in the streets. She was shot in the back and spent nine months in the hospital, leaving the two youngsters effectively abandoned.

Caught, metaphorically or literally, in the crossfire, a child's first instinct is, naturally enough, to survive. But the next impulse is perhaps more surprising: to make a better life and build a brighter future. Despair, it seems, is not something to which young people readily succumb. Even M.T. grew tired of cowering at home. "We had to face reality and get out; we did not care what would happen to us, even if they killed us.... This is the journey of life, and we have to continue it."

Gaj Bahadur Chaudhary, a soft-spoken Nepalese, went on his journey of life, fleeing from his village, where young boys like him were targeted by both sides in the war, to the capital city, where he was determined to get an education, even though he was only eleven and had to work to support himself. "Everybody should be educated," says Gaj, and recollects how he and his brothers "forced our parents to send our sisters to school." Many others we spoke with share this appetite for education—and they also share a disdain for classmates who don't seize the opportunity to learn.

For some, education is a path that can lead out of poverty; for others. It is an escape route from the kind of ignorance that fueled conflict; and for yet others, it is a way to a more just society. The experience of war has not dimmed youthful idealism. Raúl, who had seen all too much of conflict, is going to law school and working for an organization that helps the families of the disappeared to seek justice. Miloš, when he returned from university, formed a youth theater group that tries to bring the Serbian and Albanian communities closer together. Nohelia is determined to use the law degree for which she is studying to fight corruption. M.T. is a radio presenter who raises awareness of violence against women.

Youssef, who had grown up in Canada but had studied in Libya and participated in its revolution, felt that his generation had a special responsibility to keep the momentum of reform going. "The revolution was something that as Libyans we had to do to change our country," he said. "Now, it's the youth's turn to make sure we start building the first bricks of a new Libya. Maybe we won't live to enjoy it, but at least we'll know that we started up on the right track."

Liridon shared this readiness to embrace a long-term perspective and to see a key role for his generation and for future generations. "It will take time to fix this problem," he said. "The only solution would be to involve more people who are younger, have different experience, and are not so connected with [powerful] people or with political parties. . . . Maybe my generation, or even two or three generations from now. They might have more will to change things." ●

Liridon Shurdhani *(Kosovo)*

"Although I was young, I was all the time thinking, 'Oh, today we are alive just because they want it.'"

Sitting outside a café in Pristina, Liridon spoke confidently as he recalled growing up in Kosovo before, during, and after the war. He spoke in English, having recently returned from studying law in the United States.

◀◀ I am twenty-seven. I was born in Pristina, but I grew up in Gnjilane, which is fifteen miles from Pristina. My family still lives in Gnjilane.

My father used to have a transportation company, big trucks and small trucks that moved goods within Kosovo and the region. We also owned some big supermarkets in Gnjilane. Since 1982, the year I was born, it was difficult for Albanians [in Kosovo] to work in any kind of government institution, so most of them, like my father, decided to work in the private sector.

In the late 1980s, in my second year of primary school, the Albanian community or the Albanian leadership decided to organize a parallel education [Albanians in Kosovo took their children out of the official schools and organized private classrooms for them]. In my neighborhood, we didn't have a Serbian community, so the Albanian children stayed in the official school building but were taught different kinds of programs. In areas that did have a Serbian community, even if there were just two Serbian students, the entire school would be reserved for those two students, and the Albanian students, who might be two or three hundred, would go to private home schools.

University students were all the time chased by police and if they found any kind of document that said "University of Pristina" or something [else that showed that they were participating in the Albanian-organized boycott of the official schooling system], it was quite difficult. There were a lot of cases where they were beaten and tortured by police because they were not entitled to have their education in Albanian. So it was kind of like apartheid that was done for ten years by the Serbian administration, toward the Albanian community. After ten years, this generation decided that this is enough and we can never continue doing this. So they tried to be more self-organized and active, whether with demonstrations or more radical groups.

WHAT WERE YOUR EXPERIENCES DURING THE WAR?

When internationals speak about "the war," they mean just the time of the NATO bombing. In Kosovo, the war is considered to begin in 1982 or 1989, when Milošević took away Kosovo's autonomy and started doing the real discrimination, like when they fired all Albanian employees from public administration—the parliament, the schools, universities. The conflict started growing from that time, and it was 1995 when all this maybe reached its peak.

I was quite young at that time and I couldn't understand everything, but from the beginning I understood that, for instance, we are not allowed to go to school in a normal way, we have to use back roads, you shouldn't show that you're Albanian because you might be stopped by police or other kinds of forces. We were raised in that way. It was not a normal life to live. For instance, we could never think of going from Gnjilane or from Pristina to Prizren just to have fun in the city, because of the police patrols and military checkpoints that were everywhere all the time. If you were beaten by a policeman, it was maybe unusual, but it was normal. Our parents were saying all the time, "You have to be careful. Don't try to go in their streets."

During the NATO air strikes, I was in Gnjilane with my family. Everyone was asking in one way or another for NATO to start air strikes, but I don't think that people realized what that would lead to. When NATO decided to bomb military targets in Kosovo, then the Serbs started to be more active, like killings and mass killings, as revenge.

I was living in a neighborhood where it was 100 percent Albanian. The police were taking cars and trucks, saying, "We need your car for the military stuff, and we will give you [a document stating that] the government of Serbia is taking your car or your truck." But in reality we knew that it was stealing.

[Serbian militia] were driving through the streets, passing by in big minivans, masked, masked with guns. They were trying to show us, by their presence, "You see you are alive because of us. If we want to kill you, we will kill you now." Although I was young, I was all the time thinking, "Oh, today we are alive just because they want it." And all the time they were playing music, Serbian national music, on big surround-sound systems, and trying to show that they were the bosses. In the evenings, they would start drinking and start shooting in the air with AK-47s. We watched from a distance and knew that they were not trying to kill us directly, not now, but you knew that if they got drunk for an hour, then they will kill for sure.

In the last days of the NATO air strikes, a lot of people were saying that [the Serbs] were digging big holes, graves or something. It was very difficult to see those holes, but we were living in a big community where everyone was feeling the same, and everyone was saying, "This is for us," and that kind of stuff.

I think it was the last day [before the Serbs left the area] when they started massively looting the city. And in a village maybe five miles from Gnjilane, they were killing people, killing families. This was done by the official Serbian Army together with some village people who were helping them. It was difficult to live in that time, but I can imagine that for our parents and people who were more informed, it was even more difficult, because they were all the time thinking about their children and their families and their houses—that everything would be destroyed within just one day.

The members of the Serbian community who were living in Gnjilane were not so tough, not so aggressive. But there were some military volunteers who were doing a lot of bad things to their neighbors. They were older than us, but we were quite close with them, and we played basketball with them, before the NATO air strikes. After that, they were mobilized, they took guns, and then they came here in cars and were playing this loud music. They didn't kill anyone, but still their guns were loaded, and they were trying to intimidate us.

These were bad guys who were trying to show that they are strong. Now they cannot live in the same neighborhood because no one will talk to them. They don't feel safe because they think someone will come and find them.

[After the Serbian forces left], some members of the [local] Serbian community sold their houses and moved to Serbia or to a village next to Gnjilane, for security reasons. But today there is a lot of freedom of movement. You see a lot of different car license plates, including Serbian car plates, and you will see people even in Pristina speaking in Serbian, and so that's not a problem anymore.

Everyone was saying that after the declaration of Kosovo's independence it would be quite difficult for [the Serbs living in Kosovo], but it was completely the opposite. They move freely and now are taking the new documents [issued by the Kosovan government] and trying in one way or another to accept the system.

How has this progressed since the war?

In 2000, the international community started building a new country. I don't even know if the aim of UNMIK [the United Nations Interim Administration Mission in Kosovo] was to establish a new state of Kosovo, but it seems like the spirit of laws or regulations that were drafted in that time was to establish a new separate state from the previous ex-Yugoslav state. UNMIK did a lot of jobs well. It established new institutions, like the new Kosovo parliament. It organized the first democratic elections—and they were a model for the region because they were organized in a very good way. Then the local elections were held. When I voted for the first time, I never realized that I would have this kind of joy; I was very happy. People were very happy when they had a chance to vote for their representatives.

Then, things started improving more slowly. People were tired; they had thought that after having the international community here for several years that they would have better lives, they would live in better conditions, and they would have more money or find jobs. And then they realized that after nine years of the international community being here, you are not afraid that you will be killed during the night or during the day, but still you don't have what you need to feed your family, you don't have choices for your education.

The Kosovo government didn't want to change anything because they just wanted to be in power and stay in power. They didn't want to have more youth educated, for example. In Croatia, the government every year sent maybe two thousand young people abroad to study rule of law, good governance, European studies, and those kinds of things. But here in Kosovo, few students were sent abroad. Those who were sent were strongly connected with the political parties. Some didn't even know English and were not prepared for their studies abroad; they just had connections with internationals or with the political parties. Some of them didn't even return to Kosovo and contribute to the building of a new Kosovo.

WHAT DOES "RULE OF LAW" MEAN TO YOU?

Rule of law in Kosovo or rule of law in southeast Europe means something like a set of regulations that guarantees free elections and that grants people free access to courts, access to official documents, and access to decisions that the government and the local government take. Everyone has to feel safe when they want to approach the justice system in Kosovo.

WHAT DO YOU THINK IS THE BIGGEST THREAT TO RULE OF LAW?

I think many problems are related to political interference. There's a group of persons with high-ranking positions or connections to the government and the internationals—they have the power [to interfere with how the justice system operates].

The generation that is working in the courts today worked for twenty or twenty-five years in the Yugoslav regime. They have a mentality that is hard to change. This is the same throughout the system: wherever you go you see those kinds of people, and they are all connected.

[Another] serious threat to rule of law is the backlog of maybe ten thousand cases in the courts. People don't have access to those courts, especially not if they're suing for just a rent case or a small debt of, say, 5,000 euros. Judges or someone in that court would say, "You know this is nothing. Why you are coming here for just 5,000 euros?" It will take time to fix this problem. The only solution would be to involve more people who are younger, have different experience, and are not so connected with [powerful] people or with political parties.

LIKE YOUR GENERATION?

Yeah, maybe my generation, or even two or three generations from now. They might have more will to change things. **>>**

Gaj Bahadur Chaudhary *(Nepal)*

"They came to arrest me [when I was eleven], but I escaped."

Soft-spoken, intelligent, self-reliant, and interested in a career in graphic design, Gaj was interviewed in a lush garden at the back of a hotel—the kind of place, as Gaj made clear, where he would not normally be found. He comes from the Tharu indigenous group, many of whom are bonded laborers who had their land taken away generations ago. Many joined the Maoists during the civil war.

<< I was raised in the Kailali district of the Seti Zone, in the far west of Nepal. Now I am twenty-one years old. I grew up in a big family, with seven brothers and two sisters. Our Tharu community survives on agriculture. Because we have a big family, the land we farm is not enough for us. It is adequate for food but hard for clothing. Everybody must work.

Most of the people in our village work in the fields. They do not have any other opportunities. They are not educated, and they have difficulty getting other jobs. They need education to get out. My family is the most educated.

We brothers forced our parents to send our sisters to school. Everybody should be educated. Boys are not everything. Girls are also something. They also can do things—they may be more powerful than us if we give them priorities. Most people force girls to work at home. They do not want to send them to school or college.

HOW WAS YOUR VILLAGE OR COMMUNITY AFFECTED DURING THE MAOIST INSURGENCY?

It was greatly affected. The young like me and elder males either fled to Kathmandu or to India. The Maoists had told each of the houses that one person ought to join the revolution. The Maoists would come to us at night and ask for shelter. The army would come in the day and interrogate the villagers, asking why they had let the Maoists sleep in their homes. Thus, we were trapped by both warring parties.

It was very difficult to work in the farm fields. When the Maoists would detonate bombs, the army would open fire and batter us; they would blame us for the Maoists and arrest us. It was such a deplorable situation that only the children and the elderly could stay in the villages. Even a person wearing a white shirt might cause an incident [because Maoist activists wore white shirts at rallies]. The army used to arrest everyone who was wearing a white shirt in the village areas.

The security personnel who used to come during the day would not let us sleep during the day. They did not understand that it is usually too hot in the day to work. They would accuse us: "You work as Maoists overnight and you sleep by the day." Whenever the security personnel noticed us asleep during the day, they would take us away for questioning.

WAS ANYONE KILLED OR DISAPPEARED IN YOUR VILLAGE, AND IN YOUR FAMILY?

Yes, in my village, certainly—there were so many cases. But not in my family, because the younger ones had moved to Kathmandu. They came to arrest me [when I was eleven], but I escaped. I didn't go back for two years. I fled to Kathmandu. I was determined to get an education and find work. I knew the son of the headmaster of our village school, who was staying in Kathmandu. He was working as a manager at a hotel. I stayed in his home. I cooked his food, washed dishes, and studied until I passed the SLC [a tenth-grade-level exam]. After leaving his home, I worked at one restaurant and then another.

Whenever curfew was imposed [because of the civil war], we would stay at the restaurant whether guests came or not. Because of the emergency, the number of tourists coming to Nepal dropped. At any time, any kind of incident might happen. When peace was restored in Nepal, tourists flowed back into the country. Everyone was happy because it meant more jobs.

I have received many things from [the restaurant where I work]. I must thank it. I learned the computer, too. And I think the wage is satisfactory.

HOW DO YOU THINK THE PEACE PROCESS IS PROGRESSING?

People voted for the Maoists, hoping that they might do something. But [the Maoists] have been ousted from the government. Not even 50 percent of their goals have been fulfilled. I think that the conflict will start again, but from another angle, because the ethnic discrimination in the country could lead to an explosion. At any time, a civil war may erupt in the country.

WHAT DO YOU UNDERSTAND BY "RULE OF LAW"?

It means the rights of the citizens to survive and to have freedom to do everything without any restriction. But I am not feeling that in Nepal. [The people in power] make their own rules.

[If Nepal is to move ahead], the education sector should be improved. It takes years to get a qualification, and there are many delays. Students have to waste so much time, how can they contribute to the country? **>>**

Miloš Tomić *(Kosovo)*

"We grew up a lot in one year, in our heads, because we had to."

Although young, Miloš possessed a very gentle and wise spirit. He was reserved but also confident, and one could easily imagine him tossing that reserve to one side as he took the stage and entered the spotlight.

◀◀ I am twenty-one and am studying English language and literature here in Mitrovica [a municipality in northern Kosovo]. I am one of the founders of an NGO [nongovernmental organization] called Ghetto Theater Group.

I have lived in this area for my whole life, except for three years when I lived in Serbia. I went there in 1999, after the bombing [by NATO aircraft of Serbian military targets in Kosovo] ended. I finished primary school in Serbia; then I came back here to Kosovo.

Soon after the bombing ended, when I was eleven years old, I was riding in my father's truck [Miloš's father and mother are ethnic Serbs] on the road to Mitrovica, and we were stopped by three civilians who said that they were looking for any refugees who might be in the back of the truck. They started trying to intimidate my father. They said, "You Serbs took everything from us. You Serbs stole my truck, so give me your truck." Things like that. They were speaking in Albanian. My father was speaking with them a little bit in English, a little bit in Serbian, and a little bit in Albanian.

After that, my parents decided to move me and my two brothers to Serbia. They took us to Serbia and then they returned to Kosovo. They visited maybe once every two months. They would call us two times a day and say "I miss you." After one year, I told them that they should call us just one time a week, because we didn't want to speak to them so often. It was actually harder for them than for us. They thought that we were like babies, but we grew up a lot in one year, in our heads, because we had to. I was like, "I'm not little. I'm twelve years old and I'm not little."

We were living alone in our house, preparing food, washing our clothes, and everything.

After three years, when both my older brothers were at university, I came back to Kosovo. We didn't have electricity, and everything was quite scary for me. I was very confused and was wondering what I should do, so I started to go to high school. I felt that my life here was very empty. We don't have television, we don't have electricity, we don't have anything.

But then we decide—me and a couple of my friends—we decide to start a theater group. We chose the name Ghetto Theater Group because we were living in a ghetto, we were out of electricity, that was the most creative name that we could find in that moment. We don't want to change it; that's like our personal story.

We started to learn about theater, how to prepare shows, how to do rehearsals, what is the movement of a scene, everything. In the first six, seven months, we were just learning about theater skills and everything. Then we started to put on shows. We now have about twenty members, aged from sixteen to twenty-two.

We put on a lot of shows. Our only problem is our working conditions. We work a lot of times during the winter without lights and heating. But our motivation was there all the time. We are now in our sixth year.

WHAT TYPES OF SHOWS DO YOU DO?

Most we do for the kids, but also we are now preparing one serious show for the older audience. We did a show like *Beauty and the Beast*; it was adapted for the kids and also for the youth and older people—sometimes funny, romantic, and it has a story.

We have performed in many villages and towns, including Leprosavic [where the theater group was formed] and the village in Kosovo for the Serbs who are returning to Kosovo. We performed in Belgrade [the Serbian capital] in a theater festival and won a prize. We were also in Banja Luka [a Serb-dominated city in Bosnia].

HAVE YOU HAD ANY EXPERIENCE WITH THE INTERNATIONAL COMMUNITY?

I spend a great deal of time with them and have a great time. I have learned English with them.

Many of our performances have been funded in some way by the internationals, and the Serbian government has also helped sometimes. Just small things, like [money] for a van for costumes, dinner for the theater, some money for rehearsals.

WHAT WOULD BE YOUR MESSAGE TO THE INTERNATIONAL COMMUNITY?

They should pay attention to culture and art. They think that everything here is about politics. But what you need are cultural activities. What is politics to me? Politics means nothing to me. I was just eleven years old when the conflict started; I didn't see anything about the conflict. We don't want to talk just about the conflict. We can make the [Kosovan and Serbian] communities closer with cultural activities: sports, theater, and everything. You need to be tolerant.

I want to say to the international community that they need to pay attention to youth, because youth are very creative and youth can make something from nothing, like our theater group has done.

WHAT KEEPS YOU GOING?

What motivates me? This theater most of all, because my free time is always filled with something nice. We have twenty people who are actually trying to act, and we have a lot of their friends who just come to see what we are doing in our ghetto. So it's always interesting. My biggest goal is to create some kind of institution, a first theater for the youth who come after us. **>>**

Raúl Arotoma Oré *(Peru)*

"Sometimes It Is difficult to do this work, because every story I hear brings me back to my own experience."

Raúl is usually the one conducting interviews, not giving them, so he was a little shy and uncomfortable. We talked to him in a sitting room in a hotel in Ayacucho, away from the busy lobby.

<< I am from Ayacucho, from the southern province of Wankapi. I was born in 1979. When I was eleven years old, I lost my parents when they were disappeared. On April 19, 1991, the military took them away and detained them at the military base of Wankapi, and we never saw them again. That's how it happened.

I am the fourth of seven children. After my parents were disappeared, we had to grow up apart from each other. That has been one of the most negative consequences. Thanks to the support of many people, especially family members, we have tried to overcome this situation, but it has been very difficult. In my case, I had to move to Lima to live with an uncle in order to go to school. We have always tried to move forward in life. Thanks to the support of my older brothers, I went to the University of San Cristóbal, where I finished law school, and now I am doing a master's in criminal law.

DID YOU TRY TO FIND OUT WHAT HAPPENED TO YOUR PARENTS?

From the very beginning, we never stopped searching for them. We also identified the chief of the military base who was responsible for my parents' disappearance. We reported his name to the prosecutor, but the process got frozen, as he is still in the military and the state does not want to prosecute him. He has been promoted over the years as if nothing has happened. The Ministry of Defense never really wanted to subject him to the judicial authorities. First, it said that it was not its responsibility to subject officials to the judicial authorities. Second, it always denied the information on where he was.

Many people feel that impunity is the law, and they feel that there is no point in doing anything [about their disappeared relatives], that they will waste their time and money. They are also afraid of suffering reprisals against themselves and their families if they do report the perpetrators. Many people don't even dare report the perpetrators to the authorities. If they do, then the state does not provide the information to the officials and then we do not get any answers. We don't even know in whose hands our relatives died. This is a terrible problem.

YOU WORK FOR APRODE. WOULD YOU TELL US SOMETHING ABOUT APRODE?

We are a group of people who help promote and defend human rights. We help families and individuals get organized to protect their human rights. Because I am a lawyer, I am in charge of following up the prosecution of criminal cases. We have a social services network and a person who supports family members directly. We are very happy because we realize that now people have a place to go to for support. Before, when the conflict ended, people did not know where to go to seek justice.

APRODE took my family's case and has supported us. I got to know them when I was in law school. Then they took me on, first as a volunteer and later as an attorney at their Ayacucho office. There I met so many people in the same situation and got to hear their stories. We formed an association of family members who lost their relatives during the conflict to help them advocate their cases. Some of the cases, like mine, have made it to the Inter-American Commission of Human Rights.

I have been in a leadership position with this group, and it has been a wonderful experience: interacting with other family members who lost their relatives, sharing stories, and realizing that we were not stuck but were creating a community that understands that it has rights, including the right to know what happened to their relatives and that they are not alone.

Sometimes it is difficult to do this work, because every story I hear brings me back to my own experience. But this only strengthens my commitment to continue doing the type of work I do.

WHAT DOES "RULE OF LAW" MEAN TO YOU?

I would distinguish between what the rule of law is and what it should be. It should mean respect for the norms, fundamental rights, human rights, etcetera. However, the rule of law in Peru is still at an early stage. In a way, the rule of law is like a big lie. No? When people see that there are citizens who have huge economic power and are close to the political circles and that they can break the laws and commit crimes [with impunity], what type of rule of law are we talking about?

The political powers also prioritize security and leave aside other important values. For instance, since the '80s, the political powers have created or even maximized some problems. First, it was the fight against terrorism. Now, we are fighting against narcotrafficking. It is true that these have been serious problems, but when fighting against them, many liberties have been sacrificed, like freedom. There is also the opportunity for the armed forces to abuse innocent people and detain them because [the armed forces] have full powers. In other words, in the name of the fight against terrorism and narcotrafficking, we sacrifice many liberties and end up hurting lots of innocent people.

Sometimes in a year, there could be two or three attacks on military bases. And the media make it seem as if there were attacks every single day. Then, the Ministry of Defense begins blaming NGOs because they defend human rights. The political powers they don't want things [related to security] to work under the rule of law. And if there is no problem, they make problems up.

Policemen and the military are being taught about human rights, but they do not identify with the concept themselves, as if they did not have human rights themselves. People don't understand that a human being has dignity and must be shown a minimum standard of respect. Unfortunately, we have not been able to capture what human rights are and their importance within the rule of law and a democratic system of government.

WHAT ROLE HAS INTERNATIONAL COOPERATION PLAYED HERE?

I think it is very important what the international cooperation has done so far. The international community has invested in different ways in the state, in nongovernmental organizations, and in raising awareness among people on what it means to be a citizen. I think the international cooperation still has a very important role to play.

WHAT HELPED YOU GET THROUGH THE WAR?

I always dreamed about having a profession. I always wanted to study to have a career and never forgot about it. I always kept it in my mind from the very beginning, and I think I am getting there.

WHAT MOTIVATES YOU TODAY?

The family. I have two small kids and my wife. Also my siblings. We all supported one another. That motivates me a lot. Also, the people who suffered so much, like me; they are the ones I also try to help through my chosen profession and job. That motivates me a lot as well.

WHAT DO YOU WANT FOR THE FUTURE?

I would not like my children to be left without their parents. I hope to have a society with social justice so we do not have to go through the same circumstances again. **>>**

M.T. *(Iraq)*

"We broke the barrier of fear inside us long ago."

M.T.'s hands were shaking while he told us his story, and he couldn't control his silent tears. We spoke with him in the office of the director of a women's NGO in Baghdad, a location in which he felt secure and comfortable to recall his traumatic experiences. He was shy but friendly, and his fears and sadness were mingled with hope.

<< I graduated from high school in 2005–6, and was accepted at the Department of Business Administration, University of Mustansiriya, but I could not go to this school because of sectarianism. The college is located in Talbiya [a Shiite area of Baghdad], and I could not reach that area; it was the beginning stage of sectarianism and this is one of the areas forbidden to us [because we are Sunni].

So I left college and left the country. I went to Kuwait, where I have an aunt, and remained almost six months out of the country. I came back at the beginning of the next school year. I registered with the University of Baghdad, and I studied for about a month. Then, a group of students were kidnapped from the Ghazaliya area [in the west of Baghdad], and the fear of kidnapping haunted us.

[The violence in 2007–9] had a great impact not only on us but on most of the families that lived in such areas. We were haunted by fear; we could not go out or live a normal life. We were even deprived of work; we could not go to work.

I was a house painter, and we used to receive work orders but could not go to any other area. We were threatened with death if we left our area to work in another area. Our work had to be confined to a particular place, but there was no work in this area.

Frankly, the situation was devastating. We became hysterical, from staying at home morning until night, in addition to the fear of being killed or exposed to raids. We did not know what to do; no study and no work.

Sectarianism had already spread, as well as terrorist groups and militias; all of that was causing us to live in fear.

WERE ANY OF YOUR FRIENDS KIDNAPPED OR MURDERED?

A lot of my friends. I had a friend named Mohammed who was visiting me, and while he was knocking on the door he was killed on the spot and the car sped away. I found his body in front of my house. He was very close to me, as were a lot of young people who were killed.

As for the kidnapping that took place at the University of Baghdad, most of those kidnapped were my friends. They lived in the same area, including one of the girls, who was our neighbor. They did not kill her, but they harmed and raped her, after which she lived a very tragic life. She returned to her family, but it was better not to come back. Her family had to send her outside the country to be treated by a psychiatrist.

HOW DID THE ABDUCTION OF YOUR FRIENDS TAKE PLACE?

We were registered to travel from Ghazaliya to the university. It seems that they traced the vehicle. One day after school, when the vehicle was on its way to Ghazaliya, a group of cars overtook it and abducted the students. I was not with them. They took all the people in the car. Five young men and three young women were in the car. Only one of the young men returned to his family; the rest were killed. Some of the bodies were found, disfigured; they did not find the bodies of the others. The girls were raped and beaten.

[Eventually], we were thinking that we had to face reality and get out; we did not care what would happen to us, even if they killed us, because we could no longer tolerate the situation. We began to go out from our houses when everybody tried to stop us, telling us that this person or that person had been killed, but we did not listen to anyone, and we took the risk of going out once we felt that there was nothing more to lose.

This is the journey of life, and we have to continue it. I will not spend my life in sorrow and wait for change in the future; I must go out and continue my life, and continue my journey.

WHAT DOES THE TERM "RULE OF LAW" MEAN TO YOU?

I know nothing about it.

DOES THE LAW PREVAIL IN IRAQ?

No. The law is applied to the poor class of society, but not to the class that has links with the government or society—some people are not held accountable at all.

YOU ARE A RADIO PRESENTER. ARE YOU WORRIED FOR YOUR SAFETY?

I have heard a lot [about assassinations and arrests of journalists], but that has not created fear inside me.

WHY NOT?

Because we broke the barrier of fear inside us long ago; since we went through the events of sectarianism, we no longer have any fear.

There is a large demand for youth programs [on radio], especially because they discuss the suffering of the young people in Iraqi universities and the problems they face. They also deal with violence against women. Many women are subject to violence, so we try to address these issues through civil society organizations by conveying a message through our radio station.

For instance, there is the case of a woman who has three children, who wakes up in the morning to clean the house, cook, go to work, and return home. In spite of all that, when her husband returns home, the tragedy begins! He questions her and then beats her, and one time he hits her badly, resulting in two broken ribs and a broken hand. This is one of the cases that I encountered, but, thank God, [the husband] has been prosecuted for his actions.

How was he prosecuted?

The woman resorted to the law; there were witnesses, and many people supported her and the law ruled in her favor. A very diligent female lawyer helped her win the case, and her husband was held accountable.

What are the main causes of conflict in Iraq?

The cause of conflict is authority. Politicians quarrel over power, and the victim is the people. >>

Youssef (Libya)

"I saw them carrying him with blood dripping from his side,
and it was really shocking."

We interviewed Youssef in Tripoli, Libya. Yousef was born in Canada, but his father, a Libyan exile, took his family to live in the Middle East for several years before moving back to the West. While living in the Middle East, Yousef learned Arabic and began to explore his Libyan roots; he also began making friends and acquaintances with Libyans from powerful families within Qaddafi's regime. After graduating high school in Canada, he studied for a year in an Arab country and then decided to attend a university in Libya.

<< I decided to move back for a bunch of reasons. My mother was one: she really wanted me to marry a Libyan girl. And my family had a house there. And in high school I'd taken a tour all over Libya [organized by one of Qaddafi's sons for a large group of Canadian youngsters], and we were told about scholarships and opportunities, and we got pocket money and met high-ranking people from doctors to engineers.

When I first moved back to Libya, which was around 2007, it was really hard for us to get registered in the university. They didn't accept us in the beginning, because they had these suspicions: "OK, you lived abroad, what are you doing coming back, why didn't you just study abroad?" And I had to find reasons to get accepted, like "What, are you trying to kick me out of my own country?" But finally I got registered. It took me a lot of hard work to catch up, but thank God I passed that year and moved forward in university.

I graduated a month before the revolution [in 2011], but I still had to do my internship.

WHAT HAPPENED TO YOU DURING THE REVOLUTION?

I remember [a friend] in the last days before the revolution began telling me the people from the east were planning to come in [to Benghazi] to protest [against the Qaddafi regime] on the 15th [of February]. On the 15th in the morning, I went to the library and had a conversation with [friends], and they said that their mother was sleeping over today at the courthouse, her and the rest of the lawyers, to protest. So I thought the courthouse would be a good place to start.

So I headed there, and the first sign that I saw, in Birka [a neighborhood of the city], was a person with a scarf around his face, and there was this huge picture of Qaddafi on a poster. He just climbed on peoples' shoulders, and he tore the picture from top to bottom, ripping it down the middle. And the fear of just seeing that people are really willing to take it . . . people were like, "Yeah, let's go! Move around the neighborhood and start ripping down pictures of Qaddafi, and that will be a sign that we are willing to do something."

So I joined one team; we had a big number, eighty to ninety people. And we went to this other neighborhood and people started joining us from there, and there was a huge number in their group. Mostly people were in their twenties, young, youth; the old people were just looking, to be honest, but they were so supportive.

I think three or four hundred joined us, and it was so quick. They smashed the [surveillance] cameras in the streets. People wearing masks took out the cameras. In the beginning [the police] were a big help; they were telling us where to find the cameras. Once we got to Jamal Street, we were a large number. So our protest was moving from Birka to Jamal Street, and another protest was moving from a bridge that connects the rich neighborhoods to the courthouse.

I remember my friend calling; he told me: "Don't come from that bridge because they're literally shooting at us." And the first person got killed in the revolution and that's it. The people around us heard the news and were really excited to cross Jamal Street and go to the courthouse. When we crossed Jamal Street, we realized that the Special Forces were waiting for us with their armored cars and hot-water spraying. And because the street is very narrow, and you can't leave from either side, women were opening their buildings for us to just walk inside. We realized they supported this. When we left the buildings, we started hearing gunshots. That was a very scary moment.

On Jamal Street, some had already crossed the line to the courthouse. People were running through cars, and they finally reached the courthouse.

At the courthouse there were a bunch of lawyers. I still remember this moment. When I first got to the courthouse I saw a big number of people arriving. The first night, people decided that they are going to sleep around the courthouse. I went to sleep at my grandpa's house [nearby].

It was a Thursday. Really heavy machine guns were fired, and a lot of people passed away. At least seventy to eighty people were killed. One of them was hit by three shots from the antiaircraft gun that hacked him in half. So we realized, OK, now it's going to be happening.

WHAT WAS THE MOOD OF THE PROTESTORS?

They thought it was going to be like Tunisia and Egypt, where they are just going to walk around, protest, and close streets. I'm not saying that Egypt and Tunisia didn't have any kind of reaction, but not as strong as the reaction that we saw on the first day. Our neighbor was shot in the head by a sniper. There was a lot of blood, a lot of crying. And I remember walking to the mosque. It was right next to my grandpa's house. One of the people who lost his father that day was praying. He became hysterical, remembering seeing his father dead, so he started praying, again praying, again crying, again praying. People were really shocked. It was all over the news, saying that the protest has been taken to another level. People are getting shot. And there was the first video as well that was shown on the Internet.

And that night at around four or five in the morning, the Internet got shut down. Phones were shut down, and the government was taking a really strong reaction. They realized that it's going to be more intense because there is blood.

The next day was Friday, Friday prayers. We went to the courthouse. We prayed there. We took the people who passed away on the previous day, and were planning on marching all the way to the graveyard to bury them. So people were thinking, "What's going to happen when we walk in front of the Katiba [a large military compound in the middle of the city]?"

We went to the courthouse after the Friday speech. Someone gave a very beautiful speech. I was so motivated. After that speech, my friend's cousin came up to us and said, "We must do the strong reaction and show the world what Libya is really about." He studied most of his life abroad, he had a very good degree, and he was a very nice person; money was not an issue; he didn't live a miserable life. He was from a Jewish family that's considered one of the richest families in Benghazi. He had two beautiful daughters.

Right after the speech, he passed by one of those guard stations and took two big gas [cans] and put them in the back of his car. Then he came and told us to watch over his daughters and left to go to the Katiba. We didn't know what he was doing; he didn't tell us he had stuff in his car. We would have talked him into other ways. Twenty minutes after that we heard there was a big explosion in front of the Katiba gate; eight or nine people who were [guarding] the main gate were killed. Then I realized that it was the person who had just been next to us. So that was a sign that people were willing to take it to the extreme.

After that, we walked with the people, marching to the graveyard, and we had to march past the Katiba; it was a long walk. When we arrived in front of the Katiba, we stopped there. Some people were attempting to attack the Katiba with just sticks. We stopped there, and they started shooting at us.

I was there, my brother was there, my cousin Apia, who had been tortured back in 2001, was there. And I remember when we were walking he said, "Listen, you guys have nothing against the government, you guys were living abroad, your socioeconomic [status] is nice; don't do anything stupid," because they were so against the regime. "Whatever we do, don't do."

When the protest started, we hear, "Get down!" because there was shooting in front of the Katiba. Then I see my cousin Apia, saying, "Oh, so this is what you do! This is all you can do, even though we're not armed!" And they shot him in his kidney. I didn't see him because I was too scared just crouching down. And then I saw them carrying him with blood dripping from his side, and it was really shocking. I had to leave with him. I got in the car that they were carrying him in. They put him in the car and left with him. He was bleeding. He had just got married, and his wife was pregnant.

On the way, I told him, "Apia, you will do fine. Don't worry about it, it's just one bullet." He said, "Oh, it was worse when they were torturing me, I've been through worse." And he was telling me, "It's better for you to be with them, and leave me here in the car. I'll be fine because I know how crazy the other side is and you are the brains, so tell them to calm down and not to move forward. We will get guns, I know where to get guns." And we were having this conversation while he was bleeding and he was telling me, "Whatever happens, I want my daughter to be named Maha, after your sister." My sister who had passed away because of a car accident. He fainted as we got to the hospital because of the large amount of blood that he lost. They took him into the hospital and took care of him. I stayed in the hospital.

Apia had a twin brother called Abdul. We were waiting there, and I told the males in the family what happened to Apia. They were wondering, "What do we do? This is getting really intense."

And then on the 17th came shocking news. My sister, she was working in the emergency hospital, called me. She said, "I think Abdul is in the hospital dead." I thought maybe they killed him in front of the police station, as the protestors were walking toward the graveyard. They killed thirty-two people in front of the police station. They shot him with two bullets, one hit him next to the eye. I had to tell the bad news to the males in the family. Apia is still alive; he's in Greece right now getting treatment.

The Katiba finally fell, and the bad people, like Qaddafi's son, fled. Then one day we heard news about Special Forces tanks moving toward the courthouse, so it was good news because [it meant that] the Special Forces had joined the revolutionaries.

[In late February, my brother and I went with my mother on a ship to Malta. She needed treatment for a medical emergency.] When we were in Malta, my brother and I decided that we were going back. My dad was against it, my mother was against it, but we felt like it's time for us to help out with whatever we can. We are not good with weapons. We never joined the military, so we figured at least we can help out in the ICRC [International Committee of the Red Cross]. So we landed in Egypt and went in a private car to a city at the border between Egypt and Libya. Egyptian cars weren't allowed to enter Libya, so we had to do some walking to cross the border. So we walked, took a car back to [Benghazi], and started helping out a lot at the ICRC.

WHAT ARE YOUR HOPES FOR THE FUTURE?

My hope is to have a country that can stand proud in the world with its citizens having their rights to live freely and to respect each other. My dream is to wake up to a national dialogue that involves all Libyans—liberal and Islamist, East, West, and South—who sit down and leave their hatred of each other behind and put Libya in front of their eyes.

The revolution was something that as Libyans we had to do to change our country. Now, it's the youth's turn to make sure we start building the first bricks of a new Libya. Maybe we won't live to enjoy it, but at least we'll know that we started up on the right track.

People say to me, "What are you doing here, Youssef? How can you still live here? You've got a Canadian passport, an opportunity to leave the country any time you want." But Libya, with all its bad days and good days, will always be on the top of the world. **>>**

"Haseena" *(Afghanistan)*

"That was painful, not being able to live life like a regular Pakistani kid."

Haseena is from Afghanistan and spent much of her childhood as a refugee in Pakistan, but we interviewed her when she was in the United States, living in California.

◀◀ We left Afghanistan when I was really young to escape the war. I wasn't able to go to college right after finishing high school because I was living in Pakistan as a refugee. I didn't have the opportunities to pursue higher education. I had to help my family financially, because my parents didn't have jobs. I had to work and earn a living for myself and them. So that's why I decided to work for nonprofit organizations that were helping Afghan refugees in Pakistan. At the end of 2003, after the fall of the Taliban, my family decided to go back to Afghanistan.

WHEN DID YOU MOVE TO PAKISTAN?

In the early nineties, when the war started in Afghanistan. As a female, I was not allowed to go to school, and that was when my parents decided to leave Afghanistan. The war was going on, and my parents weren't able to work, because my dad was an employee of the government, a civil servant, and my mom was a teacher. For them, it was really important to have me go to school, so they decided to go to Pakistan.

It was really tragic for us, leaving our own home and country and going to a place where we did not know if we would be able to return home. When we moved to Pakistan, we had only a few pieces of essential clothing, and a little money that my parents had saved. We didn't have anything else; we left *everything* behind.

My family moved to Pakistan illegally, like the rest of the Afghan families that had to escape the war. Only my dad was working, and he was paid under the table. We made a very minimal living.

We lived in Peshawar. We moved a lot because we were renting only one room for all of our family, which was five people: me, my two siblings, and my parents. As the family expanded, we had to move to get a two-bedroom place.

Life was really difficult in Peshawar because we didn't have legal status and we were not able to go to Pakistani schools, so we had to go to refugee schools.

We had a lot of Pakistani neighbors, and we were seeing them every morning, getting up and dressing in their uniforms, and having the school bus picking them and taking them to school. They could speak English to each other, since they were taught English in school. I wanted to do the same thing, be able to go to school like those exact same kids, wear a uniform, speak English, and all that, but I wasn't able to do that because of our status.

That was painful, not being able to live life like a regular Pakistani kid lived there. Always hiding, just sitting at home if not at school, so that nobody finds out who we are, hiding our identity. This was really difficult.

I remember one moment in Pakistan: when celebrating their independence day, our neighbors were playing, singing, being happy. And this was so painful; why can't I do that? Why can't I have my country's flag in front of my house and be proud of my country and have a home and hear my national anthem played on the TV?

Yes, life was pretty difficult, but sometimes when I'm thinking about the living situation of Afghans in Pakistan, I find myself really lucky. Because my parents, they really put pressure on themselves to keep me in school so that I can get a good education.

When we returned to Afghanistan, we found that our house was all burned, all our belongings were gone, all the memories that we had built back in Kabul—everything was ruined.

My dad went back to his job and started working in the ministry. And then we gradually started to have a normal life. But of course the wounds that the war gave us, they will never go away. The war memories always stay with us. There are times when I still have nightmares about it. I was very young when I left Afghanistan, but there are memories that I still carry.

When you're a kid, you have so many dreams. You are attached to your home. You are attached to your toys. You are attached to your friends. You are attached to the environment in which you were born. So, for me, it was really hard thinking that I'm going to leave all my belongings, my friends, my dog. You know, it was difficult for me to leave everything behind.

WHAT WERE YOUR FEELINGS ABOUT THE CONFLICT?

I hate it, I hate how the entire war started in Afghanistan. And how the different regimes ruined the lives of a lot of innocent people. They got killed, they got injured, they got paralyzed permanently. Kids lost their parents, parents lost their kids. It's just so sad. As a political science major, I have always focused on finding the answer to why the war started in Afghanistan, why our own people ruined our own people there. But I never found an answer.

WHAT DOES THE TERM "RULE OF LAW" MEAN TO YOU?

For me, rule of law means having law in my country and having a functioning legal and judicial system in the country. A functioning law, accepted by all, adhered to by all. But in a country like Afghanistan, you have law, but the law is not being applied there; the law is there in the constitution, but no one really cares. It's applied only to a very few, and by a very few. And so it's not functioning. **>>**

Nohelia Mendiola *(Nicaragua)*

"We need a complete revolution."

Nohelia is of Afro-Nicaraguan descent, which is unusual in the Nicaraguan highlands. We interviewed her in Jinotega, a city set in a vast green valley surrounded by mountains, which produces most of the country's coffee crop. She is a mother and a law student who pays for her studies by making and selling fresh tropical juices in the marketplace.

◄◄ I am young, twenty-one, and I didn't come from that [era of war], but I listen to the older people express themselves, and no one has a good memory of a war where the worst affected are the elderly and the children.

My mother, having been born in 1948, was already a woman with children when the war came. She lost her house in which she lived. She had to flee to keep my two brothers alive. She lost her father, too.

In 1984, before I was born and when my brothers were four and two years old, she had to leave them inside to go out to the street to look for food. She was walking in the street and they put two bullets in her back. So they had to take her to the hospital and for nine months she was in the hospital and couldn't get up from her bed; and my brothers remained, well, abandoned.

WHAT ARE YOUR PERCEPTIONS OF NICARAGUA'S REALITY?

All of us want the same thing. Ask the same question of anybody, and they will say, "In this country, there's too much corruption." The representatives [should] earn less, because they have so many privileges and only work three days. They give them a bodyguard and cellular phones, they give them, I don't know, how many gallons of gas that they don't even use. There are people who really need help, the poor people.

We need a complete revolution, changing everything from the top to the bottom, cutting it at its root. Getting rid of the representatives we have today. Getting rid of the magistrates we have today. They only talk and talk. And they play pranks: you ask them one thing and they respond to another. A reporter asked a representative, a *diputado*, who is president of the unions in Nicaragua, president of human rights in Nicaragua, and a medical doctor, "How do you manage to do four jobs?" Four salaries for the same person. He is keeping three others from working. And what did he respond? "I can't respond to that question." So.

DO YOUR UNIVERSITY FRIENDS FEEL THE SAME?

I have some friends that, if you will pardon the expression, they show up to screw around, sit in the back row, and start mocking the class to the professor. And always, if he is questioning them, they never know anything! They never read anything! And they are making fun of older people. If you talk with them, you could be talking [to water]. Out of ten students, I think only four [are there because they want to be], and the others are there because their mothers and fathers send them.

WHAT ABOUT THOSE WHO WANT TO BE THERE, WHO WANT TO HELP SOCIETY? WHAT MOTIVATES THEM TO KEEP GOING?

The same necessity to live better. Me, at least, I want to have a good job. I don't want to continue working in the market. If I study, it is for something, not to keep working in the market. And if things are better for me, they'll go better for my son—he'll go to school.

And I want to hear people say, "Look, remember that girl who sold in the market? Look, now she is a lawyer and has a good job."

I want to become a public defender, because it helps people and you don't have to charge them anything. But it is difficult, too, because they make you defend murderers and rapists, and people will always curse you and say, "How can you defend that murderer, that thief, that rapist?" Sometimes, people only think of the good aspect [of the rule of law], not of its other face. **>>**

GOVERNMENT
OFFICIALS

Officials are often stereotyped as cold, corrupt, or callous, but there was nothing stereotypical about the officials we interviewed. If we had been expecting to meet with haughty or distant figures, isolated from the cares and lives of ordinary people, spouting the standard government line, icily professional, choosing their words carefully so as to say nothing controversial or surprising—then we would have been disappointed. Instead, we met people with distinctively different personalities and demeanors, each one a distinct—and often very colorful—individual. That's not to say, however, that we didn't discover many of the same personal qualities (such as dedication) and professional concerns (such as how to make government work better) among them.

Some of the officials with whom we spoke had recently left government service, but most still hold positions in the national or local power structure, and almost all of them were remarkably candid about the causes of war and the barriers to postconflict reforms, critical of both their governments and the international community, and committed to their work and the welfare of their fellow citizens. We heard certain common refrains on the causes of war and barriers to postconflict improvements, including failure of the government, weak institutions, and a lack of common focus and goals; power struggles; inequality; and divisions among people.

Their sense of commitment was unmistakable. U Sit Aye, an adviser to the president of Myanmar (Burma), was determined to see his country develop. He spoke of how during his time as a police officer, an inordinate amount of time was spent worrying about security. The country, he said, needed to spend time on development, but a country cannot have development and peace without security.

Mohan Karki of Nepal had sold his land, slept under a makeshift tent, and worked day and night in his role as elected chair of his village's development committee. "I carried out the functions of the so-called local government for two terms. But I [never] embezzled even a single penny, or was insincere, or deceived a person."

Jamila Ali Rajaa from Yemen was with the foreign ministry when a popular revolution spread across her country. When peaceful protestors were shot dead by the government, Jamila resigned from her government post and joined the civil society movement to try to effect change from the people's perspective. She explained that conflict was normal in Yemen, with people putting pressure on the government to take action. But, she added, killing protestors was not the Yemeni way; a line had been crossed.

When speaking of drivers of conflict and barriers to peace, failure of the government and a lack of good governance was a recurrent theme. Shrish Rana of Nepal, a former minister of information under the king of Nepal, said the war was a failure of the government and that the lack of a strong national focus allowed Nepal to be pulled apart by other interests, external and internal.

Ivan Escobár Fornos, a judge from Nicaragua, saw conflict as the result of each ruling group being for itself and leaving the people out. Mohan Karki said that those in charge at the central level governed in a feudal manner, and that the nation's leaders were "spoiled."

Another common target for scathing criticism was the international community. Shrish Rana accused foreign countries of "virtually dictating policies" in Nepal, driven by their own selfish national interests disguised as democratic and humanitarian impulses. Joko Moses Kuyon, a chief in Liberia, complained that the international community has no understanding of Liberia's indigenous culture and customs, and is stifling them in the name of human rights. A fellow Liberian, Chief Yarkpawolo Bucket, appealed to foreign NGOs to deliver on the promises they make and to make sure that the government doesn't steal the aid intended for the people.

A number of officials feared that violence would resume, because vicious cycles of political instability, economic and social inequalities, and corruption have been left unaddressed. Yet most of the people we spoke with saw some reason for hope, or at least a possible pathway to enduring peace. Some put their faith in the different sides learning to work together and to build consensus—a consensus that could be expressed in a constitution and in policies aimed at the welfare of the entire country. Some trusted that as their country strengthened its institutions, they would become guardians of justice, not victims of political infighting. Almost all saw the rule of law as an essential component—indeed, a guarantee—of a fair and peaceful society, and most defined rule of law in very similar terms: everyone equal in the eyes of the law, and no one above it. "My goal," said Nebojša Popović, a Serbian policeman in Kosovo, "is to apply the rule of law equally to everyone." ●

Mohan Bahadur Karki
(Nepal; former local government chairman)

"I was so dear and near to the people that I had no fear."

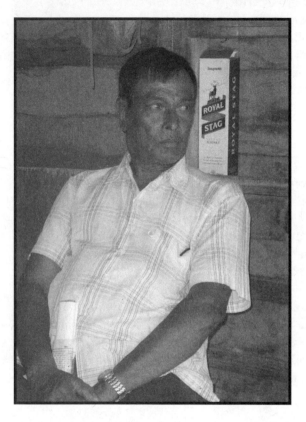

We spoke with Mohan Karki at a small roadside tea shop with an open sewer out front. A few older men sat outside, going through the daily newspaper. A woman was making tea inside and also tending a child of about three. Throughout the interview, other men in the room sat at wooden tables next to the interviewers and their translator, listening and nodding in agreement to the questions asked and answers given. As he chatted to us, Mohan held a rolled-up newspaper that he beat against his leg when he wasn't using it to swat at flies. (Sadly, Mohan has passed away since this interview was conducted.)

◀◀ I am seventy-one years old and come from Kavre. I have a son, two grandsons, a granddaughter, a wife, and a daughter-in-law.

My family is fed up with me in many ways. I have neither prosperity nor adversity. I belong to a middle-class family. I've had a hope since my childhood that the country might prosper and have peace. My hope has not yet been dreamed into reality.

YOU LIVED HERE DURING THE CONFLICT?

Yes. People were frightened—frightened and terrorized, first by the army and the police, then by the Maoists. Really, the country was terrorized.

One time, I don't remember the exact date and time, but the army used to come here and set up a checkpoint at the intersection. Buses were stopped, and passengers were checked one by one and had their pockets searched. It was about eight in the morning. Some soldiers were wandering into the jungle and some were at the checkpoint. They were scattered here and there. Just then, a vehicle came around and sounded its horn. Some students were standing nearby. Some small children were there, ready for school. Immediately after the vehicle sounded its horn, to our surprise, gunfire opened up. I looked to and fro, but there were no army men—they had fled the scene. Perhaps it was about five minutes of firing. I found bullet holes in the wall of my house. I was standing near the spot where this happened, but luckily I escaped. All my family members escaped harm.

There were about twenty-five soldiers and forty to forty-five Maoists. The [Maoist] combatants looked young, sparrow-like. Most were about seventeen to nineteen years old. They were fast enough to catch the soldiers, who had boots that kept them from running quickly. They were chasing the soldiers; but we did not see any die or be killed. Later, we heard that one of the soldiers was shot three times and died. An army helicopter collected the corpse of the soldier. When the gunfire stopped, we headed down to the village. That's all.

WERE YOU WORRIED FOR YOUR OWN SAFETY DURING THE CONFLICT?

I was then a representative of the people. I had been elected as a chair of the ninth ward's Village Development Committee [VDC] from the Nepali Congress Party in 1992. I performed very well. I helped the village to develop. I worked so hard for the interest of the people that I gave up my household work, and I sold my paddy-field to serve the people, but I could not accomplish my goals because of a shortage of capital for development.

I was so dear and near to the people that I had no fear. Neither the army nor the Maoists dared to kill me, nor did anyone come to ask me for a "donation" [a euphemism for extortion]. I would sleep fearlessly under a makeshift [shelter] a short way from the village. The incident that happened here occurred in the morning, but I stayed there that day and slept there at night.

I was self-reliant. I am still self-reliant. No one dares to harm me. I am not afraid of anything. I have the conviction that no one can blame me. I operated the VDC for ten years. It was a small government. Now it is called a local government. During the Panchayat system, the VDC chief was called *pradhanpancha*, but now it is just "VDC chairman." I carried out the functions of the so-called local government for two terms. But I deceived no one. If any person accuses me, or even makes a sound against me from any corner, that I embezzled even a single penny, or was insincere, or deceived a person during my terms, then I do not want to live even for five minutes. I would rather kill myself.

WHAT DO YOU THINK ABOUT THE CONFLICT NOW?

Looking back, we realized that the conflict was not adequate to root out feudalism, not enough to finish off the badness that obstructed the nation-building process. There are people who will never let the nation go forward. We still feel like they have dominance in all sectors. We hoped that the nation could be built in one turn or another. We felt that the nation would become prosperous and we would breathe in peace, but the nation is still as rigid as a statue since the conflict ended.

[Back when the peace agreement had just been signed], we felt that peace was necessary for Nepal to become an established country. People would become happy. Sounds of gunfire and bombs would be halted. Both armies would go back to their barracks. Even the Maoists would compete in elections, and peace would be restored no matter who won the election.

YOU WERE REALLY OPTIMISTIC?

Yes, I was; but now I am saddened. I expect the conflict to start again, at least one more time, because the remains of feudalism have not been rooted out completely yet.

We should chase feudalism out of the country through conflict, but a conflict without arms. Killing does not settle the problem. Better to have a kind of conflict that chases away rather than kills.

HOW IS THE SITUATION REGARDING THE RULE OF LAW IN THE COUNTRY?

In my opinion there is no law functioning at all.

Nepal has been considered a brave nation in history. So why are the Nepalese experiencing sorrows and adversity? What demon-like people cause these sorrows? I would appeal to friendly countries: "Please mend our spoiled leaders' bad habits so that this country may turn into a garden for all communities."

WHAT DO YOU WISH FOR THE FUTURE OF NEPAL?

I wish that all the Nepalese may be happy. That all may prosper. That all may receive an education. With no discrimination. That all may exist on an equal footing. **>>**

U Sit Aye *(Myanmar [Burma]; retired police colonel)*

"Whenever there Is peace, development follows."

We interviewed U Sit Aye in the lobby of the Kandawgyi Palace Hotel in Yangon. He was rather stiff and formal at the start, and although he had relaxed a little by the end, he never let his emotions color his answers. But his dignity and wisdom shone through during the entire interview.

<< I am a retired police colonel. I am sixty-seven years old and have forty-six years of police service. I have a bachelor's degree in law from Yangon University. At present, I am the senior legal adviser to the president. I'm responsible for giving legal advice to the president, as well as advice on the rule of law, legal reform, and police reform. It is a very good opportunity for me to share my experiences for the best interest of the country and the people.

How did the conflict affect you and your family?

I worked in an area in southern Shan State where insurgents came in and out; I was a township police commander for one year. After that, I was nominated as a township judge. It was a four-year term. This was in an armed conflict area, where insurgent groups took property, rice, money, and other things. So government troops were permanently stationed there. Peace and stability were very difficult to acquire during this time.

When I worked as the township police commander, I had to travel around the whole township. Some of the insurgent groups occupied the border[ing] areas. Whenever I had to accompany a party committee or town council as the security officer, I had to take police personnel for security, and the military officer went in advance. It was very hazardous, and my family was always anxious about what would happen. And children [of government officials] attending school could be kidnapped, so that kind of anxiety was always there, too. Finally, we sent our children to Yangon to stay with the grandparents and to attend school in Yangon.

HOW DID WORKING IN THAT ENVIRONMENT SHAPE YOUR VIEWS?

We had a technical arrangement with the leader of the insurgent groups. His people needed jobs, rehabilitation, and a resettlement program. We tried to facilitate this as much as possible. For instance, I made a survey of the water supply and small dams for the purpose of cultivation, water supply, and water sanitation. It was very difficult but a good opportunity for me, and I was quite happy to be able to benefit the populace. They created more arable land and produced more rice. So it was good. Whenever there is peace, development follows.

During my tour of duty in Namsan township, an incident occurred where some insurgent groups came into the market. One of the police sergeants recognized an insurgent. He tried to hold the man, who shot his pistol and then ran into the forest. It threatened the peace and tranquility of the general public in the market. In Shan State, every five days there is a market day. It is crowded, people come from all the villages and sell their products and purchase whatever they need for their home. It is a very peaceful and happy occasion. But with these insurgent incidents, the general public grew alarmed and complained. I didn't want this situation anymore. We were wasting a lot of time and money and energy, instead of making a development program.

So, I didn't want it anymore. It was nonsense. I thought that we should be working directly on village development, road construction, and other infrastructure development; the government should be joining hands with the community and the local people. Instead of always being threatened by this security [problem], we should be peaceful and they would be quite happy. Our township authorities are responsible for development programs. I went back there last year. I wanted to see how much development had taken place. We still need to do a lot of things, but a lot of infrastructure and buildings have been constructed, and community development is occurring. It is very good indeed.

The roads are more developed there now. Formerly, the military government thought that if the roads were good, the insurgents could come and go more easily. This became an obstacle to development. Without the development of roads, the community could not be developed. So now with new roads, the community is making a lot of development progress.

But we need to do more. We need to develop our whole country. We are lagging behind ASEAN [the Association of Southeast Asian Nations] and the Asia-Pacific region. We need to do a lot of things.

Previously, the international community could not access our country directly, so they relied on media reports. And all the media were negative. But seeing is believing. They need to come and deal directly with our people, to understand the feeling of the people, to know how much they have suffered for a long time, to know how different the situation today is from before.

You should come, investors should come, even though we still have some difficulties. We have new mechanisms. Our president wants everything to change and he's made a lot of reforms: economic reform, political reform, legal reform, rule of law—everything. If this fails, the senior leaders of the previous government will be held responsible, so there is still a kind of reluctance. But our president has forged ahead bravely with wholesale change. For the best interests of the people, he wants to change everything. So that's the reason that so much has changed within such a short period of time. **>>**

Jamila Ali Rajaa
(Yemen; former Foreign Ministry official)

"The price of war is borne by women."

When Yemenis socialize, they usually do so at home, and often in the mahfrag, a private room usually found on the top floor. On the day of her interview, Jamila was hosting an all-girl "qat chew" (a common daily event at which people get together to chew qat and socialize) in her mahfrag. We chatted before her guests arrived for the evening. There were biscuits, mini pizzas, and sweets from a local bakery on the table, together with sweet mint tea and soft drinks. Her daughter, who had just returned from studying overseas, was there, as was one of Jamila's friends, a local artist who had come by with some of her paintings. At the time of the interview, Jamila was an activist for women's issues, pushing for quotas for women in government positions.

<< HOW WOULD YOU DEFINE THE CONFLICT IN YEMEN TODAY?

Yemen is not in a war, a violent conflict, now after the revolution. Is it in a conflict of interest? Yes. A conflict between different religious backgrounds, ideologies, and theologies? Yes, we're there.

DURING THE 2011 CONFLICT, DID YOU EVER FEEL PERSONALLY THREATENED?

Oh, definitely. But we always felt like there was a line, a limit. It didn't affect us in the sense of killing or injuring our immediate family, but it affected our daily lives—attacks on electricity sources, the Internet, and such. It also affected most small businesses, and security and stability. It's not necessarily combat in terms of physical forces, but political conflict. That's the part of the conflict that affected me. I wouldn't drive alone. Not even men would drive alone. Yes, it's affecting us, definitely. You can see by the number of beggars on the street, whole families on the street. If you go out to Sanaa, you will see the signs.

WHAT IMPACT HAS THE CONFLICT HAD ON WOMEN?

Men make the decisions of the conflict and the women are not part of that decision. They suffer the conflict, but they can't take part in the decisions. A woman from Saada said, "We are the killed, the injured, the widows, the caretakers [of the injured]; we take on all the responsibility of the deaths, but we don't have the responsibility for our own fates." That summed it up for me. There's a high impact on women in conflict, but when there's political conflict, too, the effect is even greater. The price of war is borne by women; the trophies of war are given to the men, but not to the women.

YOU WERE WORKING FOR THE MINISTRY OF FOREIGN AFFAIRS, BUT YOU RESIGNED IN 2011 WHEN THE PROTESTS STARTED. WHY?

Dignity Friday—March 18. All the reports of youth being killed and photos started coming in. I felt there was a hole in my heart that would not be filled, that the only little thing I could do for the youth was to resign. There was a red line. Yemenis don't kill in cold blood. We kill each other in combat. You don't kill innocent people. Everything looked gray. The next day we went back to the square [where the protesters were killed]. We saw those who were injured. There was this grief and sadness in the square. It was the saddest point of the revolution, the killing. It made the youth resilient and the women as well. I was an adviser to the ministry at this time.

DID YOU EVER WORRY FOR YOUR PERSONAL SAFETY DURING 2011?

To be honest, no. I never knew that I was that strong. Many in my family were worried. My brother called from the States. He had seen me walking in the square on TV on Al Arabiya and said, "Are you crazy?" I said, "It's history." Everybody in the square felt that way. We were to some extent fearless. But everyone was fed up. Change, change, change. It was something that kept nagging at you. Something you can't suppress by looking the other way.

A revolution does not have to be in a way of action, it can be in a way of thinking.

When the separation of the south was announced in 1994 it was different. There were missiles falling in both directions. It was terrifying to both groups and it was not like the revolution. It was like a war. It was the power of a state against another state. People were trembling.

WHAT DOES THE TERM "RULE OF LAW" MEAN TO YOU?

You start with everyone being equal under the law. But the powerful people are above the law. When the electricity was cut, my house was dark. But nobody dared to cut it in the neighborhood of al-Ahmar [a powerful military leader]. That's the rule of law in Yemen.

If I go to court, it takes me years to get my rights. After the revolution, I wanted to test the courts. I had a few incidents—simple car accidents, a financial director embezzled money from me, and such—and I took them to court. I still haven't gotten my rights, even today. "What a failure," I said to myself. "This time I'm not going to pay the bribe." But that's rule of law in Yemen. What law is going to stop corruption? First comes good governance, then rule of law.

Yemenis want to see a beginning of hope. Until now, they haven't seen anything. People are getting worse and worse. That creates a lot of national frustration. It's affecting youth. It's killing the spirit of the whole nation. Give us hope.

WHAT DO YOU HOPE FOR IN THE FUTURE?

I have an optimistic nature. Maybe because we Yemenis have been through a lot, we're resilient. And we want a better future for ourselves and our children. What motivates me is that glance from the eyes of the ordinary people. The blessing of the simple people—that they hope you're doing the best for them [in the National Dialogue Conference, a ten-month gathering of political and tribal leaders and civil society representatives that sought to reach a consensus on reshaping the country's political system].

I'm a simple person, but I know that radical change is not the answer. The end of the National Dialogue should not be the end of the dialogue among Yemenis. Not working together stalls progress. We will not be safe until the old guard leaves. If those old guards leave, maybe we will be safe and have a fresh breath of progress. A change of faces. But if we have radical change, without discussion, we will have another period of war, like Syria, like Egypt, maybe like Libya.

Let's fight at the table; let's fight with our minds. But militias and Houthis [an armed political faction that controls parts of northern Yemen] are still fighting. Killing by the security forces and the armed forces is another major problem. Then you have the issue of al-Qaeda and sponsorship of Wahhabism and Salafism from neighboring countries. All this is creating layers and layers of politics in Yemen. But still I believe there is space for a national common ground. **>>**

Shrish Rana *(Nepal; former minister of information)*

"Western democracy has been used to erode our nationalism."

We met Shrish Rana at his home in Kathmandu, which sat within a walled, well-manicured, and peaceful garden. Initially, we were ushered into a waiting room outside his house, and then into his elegant home, adorned with portraits of relatives from the past. The interview was conducted in a large and very formal living room. He was soft-spoken, confident, and gracious throughout.

◀◀ I'm fifty-eight. I began work as a journalist and still consider myself to be one. Somehow I have ended up in politics. I was minister of information for King Gyanendra in his last months [in power—the king was stripped of his political powers in 2006, and the monarchy was abolished in 2008]. And right now I write about politics and development.

LOOKING BACK, WHAT DO YOU THINK ABOUT HOW THE CONFLICT DEVELOPED?

In the 1990s, there was an agitation for a multiparty system, and the new constitution was drafted. It was a very partisan approach to democracy, and it actually encouraged the extreme Left to take up arms. When the conflict took an upswing, the state did not react to it as a security problem properly.

And whatever happened after that was a partisan problem. If you look at it politically, the various actors pursued opportunistic partisan lines. They didn't contribute to solving the problem constitutionally, and the solution they have sought now has actually rid the country of any semblance of constitutionalism. Theory will tell you that a democracy we are not. We are a three-party country. The three hold a monopoly over politics and the constitution. And when they dumped the monarchy, they actually made sure the solution [to the constitutional impasse and political deadlock] would not come from that place. So any indigenous solution now appears lacking.

The conflict is still impacting everyone. In terms of daily life, you find that the price of the cost of living has probably doubled. In terms of security, I don't think that anybody feels secure. Things are not normal. They have not been normal since this partisan approach to policymaking was introduced in 1990 and since it expanded. I don't think anybody in Nepal feels normal. If they are saying that things are normal, they are lying. [Laughter.]

WHAT HAS BEEN YOUR EXPERIENCE WITH THE INTERNATIONAL COMMUNITY?

Well, I try to shy away from the international community because I find their presence here increasingly [problematic]. The international community has stepped in very conveniently; NGOs [nongovernmental organizations] and INGOs [international NGOs] formally and informally supporting one or another of the parties. And their say in politics has increased. And it has been at the expense of the nation. I know there is a lot of do-gooding, but we have been robbed of our policy choices, of deciding policy for ourselves, in a very surreptitious manner. What you see here is the international community virtually dictating policy. I think it should be Nepalese saying what they want to do, and then seeking international help where it is needed. That is what foreign policy is all about.

Nepal is a strategically located country, where international interests can compete. And if [Nepalese] institutions are lacking that can keep these competitive interests apart, it will be us, the people, who will suffer. Ultimately, this competition will expand to the region. Perhaps there will come a time when we will not be in a position to keep this competition out of the country. And I think this is slowly approaching.

When the West and other countries supported [in 2006] what we call the "peace movement" by overthrowing the monarchy, the actors they supported were competing themselves. And that has given ground for further competition from outside the country, too. The more the Chinese spend here, the more the Americans will have to spend, and so on. And that will contribute to more conflict. And it will be us—this population—that will suffer most.

Basically, I think this country must be able to decide for itself. So, how are we going to do it? That is the major problem now. The constitution is, at the moment, what the three parties say it is. We won't have a new constitution until the three parties agree what that constitution is. So what you are talking of is perpetuating the same disorder that contributed to the conflict in the very first place and weakened order. But the monarchy actually had the ability to resist this international intervention.

I don't blame other nations for having a national interest. I blame ourselves for not having one. It is for the state to assert its presence, but we have been disabled on that front. We have virtually been disabled in the name of democracy.

This is the oldest independent sovereign county in the region, and we are neither independent nor sovereign now, in real terms. Western democracy has been used to erode our nationalism. You have introduced a democratic system of competing political parties, which in the West must declare their assets, but in Nepal we refuse to even consider disclosing our economic transactions.

WHAT DOES "RULE OF LAW" MEAN TO YOU?

The rule of law means that nobody, including the politician, is above the law, including international norms. Everybody must abide by the law. And that includes international powers, which tend to be above the law at times. **>>**

Yarkpawolo Bucket (Liberia; town chief)

"When our children learn and are educated, war will not come back."

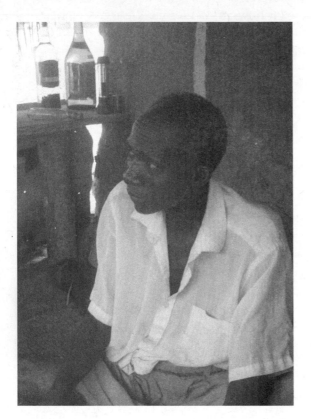

We interviewed Chief Yarkpawolo in a small village several hours' drive outside the city of Gbarnga, which is in the north of Liberia.

<< My name is Chief Yarkpawolo Bucket. The town is for me, I was born in this town, and this is where my generation came from; there is no embarrassment in this town.

How is security locally?

Since the cease-fire, there is no problem here. The place is calm in the night. People don't come here to give problems. But one thing we don't have here is a school building. Someone came and said that he was going to build a school. Since that time, he has not come back. They are in the process of fixing the bricks. So we are asking you to come and help, and other organizations to come and help us build the school.

What motivates you?

What really motivates us is that we want our children to learn and don't want war to come back to Liberia. Because when our children learn and are educated, war will not come back to Liberia. So what they want is a school to be built here and some facilities so their children can be educated.

WHY DID THE WAR COME TO LIBERIA?

I'm not educated. The devil is in the hand of the educated ones; that is why the war came. Because if people were educated, they should not allow war to come here.

NOW THAT THE WAR HAS COME AND GONE, WHAT IS YOUR HOPE?

My hope is for the government to help. This is a thatch house I'm sleeping under; the roaches from the latrine are in the drinking water; so I'm appealing to the government to bring down the price of zinc and cement so that we will be able to purchase them to build these houses. But when the international community gives the money, the big people put it in their pockets and do not use it for the intended purpose. So I'm appealing to you people that when you go you should tell [international donors and humanitarian organizations], so that they should make sure that the money will reach the little people down here.

JUSTICE IS NOT DONE, BECAUSE THE PEOPLE DON'T GET MONEY.

I'm appealing to the government to give the money to people who have feeling for us and know that we are suffering. That is the kind of people who should be in control of the money business for the people, so that they will be able to hand-deliver it. Even people who are working for the NGO, when [donors] give them the money to come and fix the hand pump, they will say that we are coming next week and will not come. **>>**

Joko Moses Kuyon
(Liberia; director of culture and native affairs)

"The first thing you need to learn is to respect us for who we are."

Joko Moses Kuyon is director of culture and native affairs for Bong County, and the vice chairman for men's affairs of the National Traditional Council of Liberia. He was eager to be interviewed and spoke passionately about the importance of African traditional religion and practices.

<< *WHAT DOES "RULE OF LAW" MEAN FOR YOU AND FOR YOUR PEOPLE?*

Traditionally, rule of law is very, very important to us. It's so important that we don't joke with it. We take an oath that has been implanted and embedded in our culture. When we swear to God, we mean what we say. We are not those who can just kiss the Bible and lie under oath. When our chiefs lay down the rule of law, we obey it. Although we are traditional people, we are also citizens of a country, and the rules that have been set by the elected government of that country we obey. So the rule of law means a lot to us.

IS THERE RULE OF LAW IN LIBERIA?

The justice system is doing the best it can. It is not where we were expecting it, because in the villages there are no police stations, no courts. But through us, the traditional people, not the government, rule of law still maintains peace and security. The government, in its own weak way, is helping nationwide, but it can go only so far. We are enjoying the peace through the help of the international community and of the government. Security is not too bad, but the night-time boys—the boys who move at night like rogues and armed robbers—they are giving us problems, and the government has not been able

to fully deal with the situation. So when it comes to security: war, n
harassment from criminals, yes.

*DO YOU THINK THE GOVERNMENT AND THE INTERNATIONAL COMMUNITY RESPECT YOUR TRADI-
TIONAL LAWS?*

The first thing you need to learn is to respect us for who we are. People [some
national legislators and members of the international community] show little respect for our tradition and culture, and we are feeling threatened. In
the same way that the constitution was written without the involvement of
the traditional people, that's the same way we fear these [formal] laws [that
are being introduced and that ignore or outlaw traditional practices and be-
liefs]. If you don't speak out about these things, people are prepared to take
our culture away from us. And then you will have to rename this country,
because it is our culture that kept us together as Liberians. If you strip us
of our culture, you have to rename this country. That is one thing you all
should learn.

The second thing is we are a people who are disciplinarians. We discipline our children. The law is not to be tampered with.

The spirit of coexistence should be encouraged on both sides. For us, we
have no problem with the [formal] legal system, but the legal system says we
are adjudicating cases that belong to it. They are the ones who say that they
have a problem with us. We are a civilized group of people.

The international community understands none of these things. But I
do not blame the international community. I blame our so-called elites who
are misinforming the international community. They are misinforming you
people. The women's rights, child rights, all these rights you're bringing, they
are foreign to us.

They say, "You must be paid before you do any piece of a job." But we
don't have money to pay our people. [In many rural communities, the chiefs
and elders assign communal tasks for all the members of the community,
particularly young men.] We go and sit under the palaver hut or under the
kola tree. We say, "Next week we will be clearing these roads and bridges.
OK? One cup of rice and a small bottle of oil, this and that. OK?" "OK, yes!"
We work, we eat, and the job is done. But now [civil society organizations]
and other groups say that before anybody does anything, you must pay them.
As a result, the bushes close the roads to market. All bridges are cut off. Because we don't have money to pay [people to do that work], you see?

So, some of these laws that have been introduced to us have been misin-
terpreted by our people and have carried us backward. The chief doesn't have
a police officer assigned to him. He doesn't have a messenger, he doesn't
have a clerk. He doesn't pay. We are doing official jobs just to maintain
peace and order in our localities. But with the new messages that have been
preached over the radio, the people have gone wild. We've got little control
over them, except through our secret society, which forbids certain things,
which says, "If you do it, we will move on you. As soon as you start, we come
for you." So you stop doing it.

DO YOU HAVE ANY ADVICE FOR THE INTERNATIONAL COMMUNITY?

Move closer to the chiefs and elders, and then they will tell you what's on their minds, and you make use of what they are telling you. You can't just make law from outside and bring it to a group of people who really don't live the way you live. Your country is different from ours. We should respect each other for who we are and deal with each other according to the situation on the ground. And in that way, there will be no conflict. But if you want to make your culture degrade mine, I will resent you.

DO YOU THINK THAT THE FORMAL LAW AND CUSTOMARY LAW CAN COEXIST?

Oh, yes. I have hope because President Ellen Sirleaf is the first in our history who is beginning to turn to the traditional people and tries to dig from the well of knowledge that they have. So the old mom [Sirleaf] looks into it and says, "Let me go back to the traditional people." That's why the Traditional Council was formed. We are peacemakers. You see, while making peace, you have to be willing to listen to people. Otherwise, you will just impose yourself on the people and they will soon hate you, and then things will not go on in the right way. **>>**

Nebojša Popović *(Kosovo; police lieutenant)*

"People were not guilty. Politics messed it all up."

We met Nebojša at a café in a mainly Serbian village outside the capital, Pristina. There were very few people in the dark café, and very few foreigners visit the village, so we attracted some stares. We walked through the café out to the outdoor seating area that looked out over a small garden. It was morning and very cool. Although a little cautious in how he expressed himself, Nebojša was very open and friendly, with a smile and sense of humor. It was easy to see how, although he is Serbian, he was able to gain the trust of his Albanian neighbors.

◀◀ I'm fifty years old and a lieutenant in the Kosovo Police Service [KPS]. I have been working in KPS since 2000. For eight years, I worked in the Gnjilane region of the Kosovska Kamenica area. Since last year, I've worked in the Gracanica station as a commander.

Before the war, I worked in a construction firm in Kosovska Kamenica as a bookkeeper. I am married and have three children. My elder son is also a member of the Kosovo Police Service. My second son is studying at the University of Communication here in Gracanica. My daughter is married and lives in the United States. I also have my parents. We are a family of eight members.

During the conflict, I was mobilized [as a member of the Serbian forces]. I was not motivated to fight, but if I had refused, I would have been sent to jail. I was deployed in the Gnjilane region. I was not happy with the war, but what can you do? People were not guilty. Politics messed it all up. Fortunately, there were no casualties in my family or in my neighborhood. My neighborhood was relatively quiet. I think there were no losses on the Albanian side either. After the war, we had no problems with Albanians. Immediately after the war, I was looking for a job. Because there were not many positions to choose from, I decided to apply to become a member of the Kosovo Police Service. I was not accepted immediately. I got the job after my third application. As far as the job is concerned, I have never had any problems or difficulties, either here in Gnjilane or in Kamenica.

The difficulties that I had in my daily work were with parallel Serbian police forces. They filed various charges against me, saying that Nebojša was using excessive force against civilians. The Serbian authorities sent these charges to UNMIK [the UN Mission in Kosovo] and asked UNMIK to investigate these supposed abuses of power. The Serbian police filed charges against me in courts in Serbia because I was serving here in the Kosovo Police Service and enforcing Kosovo laws. This is the main reason that I've never crossed the Serbia-Kosovo border since 2001. There is an arrest warrant for me, which is completely unnecessary and silly. Otherwise, here in Kosovo I have no problems whatsoever, especially with Kosovo institutions.

WHAT HAS BEEN YOUR EXPERIENCE IN GRACANICA?

I've been here for one year, and during this year there have been no interethnic problems. The only problems are with regard to property rights and disputes.

WHAT DOES "RULE OF LAW" MEAN TO YOU?

Rule of law means equal rights for everyone and respect for the human rights that are guaranteed by UN charters. My goal is to apply the rule of law equally to everyone.

I respect everyone and am respected by everyone. When other Serbian policemen left the Kosovo Police Service [the Serbian government called on them to quit, and almost all did so], I didn't leave, because I thought about the future. I didn't care about others' decisions.

WHAT DO YOU WISH FOR THE FUTURE?

Peace and jobs. Everything else will come naturally. **>>**

Ivan Escobár Fornos *(Nicaragua; judge)*

"Democracy is a permanent fight, like Independence—every day."

A former president of Nicaragua's Supreme Court—and thus the country's most powerful judge at that time—Justice Fornos still served on the court, hearing cases on the country's constitution, when we spoke with him. We went to the Supreme Court building in the capital, Managua, to interview him, and met him in his office, a large, well-appointed room with a sitting area where we conducted the interview. He was a gracious host and clearly held a deep passion for the law and jurisprudence and enjoyed conversing with like-minded guests.

<< LOOKING BACK, WHAT HAPPENED TO THE RULE OF LAW DURING THE REVOLUTION?

The fall of Somoza created a fundamental change in Nicaragua. Everything changed, as much in economic aspects as in the organization of the state and in relations between the state and society. The revolution occurred in 1979, and the constitution wasn't [enacted] until 1987. So that period was a revolutionary period. It was believed that it would be permanent. One thing would be said one day, then the next day it's something else. "This day we'll confiscate five businesses, tomorrow we'll do something else." They [the Sandinista regime] began to confiscate from the outset. Properties were seized, everything was seized. Who knew where we'd end up? The rule of law didn't operate.

In the Esquipulas [peace] Accords, they agreed to establish the rule of law, to have free elections, to honor human rights, to do a division of powers, and that's how it went. But the first constitution enacted, the one in '87, did not guarantee the rule of law. It was practically a dictatorship: state, party, army. At first, there was no real separation of powers.

In 1995, a great reform took place when a constitution was finally issued that had a democratic switch. It included the division of powers, established the control of the constitutionality of the laws, and the [authority] of the magistrates. It was all much clearer. But afterward, other reforms followed [that muddied the constitutional picture]. In Nicaragua we have lived in this way since independence. It's been a permanent pattern: advance and retreat of the rule of law. And it follows that with this, there's been corruption.

Power has stayed in the hands of just a few. The struggle for power has been waged by those who dominate, by those small groups who fight to maintain their status and power, [leaving] the people poor and deceived. And all the intellectuals help [preserve] that status, the information media helps that status; all the economic and political powers are encircled by institutions that succeed in maintaining that status. That is the history, the poor history, of this country. And we are all still living it—although it does seem that there is an awakening in the population to challenge this.

Things are different in a country where all the institutions work. Our institutions, because of the endemic situation in which we live, simply aren't strong. I wrote a book about the endemic evils, the fraud, the constitutional violations, and the rule of law in Nicaragua since independence. We don't know where or on whom to lay the blame, so it is a collective blame.

Latin America has had more than two hundred constitutions. You can imagine the instability of institutions and the rule of law. One constitution is pretty similar to another. One a little better, one a little worse, one medium-well done. That's the way things go. One president leaves and another comes in and destroys his predecessor's work, and on and on and on. I hope that this cycle, this endemic, stops. The presidential elections are coming, as are elections for magistrates and various officials. Maybe, instead of tearing up the whole country, we'll leave something of the good that functions, so that things start improving. Improve things instead of breaking them.

WHAT, IDEALLY, WOULD RULE OF LAW LOOK LIKE IN NICARAGUA?

First, there would be a judicial power that is respectable and respected—which depends on who is nominated to be magistrates, their capacity, and their independence. Also, there has to exist a clear division of powers, and a balance among powers. And there must exist a complete list of human rights and an effective system [for the defense] of the constitution and those rights.

Of course, all of these are elements that can improve, little by little. Democracy is a permanent fight, the same as independence—every day. This is not a matter of some law or decree that states, "It is done," or of a constitution that states, "There is rule of law," because many constitutions say a whole lot of wonderful things, but we've got nothing.

And we must speak directly with the people, find out what they think. And educate the public. Issues of health and the observance of social rights are also very important; a person who does not have work, medicine, property, and is not well nourished is easy to manipulate. As you say in the US, for individual or civil rights to function, social rights have to function. We have to focus on that part. We also have to create wealth. Of course, all these constitute a very large challenge. But I think that the key rests in the civic role of the people, and in patience, and in persistence. **>>**

RELIGIOUS LEADERS

Religion is often blamed for driving conflict, but from our conversations with eight religious leaders from a variety of faiths, religion is often a driver of peace.

Not surprisingly, those we interviewed cited their own religious doctrine as central to their personal belief system. What was less expected was the extent to which they emphasized the shared principles that lie at the core of all religions. Nepal, like many conflict-affected countries, is pluralistic and diverse in terms of ethnicity and religion. Keshab Chaulagain, a Hindu leader from Nepal, said that in such multicultural situations, the key to working together is to find a shared foundation of belief. "The common element among us is that every religion talks of peace," Keshab explained. "Hindus call it *prithivi shanti* (world peace) or *daha shanti* (inner peace), whereas "Islam" itself means peace. Likewise, Christians talk of peace, love, and justice. And love and tolerance are deeply rooted among the Buddhists as well. The same goes for Jainism. . . . We united on that."

Anoja Guruma, a Buddhist nun from Nepal, saw religions united not only by desire for peace but also by their compassion for others. Whatever the religion, she said, "the welfare of others is enshrined" in its principles. "If you go deeply into all the religions of the world, you will find there is goodness in each of them."

All the interviewees expressed their support for the rule of law, which they saw as vital in an imperfect world: imperfect either in a spiritual sense, because, according to Anoja, people do not yet have "good souls, good ethics," or imperfect in a political sense, because the government in their country is not yet strong enough to ensure peace and justice. As Shaikh Ahmed Zabeen Atiah from Yemen said, "When Yemen has a government, a state, we can ask about justice. Currently, there is no government in Yemen." Anoja was similarly critical of the current state of her country: "In Nepal today, there is no justice. There is no justice in our conscience in Nepal. And so you need law. People cannot distinguish between right or wrong."

The rule of law was seen as a guardian of justice, which in turn was seen as rooted in protecting rights and discharging responsibilities. "Justice," said Shaikh Ahmed, "means that whoever has a right should get that right, whether by Islam, by law, by custom, by the Christian Bible, or even by the Jewish Torah." "To me," commented S Lont Mon, a Christian peacebuilder in Myanmar (Burma), "the rule of law means that we, the people, participate: in creating the law, in the checks and balances." For her part, Anoja commented that the "rule of law is the soul of democracy. . . . All religious groups always pray that the rule of law shall be a priority."

The interviewees' desire for peace and justice is rooted not only in doctrine but also in painful personal experience. Several have lived on the frontlines of conflict. "This hall," remarked Mother Covadonga, as she showed us around her convent in the highlands of Peru, "now used for Ping-Pong, used to be the home of all of us when we were trying to hide from bombs, threats, terrorists, and so many difficult moments." Anoja's monastery "was like a cemetery during the People's Movement. One time, the Maoists came to kill me with a knife." During the Liberian war, Pastor Wallah Wilsitow's town was overrun by rebels. "Many people were fleeing, because there were mortar shells dropping, rockets, and shooting. I saw people killed right in front of me." He spurned the chance to flee and instead stayed to try to protect the three hundred people who had taken refuge in his church compound. He felt that it was his duty to "encourage them, because their hope was gone. They didn't know what to do, but because of the passion I have for my people, I decided to stay with them."

Other interviewees worked to resolve conflicts at the political level, hoping to defuse them before they escalated into religious violence. "We religious people thought that we should not sit idle amid widespread killing," remembers Keshab. He worked with other leaders to establish an interfaith council of Christians, Muslims, Buddhists, Hindus, and Jainists. Together, they researched the causes of the conflict, urged their communities not to retaliate in the face of violent provocation, and sought to encourage dialogue among political leaders.

Others work to reduce conflict at the community and family levels. Anoja leads a campaign to combat violence against women. George Paye, a pastor in Liberia, helps people in his poor parish resolve their disputes (their "palaver," as they call it), and thus avoid the corrupt police and official courts. Shaikh Ahmed works as an arbitrator within the customary and religious justice system. Father Solomon, a Jesuit priest in South Sudan, is establishing a peace studies program at his local university, so that "maybe the students will go out from the university and teach [conflict resolution] to their own sisters and brothers at home. In maybe another twenty years, maybe fifty, we can produce a society of people who are more aware of themselves and can move ahead."

For most interviewees, if a society is going to "move ahead" and away from violent conflict, peace must be made not just at the level of society. Peace, they said, begins with each individual, within each individual. You must "fix" yourself before attempting to work with others. You must first cleanse your own heart, mind, and soul. "I do need to know myself so I can know others," said Mother Covadonga. She went on to say that things will change "the day people change their minds. . . . As long as we get closer to our God, things will change. The world will change. The more away from Him we get, things will get worse."

Shaikh Ahmed cited a Yemini proverb: "Nothing can scratch your skin like your own fingernails." And he added, "If we don't take off our partisan, regional, and religious garments—nothing will change." ●

Mother Covadonga *(Peru; Dominican nun)*

"As long as we get closer to our God, things will change."

Mother Covadonga belongs to the Congregation of the Dominican Missionary Sisters of the Rosary, which was founded in Peru in 1918. We spoke with her at her convent in Ayacucho, where she leads a busy life, meeting with local people who come to seek her help. Despite her hectic schedule, she set aside three hours to speak with us, taking us on a tour of the order, showing us her books, and talking with joy and passion of her work.

<< I was born in 1922 and grew up in a beautiful area in Asturias [in northwest Spain], surrounded by mountains and trees. My father was a miner and farmer, my mother a housewife; I had ten siblings. One of my most sacred memories of growing up was of how much we loved each other. I never saw my parents looking stern. It was when I came to Peru that I learned about suffering and violence in people's lives.

When I was twelve, I had an accident where a big rock fell on my head. I was unconscious for three days in the hospital. When I woke up, the first thing I saw was a nun with a beautiful smile, and that was when I felt the first call to religious service. After the [Spanish] civil war, when I was nineteen, my mother began taking me to mass every morning. During one of those masses, I heard a voice tell me, "You have to leave and go far away."

I told my mother, and she said that if I really wanted to go far away, I would have to prepare myself to suffer a lot. A month later, when I heard the voice again, my mother knew I wanted to be a nun. In preparing myself to be a missionary, I had to change my name, and I became Sister Covadonga. Early in my religious studies in León, I heard a priest naming countries where missionaries would be assigned. That is where I first heard "Peru," and my heart began beating madly. That was when I realized that Peru was my destiny. So for five years I secretly prayed to be sent to Peru. When I was finished with my studies, I was given my destination: Peru. I started jumping and was so happy. I arrived in Lima on September 29, 1949.

My first assignment in Peru was teaching sixth-grade students. I taught them in all subjects; I even taught them to play music. Then, in 1971 I was sent to Ayacucho. I cried all the way because I'd heard people were not nice there. Even the driver tried to help me, I was crying so much. When I arrived I was not in a good psychological mood. The weather affected me as well. So did the behavior of the teachers and parents there. After fifteen days, I told myself I was being dumb and was there on a mission because God sent me. So I changed my way of looking at things and got myself to work. I went to school and started working with the children. That was when I wrote my first booklet, "Let the Children Come to Me." Peru needed people to realize how beautiful life was.

My mission was and still is to work with very humble and human people. You have to be very educated and very human. Educated to understand what people are going through, and human to be able to have sympathy and understand how people's hearts feel. In 1980, I became the director of religious education. That is when I wrote my second booklet, "If You Want Peace, You Must Educate for Peace." Five thousand copies were widely distributed. My dream was that all teachers could educate for peace, freedom, justice, and forgiveness.

I followed my mission: to "go far away because you have something to do." That was my motivation and strength. In the midst of the terrorist years, I always said that we all were siblings and had to build a house where God lived. I was everywhere, trying to help everyone regardless of their political affiliation, religion, or even their activities. Caring for human beings was all I would do. Then, we could talk only about violence; today, we talk about peace.

In 1984, there was a conference in Ayacucho, and I remember telling participants that things would change only the day people change their minds. It is important to raise your own awareness that we are here to be happy. However, in order to be happy, I do need to know myself so I can know others.

As long as we get closer to our God, things will change. The world will change. The more away from Him we get, things will get worse. Money drives us to chaos. We need to become aware that we are human beings. If you want to change, focus on the person instead of the money. These messages do come from the wisdom of Christ.

In 1987, I saw a lot of violence and blood. I went to the cemetery once and saw a father burying his son. He asked everyone to join him in a common prayer asking for forgiveness and love. I continued working, developing teaching materials and programs. I used the problems I saw in society and turned them into messages, songs, and lyrics. Nineteen eighty-seven was a very difficult year and affected me tremendously. We were unsure whether we would survive the day, with the threats, bombs, and so many horrible things. But I also wanted to see things in a positive way. I would open the doors no matter what. That is how one day, when someone came asking for help and money because his wife was in labor at the hospital, and I was strongly advised not to open the doors, I did it anyway. I gave him all I had at that time. Days later, he returned to thank me. He was a terrorist. You conquer war and achieve peace by conquering people's hearts. It starts with yourself, and you have to be very coherent. Peace, education, and love are fundamental.

I have lived through many difficult moments and situations here in Ayacucho. I keep working hard, helping people resolve their disputes, meeting with authorities, sometimes to help them reach a consensus instead of fighting. This hall, now used for Ping-Pong, used to be the home of all of us when we were trying to hide from bombs, threats, terrorists, and so many difficult moments. Today, we use it as a space to work with disabled children and to continue with our educational activities.

WHAT DOES "RULE OF LAW" MEAN TO YOU?

Rule of law means that you have the opportunity to lead a full life as a human being. If you don't have that possibility, there is no rule of law. **>>**

Wallah Wilsitow *(Liberia; pastor)*

"There are three Gs that rule the world: God, government, and guns."

Wallah is an affable jokester, but also a man of deep convictions and profound faith. He traveled with us during some of our time in Liberia, helping us to arrange interviews as well as sharing his own story and views on the war, the international community, and the need to combat corruption. We recorded this interview in the car as we drove through the country.

◄◄ I am forty-four years old, and a pastor and a teacher. Being a pastor is not a profession, it's a passion. You must have a passion.

During my early days, after high school, I had a calling to be a lawyer, but then I didn't know that the chief lawyer, Jesus Christ, was calling me to be a pastor. So, because of that passion he gave me, I decided to go to Bible school and then have some formal training in that area. I felt that God was calling me to really change the lives of people, because the overall aim of church teaching is to change lives, behavior, and attitudes within a given community.

WHAT DID YOU DO DURING THE WARS IN LIBERIA?

I didn't move out, I was here, in Liberia. I lived in Lower Virginia, outside [Liberia's capital] Monrovia. During the first phase of the war, which began in 1990, we had to move out, but then the fighting subsided and we moved back.

In 2000, I had a scholarship to go to the United States and do some training. I went and then came back.

During the last stages of the war, which started on June 6, 2003, it was more brutal. There was a time when the rebels came and captured the area. Many people were fleeing, because there were mortar shells dropping, rockets, and shooting. I saw people killed right in front of me.

A friend from Ghana, he wanted me to leave, to go with my family. But I said, "No. If I die, I'm going to die right here." People were taking refuge in churches. I had three hundred people, mostly women and children, with me at our bible college, Jacob Memorial Baptist College. I was really challenged to stay with them and encourage them, because their hope was gone. They didn't know what to do, but because of the passion I have for my people, I decided to stay with them.

Was your family with you at the compound?

Yes. That compound is named Jacob Memorial Baptist in honor of an American missionary who was serving as a volunteer. He didn't want to go when the Americans said that all their citizens should leave Liberia, because of the war situation. He had a passion for us and Liberia. Then one night, a group of men—they didn't have respect for the church compound—shot him and he died. And so he's dead and gone, but we as national pastors and educators decided to establish a college in memoriam.

What do you think caused the conflicts in Liberia?

There are several factors that led to the war, but the main [reason was that] justice was not done. The natural resources of the country were being manipulated by a certain group of people. And the international community wasn't really paying attention to Liberia, although it saw that the justice sector was being tampered with under the regime of President Taylor and needed a change. And that change came by the power of the gun, unfortunately.

There are three Gs that rule the world: God, government, and guns. And the power of the gun is very detrimental, because under the gun there will be no justice. The one who has the gun holds the power. And as a result, justice is not done, and the rule of law cannot take its course. Jungle justice is going to take place. Violence increases. There can be no peace.

What is your experience with the international community?

I want to praise the international community, because there are lots of [international aid workers and peacebuilders] coming into our country and bringing sanitation and other improvements to the lives of our people. But they may think about giving up, because our people have so many needs. The need to have clinics, the need to have more education, and the need to improve our justice system. In a nutshell, what the international community is doing is awesome, but they need to do a lot more.

Sometimes, you see the international community donate billions of dollars, but then they don't make sure that the assistance is given to those who it is intended for. They give aid, but sometimes they don't follow up and make sure it reaches the people. They leave it to the government. But the international community needs to be involved in the process. If that means that they're going to have to go to the villages, let it be; their representatives should make sure that the items that are donated for poverty-stricken people reach them.

When people are corrupting the government, they should be dealt with. Brought to justice. What happens if a man steals millions of dollars from the government? He should be booked and brought to justice. You may not be able to annihilate corruption, but you can minimize it by making sure that the perpetrators are being brought to justice. But if that is not done, we'll be giving more room to those who are involved in corruption.

We must put in a mechanism that will be able to really serve as a watchdog for the Liberian government and also the international community. The mechanism would be decentralized to the various counties [within Liberia], so that transparency can prevail. If each county has control over the aid money, then the funds can be spent on things like road building, not put in somebody's pocket. **>>**

Shaikh Ahmed Zabeen Atiah

(Yemen; Islamic judge)

"Justice is the strongest guard for the judge."

Shaikh Dr. Ahmed Zabeen Atiah is normally based in Shabwa, a province to the east of Yemen's capital, Sanaa, but he was in the capital to participate in the National Dialogue Conference, a gathering of influential Yemenis trying to agree on a new constitution for the country. We spoke with him away from the hubbub of those negotiations, in the office of a nongovernmental organization. He seemed relaxed, joking around for the first few minutes and staying well beyond the hour he had originally scheduled for the interview.

≪ I have a bachelor's degree and a master's degree in sharia and law, and a PhD in forensic analysis. Twenty years ago, I began working as an arbitrator, what some people call a "judge by selection"—by the selection of the two sides to the case. The fee for arbitration is paid by both sides, and in most cases they actually follow through on payment [laughs]. I was later appointed by the president as a judge of arbitration in the Shabwa area.

I've overseen some four hundred judgments. The first case I arbitrated was a commercial case. But I soon widened the scope of my work to include civil matters, criminal cases, and personal status. In making decisions, I take into consideration customary law, Islamic law, and civil law.

In one instance, I remember a woman who came to my house complaining that her husband beat her with an electrical wire, hitting her four times. She and her husband asked for my arbitration. She was in her ninth month of pregnancy and was originally from India. I told her husband that from a human standpoint he was everything to her: a father, son, mother, and brother, everything. He got angry and told me, "I want arbitration, not advice," so I ruled the following [laughs]. I gave the husband two options: that his wife would beat him with a wire, giving him eight strokes, or that he pay a big fine. I was angry, because the woman was a stranger to our land and pregnant. I always see women as oppressed. The husband pointed out that he had given his wife only four strokes, but I told him, "You whipped two human beings, your wife and her baby, and this is an insult to the human being."

I issue a ruling of punishment, but I entrust implementation of the punishment to the state. There is a kind of cooperation between us, police and prosecution, because the courts have become almost crippled and litigants rarely turn to these courts in cases of divorce, marriage, or personal contracts. The reason that litigants turn to tribal leaders, sharia elders, and arbitrators like me is, above all, the delays in the formal courts. A case that takes me one week to rule on sits ten years in the court, and that costs litigants money. Some judges and prosecutors take advantage of the problem and take bribes. But we arbitrators close the door of bribery completely. It usually takes one to five hearings to reach a judgment. Recently, I was given a case that had been in the courts for twenty years; I finished it in three days.

DO YOU HAVE A FAMILY? DO THEY FEAR FOR YOUR SAFETY?

When I was eighteen years old, I got married to a thirteen-year-old girl. Today, I call for the prevention of marriage of underage girls. I believe that a law should be enacted so that a girl may not get married under the age of eighteen years, because marrying younger leads to disasters. But my wife got married to a judge, and therefore he was merciful and treated her like his own daughter.

My wife and I have five children: four boys and a girl named Manal. My love for the girl is 90 percent and the remaining 10 percent is for the boys [laughs].

They fear for my safety because of my job in the judicial system and because they hear in the media about assassinations and killings. I appear on television often, give statements and interviews in newspapers; fame has its own price, it is not for free. But when they feel fear, I ask them to pray to God for protection.

DO YOU HAVE ANY SECURITY PROBLEMS WHEN YOU TRAVEL AS AN ARBITRATOR?

When I go to a case, I take three carloads, nearly twenty men, as guards. Their qat and food is paid by the litigants. In our tribal society, even if the judge is fair and straight, if he doesn't have many guards, he will be belittled by the parties. I don't really need so many guards, because justice is the strongest guard for the judge, but the environment forces us to act like that.

WHAT DOES "RULE OF LAW" OR "JUSTICE" MEAN TO YOU?

"Justice" means that whoever has a right should get that right, whether by Islam, by law, by custom, by the Christian Bible, or even by the Jewish Torah.

Caliph Abu Bakr (may Allah be pleased with him) says, "The weak among you shall be strong with me until their rights have been vindicated; and the strong among you shall be weak with me until, if the Lord wills, I have taken what is due from them," and this is a great rule.

WHAT IS THE ROLE OF THE STATE, THE GOVERNMENT, IN GIVING THE RULE OF LAW?

When Yemen has a government, a state, we can ask about justice. Currently, there is no government in Yemen. If we are successful at the National Dialogue Conference [NDC] and establish a state, it would be enough. We want a state. Yemeni citizens do not only want to eat; they also want a state. When the state exists, I will not go to Shabwa with guards; I will drive my car by myself.

ARE YOU OPTIMISTIC ABOUT THE NDC?

I'm 95 percent optimistic about the outcome. But there is one problem: what are the guarantees that the outcome we decide on will be implemented? I guarantee you that whatever support the international community gives to the NDC, it will not be enough to guarantee implementation. There is a Yemeni saying: "Nothing can scratch your skin like your own fingernails." If the will [to put into practice what the NDC decides] does not exist among the Yeminis—and if we don't take off our partisan, regional, and religious garments—nothing will change.

The international community has a strong interest in Yemen, but it is their own interest, not Yemen's. The UN Security Council didn't turn its attention to Yemen because it loves Yemen; it did so for its own interests. As Islamists, we believe in partnership and mutual interests, but we don't want the international community to be more majestic than the king. And in Yemen, we don't want to see the United States changing its opinions, as it is doing in Egypt now. What is said in the morning is changed at night.

If I could advise the Americans and the international community, I would say, "You are the sponsors of democracy, and you are talking about human rights. But are you serious about these slogans? Are they applied equally to all of the Arab countries?" If they say yes, we'll give them a long list of contradictions [laughs]. But we Yemenis still have to take this opportunity offered by the international community, so we don't end up like Syria or Egypt. We must put away our partisan and sectarian garments.

What happened here in 2011 was an extension of the revolutions in the other Arab countries. We were searching for a way to change before those types of revolutions occurred. Traditionally, changes of rule happen in one of three ways: military coups, heredity transitions, or elections. As Islamists, we don't approve of military coups because of the blood spilled, resources wasted, and chaos caused. We see hereditary transitions as a form of tyranny. And elections . . . in Yemen we failed, because the military was used to repress democracy. When the sit-ins occurred [mass demonstrations in Sanaa and other cities], we were happy; the young people came out, just as in other nations.

I gave Friday sermons throughout the period, preaching provocatively for peace, for peace, for peace. And for this we faced bullets. But the Yemeni people have benefited: we got to chew more qat [i.e., to make the time to discuss and debate] and gain more political experience.

It started as a revolution and ended with a settlement. In my view, the revolution did not continue to the end, as happened in Libya, where the regime was fully uprooted. But the wisdom of the Yemeni parties meant we avoided [further] bloodshed.

WHAT MOTIVATES YEMENIS TO PERSEVERE?

The nature of the Yemeni people is different from any other nationality. They don't give up in the face of injustice, mistreatment, or poverty. During the events of 2011, there was no fuel and no food, yet they still found alternatives, and one could buy fuel in all the markets. If this nation weren't so strong, it would have withered by now. And there is another characteristic: mercy. When things get worse, you feel a kind of empathy among the people.

As for the future, I hope for the best, but Yemen's problem is not with its people or with its second tier of politicians. The problem lies with those politicians who have grown too old to deal with politics: the first tier. If only they would leave the country, so that young men and women could take over—a new, mature, clean, immaculate generation [whose hands have] not been contaminated with blood. Only then will Yemen be better.

After the revolution, some of the old faces are still there; the same people but with different robes. **>>**

Anoja Guruma *(Nepal; Buddhist nun)*

"Leaders, political or spiritual, must cleanse their ethics, their soul."

We met Dr. Anoja by a huge statue of the Buddha outside her monastery, which sits on the road to the ancient city of Kirtipur. She showed us her library; opened the door of her yoga room, which lies under the monastery dome; walked with us through her carefully tended kitchen garden; and served us a traditional Nepalese lunch of steamed rice, lentil soup, vegetable curry, spinach, and homemade yogurt. She could not have done more to make us comfortable.

<< It has been thirty-eight long years since I became a nun. I have been wearing this red costume since 1972.

I came to Kathmandu to start this monastery in 2063 BS [2006 AD; "BS" stands for the Nepalese lunar calendar, Bikram Sambat]. I came after I had spent nine years in India completing my PhD and, before that, ten years absorbed in mediation.

So you were studying in India during the conflict here in Nepal?

Not all of the time. For instance, once when I was in Kathmandu, I happened to go to someone's house where a bomb exploded, and I survived by only a second. Many people were hurt. Some were blinded; some lost limbs. I felt that it would have been better to have been killed than mutilated. I felt the people's sorrows as though they were my own. Who could not be absorbed in sadness when peace was disrupted because of conflict in a country where Gautama Buddha, an apostle of peace, was born? Peace is lost then.

In India, too, I would feel intense regret over people's sorrows and want to share them. Whenever I went to India, I used to see so many poor girls with so little education. How to relieve them of their sorrows?

And today, the leaders of Nepal are ruining every aspect of the country's life. I feel regret for that. Leaders, political or spiritual, must cleanse their ethics, their soul. If your soul is not cleansed, you can't cleanse others' souls. First, you should cleanse your own soul.

HAVE YOU FELT SECURE HERE, IN THE MONASTERY?

From a security perspective, this location was like a cemetery during the People's Movement. One time, the Maoists came to kill me with a knife. They came here sometimes to scold me and spoke rudely to me. They came here for extortion, too. Hundreds of young Maoists came, and complained when I could not give them food and shelter. They came here three or four times, to my surprise, to hide their bombs in the monastery. Everybody knows that this monastery has harmed no one. This is a sacred place, a hub for acquiring knowledge for all. Nor have I done anything. I have served the monastery as well as I can. I have toiled hard.

Why did they want to kill me, a nun? It is because of a lack of enlightenment. I don't blame them. If they were enlightened, they would not have any idea of killing me. You know that they killed a Japanese monk in Lumbini. It is because of nonenlightenment, because of greed, because of hatred, because of passion. Had they had enlightenment, they would not have done so much damage. It is because they lack education. It is because they have not yet realized that one day they will die.

HOW DID YOU FEEL WHEN THE PEACE AGREEMENT WAS SIGNED IN 2006?

It was good that the peace was declared, but it would have been better if words had been translated into actions. Yes, it is peaceful compared with the days of conflict when bombs were exploding. But Nepal can't go forward until and unless a campaign of punishment is imposed on the perpetrators [of violence and human rights abuses].

WHAT MESSAGE DO YOU HAVE FOR THE INTERNATIONAL ORGANIZATIONS WORKING IN NEPAL?

Let all of us work together, behaving as brothers and sisters to each other, and cooperate for the well-being of all. Not only in Nepal but also at the international levels, may the soul be cleansed and all people reconcile with one another, so that peace may be restored and their lives may be led to peace. Reconciliation will boost prosperity and establish stable peace.

WHAT DOES "RULE OF LAW" MEAN TO YOU?

You don't need any law if the people of our country have good souls, good ethics. If they have good souls and follow Panchashil [a Buddhist code of conduct for personal behavior], you do not need to observe any law at all—no counsel or court is needed. Panchashil embraces five elements: no one shall kill any creatures; no one shall steal others' belongings; no one shall discriminate, because there is always violence in discrimination; no one shall tell a lie; and no one shall be addicted to drugs. It is imperative to observe these five things, and to pursue them throughout the world.

In Nepal today, however, there is no justice. There is no justice in our conscience in Nepal. And so you need law. People cannot distinguish between right or wrong. They do not understand even the difference between what is good and what is bad. People have neither conscience nor wisdom. There are very few people who are wise, who can understand things. I very often say that when enough people understood things well, then our country, Nepal, shall turn into heaven.

Rule of law is the soul of democracy. Religious people know that the rule of law should be maintained in the country. All religious groups always pray that the rule of law shall be a priority.

In my opinion, religion is an action, religion is a duty. No matter what the religion is, whether Hindu or Christian, the welfare of others is enshrined in the religion's principles. If you go deeply into all the religions of the world, you will find there is goodness in each of them. But if the ethics of the religious leaders and observers are not good, you cannot find any goodness. Gurus should preach only after first cleansing their souls.

In Nepal, the religious communities have come together to work for peace. While we were forming the Inter-Religious Council, we Hindus, Muslims, Christians, and Buddhists came up with a common agenda that included our interest in peace and justice. We did not focus on our differences, on things we could not resolve, but on things we could all endorse. Once the common agenda was concluded, affection hit the roof among us! Each of us began to share ideas with the others. And then, while working together, we began to exchange our differences, too.

DID YOU USE A SIMILAR APPROACH IN YOUR WORK TO COMBAT VIOLENCE AGAINST WOMEN?

Yes. Before understanding or identifying any social problem, [one must] first come to the community and work toward a common agreement. If there are any dissenting views, we must discuss them so that they can fade away and we can conclude with a common goal. When there is unity, the misunderstanding between and among us can be washed away. Then we can understand each other and come to know each other's nature. This promotes mutual welfare and enhances unity.

As you know, I have been working in the Kathmandu valley to tackle the violence of mothers-in-law against their daughters-in-law, and of husbands against their wives. They use violence because of their ignorance. Some of them—young and old women, as well as men—have realized their ignorance and confessed their blunders. I believe that they will understand from now on. There must be mutual understanding between men and women.

It is said in the Hindu religion that where women are honored, even gods are happy. In Buddhism and Christianity, too, there is high regard for women. Society is, indeed, an equal creation of man and woman. If we bring both together, the well-being of society will grow. There will be good in every family, people will be happy, and society will be good and peaceful. And the nation itself will be good. Ultimately, there will be good in all three: family, society, and nation. **>>**

S Lont Mon
(Myanmar [Burma]; Christian peacebuilder)

"Be with us, don't let us be alone, . . . [but] don't rush us."

S Lont Mon chatted as we drove through the countryside of Mandalay to meet a group of monks and nuns. Although we sat awkwardly in the back of the van, the conversation was full of laughter and warmth, and his face lit up when he talked about his two daughters. S Lont Mon exudes a genuine belief in the goodness of humanity.

<< WHAT IS YOUR OCCUPATION?

I am a peacebuilder, although my official job title is programs facilitator for the Hope International Development Agency.

Originally, I trained to be a veterinarian. When I finished my studies, I practiced as a vet in my neighborhood, but I also started doing development work. Then I thought I wanted to be a minister, a preacher, but that plan fell apart. Even so, I still went to the seminary. I spent two years there. After finishing, I worked in the development section of a church organization. I needed to improve my skills, so my organization sent me to Canada to attend a six-month course on social development and leadership. Then I received a scholarship from the [US] State Department and went to the University of Minnesota. I spent two years there studying human resource development.

Then I came back and worked with the church. But I ran into some conflict, and with a friend's assistance I was able to go to the Eastern Mennonite University [in the state of Virginia], learning conflict transformation and peacebuilding. I spent two years there. So that is my educational background—different disciplines every time.

In almost every community, we see conflict. But we did not have the skill and capacity to deal with conflict at the community level, partly because of our religious teaching, our cultural values, and the education system. And then there is also the diverse nature of our country—the way we look at our own identity group and other groups. All these things congregate to create the conflict situations.

When I [do conflict resolution] work with the communities, I work within one identity group. But people identify themselves with other groups; people separate themselves by identifying with other groups. It happens all the time. If I see Kachin men, I say, "Oh, we're the same because we live in this country." And the next moment someone might say, "Oh, we're not the same because I'm Kachin and you're Karen." Even when I'm working with one village, the same race, they can still separate themselves. "Oh I'm from the southern part of the village, and you're from the northern part of the village." Or, "I am the relative of the village elders, and you are the relatives of the religious leaders." So we separate and we identify ourselves all the time.

HOW HAS YOUR RELIGION AFFECTED YOUR WORK?

There are many dimensions. One is narratives [the stories we tell ourselves about our history and experiences]. Another is the labeling, the naming. We grew up Christians, who are a minority in Burma, and we were so afraid that our identity would disappear. So we developed narratives to protect our identity. We had good intentions, but we didn't understand the whole picture. Our limited understanding led us to isolate ourselves. Until I reached a certain age, I had never been to a [Buddhist] monastery, because we'd been told that these places are not appropriate for you to go to as a Christian, that if you went, you would destroy the purity of your practice. Those kinds of narratives. When I listen to the Muslim group, it's the same thing. I don't want to blame those people who created these narratives, but they just don't understand the dynamics. We will better protect our religion if we understand other people's, and if other people understand ours.

Another problem is the labeling. It looks like a small thing—what we call other groups—but it creates a lot of misunderstanding and conflict. It is very widespread in our communities for Christians to call Christians "believers"; they call other people from other faiths "nonbelievers." And this creates conflicts. In my village, when I was growing up, we called ourselves *sachu*, "white letter," and we called other people [Buddhists] "black letter." That term we inherited from the missionaries.

MYANMAR (BURMA) IS GOING THROUGH A TRANSITION. ARE YOU HOPEFUL FOR THE FUTURE?

There are still a lot of uncertainties; overwhelmingly we have uncertainties. But there is hope. That is why we are working for peace, engaging in peace. I trust in the human capacity to do good things. We see all the time the goodness of the people, the goodwill of the people.

But in terms of safety and security, our situation is getting worse than before. In the past, we didn't have open media, so we couldn't hear things that happened in other places. But now we're opening up and we hear more things. So in terms of safety and security, I wouldn't go out at night, after nine or ten, because I don't feel very safe in Yangon or anywhere now.

WHAT DO YOU TELL YOUR GIRLS ABOUT THE CURRENT TRANSITION?

Actually, I don't know if they're interested. Before, I used to tell them a lot of things; but now, they hardly ask me anything—maybe because they're very busy with Facebook and curling their hair, taking pictures of themselves, doing things like that. It's fun to watch. I'm the only man in the house, so I behave myself. I'm the minority!

WHAT DOES "RULE OF LAW" MEAN TO YOU?

To me, the rule of law means that we, the people, participate: in creating the law, in the checks and balances. We need to use the power of the people very carefully. For people to participate, [they have to have] a good relationship with each other and also with law enforcement individuals and groups.

Whenever I hear top political leaders use the phrase "rule of law," I feel like it is incomprehensible, unreal, like putting makeup on the face. I like the president; I like Aung San Suu Kyi [the leading opposition figure]; I appreciate their efforts to build the nation. But at the same time, if they don't say "rule of law," I will appreciate it more.

WHAT DO YOU THINK ABOUT THE INTERNATIONAL COMMUNITY'S INVOLVEMENT HERE?

The international community can contribute so many valuable things to nation building, to building a better society in our world. I always appreciate the assistance and the contribution of the international communities. But at the same time, I would say that one must understand the conflict and the context, not have your own agenda, and don't go too fast.

Be with us, don't let us be alone, be with us and be attentive to the needs, focusing less on your own pride and your own ego, and let's work together. Let's take this journey together, let's build together. Thank you so much for your time and resources, but be with us. Don't rush us.

YOU'VE SEEN A LOT OF CONFLICT IN MANY DIFFERENT FORMS. WHAT HELPED YOU GET THROUGH THOSE CONFLICTS?

Actually, personally, I don't like conflict; I avoid conflict. I don't want to be caught up in a conflict. I just want to stay away from the conflict. But now, through my work experience, through my study, through my practical experiences, I've learned that [approach] is not going to help. To be in a better place, to be in a better position, we have to deal with conflict. That is my main motivation.

Another thing is I'm always hopeful. When I experience some serious conflict in my own life, and when reconciliation happens, that feeling, there's nothing compared with that feeling. So I'm longing for that moment, and I'm hopeful for that moment. **>>**

Keshab Chaulagain *(Nepal; Hindu peace activist)*

"We can say, 'At least let's sit at the table.'"

A forceful and loquacious man, Keshab is involved in a well-maintained Hindu temple in Machhagaun, in the north-western corner of the Kathmandu Valley. The author of several works on spirituality and a high-ranking member of numerous organizations, he was the founding general-secretary of the Ne-pal Interreligious Council, which was formed in 2004. We interviewed him at the USIP office in Kathmandu.

◄◄ In the 1990s, the Maoists had launched an armed rebellion in Nepal. We [religious peacemakers] had thought that the reason behind the conflict was political, and hence we had ignored it. We were simply talking about peace. But, day by day, despite our denial, we were hurled into the conflict. Soon, it was not only a matter of national concern but also a concern for the international community. A lot of lives and properties had been devastated by then. A few political initiatives had been taken, but all were in vain.

Therefore, we religious people thought that we should not sit idle amidst the widespread killings, and I took the initiative to investigate our role in resolving the conflict. The theme of my research was how Nepal's diverse religious communities could work together on a solid program in order to transform the conflict and restore peace. That brought other religious com-munities—like Christians, Muslims, Buddhists, Baha'is, and Jains—into con-tact, and we came closer. It also brought together little-known intellectuals.

Nepal is largely pluralistic and diverse in terms of ethnicity and religion; it is a multicultural and multinational society. Because of this cultural di-versity, if you initiate a conflict management campaign, you should strive to grasp what is common among us. The common element among us is that ev-ery religion talks of peace. Hindus call it *prithivi shanti* (world peace) or *daha shanti* (inner peace), whereas "Islam" itself means peace. Likewise, Christians talk of peace, love, and justice. And love and tolerance are deeply rooted among the Buddhists as well. The same goes for Jainism. When we put this [shared emphasis on peace] in writing, there was no question of anyone objecting. We united on that.

We tried to find the root cause of the conflict and analyze it. We concluded that the reason for the conflict was indeed a political one, and hence we should attempt to address it in terms of a political perspective, without criticizing [any particular political party or philosophy] but by putting forward our thoughts in front of the political arena. To this end, we made public announcements, organized meetings, interacted with organizations that came to us. And we said what the cause of the conflict was.

To the CPN [Communist Party of Nepal; the Maoists], we gave the message that they were not doing a great job by killing their fellow countrymen, and that we were not in favor of bringing peace by annihilating them. Everyone must exist in peace and reconcile. And we said, too, that because it is a political movement, their political rights must be addressed. But giving people their rights should not be achieved by killing people.

To the state, we said that you can't end the conflict by killing the rebels. We insisted that all their feasible demands should be fulfilled, and that those demands which cannot be fulfilled immediately must be addressed through dialogue. We took the initiative of creating an environment for dialogue. In that context, we religious people tried to address a political conflict in a political way with impartiality and audacity; and we identified ourselves as independent.

In the process, one of our people was killed; pundit [learned scholar] Narayan Prasad Pokhrel, chairperson of the World Hindu Council, was murdered. He was killed mainly because of his religious stand and his popularity. His popularity hit the sky very high. He started to recite verses from the holy books—the Bhagavad Gita [a Hindu scripture], interestingly—and thereby raised an enormous amount of money, which he used to build bridges and roads, and do other social works. He delivered a message: that to create change, you don't have to kill anyone. This seemed to contradict the Maoists' armed movement. His movement of social welfare was peaceful. But the Maoists fought for the same issue with arms. It seems that when the Maoists saw masses of people rallying for development projects under him, they sensed that it might affect their ideology and influence; so they killed him. In other places, low-profile pundits were banished from their villages. They are still in Kathmandu. They were not able to go back home.

His death was a great loss. But although we lost something, we [did not abandon] the work. The Maoist intellectual Dr. K. B. Rokaya, a Christian leader, came to us. So did Vikshu Anand, a lawmaker from the Maoist party. Najir Miya, the lawmaker from the CPN–UML [the Communist Party of Nepal–Unified Marxist-Leninist], helped us, too. We created the Interreligious Council by bringing in intellectuals who supported the rebels. We have been working with religious leaders who support the ideology of the rebels.

We told the rebels that they should not attack the religious sites, and we told the religious groups that were trying to retaliate that this is a political problem. It will be resolved one day. So we remained peaceful. Because, if the political conflict ever turned into a religious conflict, the country wouldn't be able to bear it. The Interreligious Council went to different communities and insisted upon not retaliating.

When a Muslim man was murdered at Kapilvastu—which led to a Hindu-Muslim riot—we organized a goodwill rally. In Kathmandu, we insisted that religious issues should not be mixed into the unhealthy political debates.

What can the religious communities, especially the Interreligious Council, do to help keep the peace process going?

We can play the role of creating social harmony and making peace in religious terms. There is a lot of misunderstanding and ill feeling among the political parties. Reality [in terms of a realistic understanding of the problem and a search for realistic solutions] can be reached only after discussions. But the parties are fighting before they can reach the reality. This can be prevented by developing friendship, and we can initiate that process. We can say, "At least let's sit at the table." If there are problems that can be dealt with lawfully, then let's talk about them. In some instances, our voices have been heard. For example, we told the Maoists that a six-day protest would not bring good results, and it did not. The prime minister called us to talk with him. A few days later, Mr. Prachanda [the CPN leader] invited us to talk [with him and his colleagues]. We talked about it in religious terms in the party office and they listened. This has led me to believe that we can approach the leaders directly. **>>**

Father Solomon *(South Sudan; Jesuit priest)*

"At the end of the day, the good will always come out."

We interviewed Father Solomon before South Sudan became a separate country from Sudan, but after a peace agreement to end the civil war between the north and south had been signed. He showed us around the town of Wau's university, a concrete building containing four classrooms and little else. The setting was very hot and very Spartan, but Father Solomon, despite or perhaps because of his advancing years, radiated spiritual intensity.

<< I am a priest, and my work includes working in missions and in houses of education. I started working here two years ago, when we had just twenty students. We have forty students this year. I very much like teaching. I like people to have knowledge, especially indigenous knowledge—knowledge that is oriented to them.

But in South Sudan, a generation is doomed because, as a result of the conflict, it is not getting educated. The conflict has been going on for two decades; that's a long time, and it means that a generation is not being educated, is not even aware that it's not getting educated.

Also, people are traumatized. One boy told me, "I was born in war and I have been doing war." He has had a gun all his ten years. Such a person's reasoning is a little complex. So there needs to be help for these people.

I'm trying to establish a faculty of peace studies in the university. The way to peace in our country is conflict resolution. In Sudan, there is conflict because of racism and religious issues. It's a very, very complex situation, even more so because of the issue of Sudan being both Arab and African, and both Muslim and non-Muslim.

We know in Sudan or South Sudan that for ten or fifteen more years we are going to have conflict. Whatever is coming, I hope that every student in all the universities can have this course on conflict resolution. They should have ethics, too. People are conflicted, they are angry, but if there is really a way of working out what the problem is, maybe the students will go out from the university and teach [conflict resolution] to their own sisters and brothers at home. In maybe another twenty years, maybe fifty, we can produce a society of people who are more aware of themselves and can move ahead. That's my hope—that we will move ahead.

There are two forces in the world, the forces of good and the forces of evil. And they have always existed and they will always be there. That's why we say the human society is both divine and human, meaning that there is always good and there is always bad, but at the end of the day, the good will always come out. It was evil when these people [northerners and southerners] were put together [in one country, Sudan], thinking that it was going to work. But unfortunately there was no way, no institution that could make everyone equal, that could give them the same opportunity.

The South is going to face many challenges [when it becomes independent]. Building a nation is a great challenge. In South Sudan, we have tribal conflict. To bring these tribal people together in one nation is a great, great challenge. And we don't have enough people [who have been educated to secondary school level]; when one employs someone who is not qualified enough, the quality of the job and the product will not be so good, and I think that's going to be a challenge in South Sudan. The transport system is also very poor. There are many challenges. But it is better to be poor when you are free than rich when you a slave.

In South Sudan, we call ourselves a "country" because we are not a "nation" yet. A country is just a land, a demarcated land, but a nation is made up of people with the same history and the same values. So, to build a nation, I think it's going to take a long time, and of course there's a lot of sacrifice that will be required. **>>**

George Paye *(Liberia; pastor)*

"In the midst of confusion, we still have God here to guide us."

We interviewed George in Careysburg, a suburb of the capital, Monrovia, in the backyard of his home, which was literally on the verge of crumbling. His church was on the other side of the street. Several chickens and a sad-eyed puppy were in the backyard, as were several men, his wife, and a girl beginning to make dinner. George was very straightforward and very serious the entire time.

<< I was born in Monrovia and have lived here in Careysburg for thirteen years now. I came here before I got married and had my children here.

I'm a pastor. Presently we have about fifty active members in my church. I have also opened a Bible school with the Living Water Ministries, and a couple of Bible training centers. We train pastors and church leaders. Some of them are bishops; some of them are overseers; some of them work with local churches.

THE BIBLE TALKS OF "JUSTICE." IS IT THE SAME AS "RULE OF LAW"?

Rule of law, justice: they're almost the same, because if you have rules and you have laws, then of course you will have justice. I believe that in every institution, every organization, every country there must be a rule of law that will help to regulate the activities of the people, so that everybody will know what they should do. I see the rule of law as being there to guide decisions and to help with the process of bringing the objectives of the nation to pass.

HOW DO YOU HANDLE PARISHIONERS WHO COME TO YOU WITH PROBLEMS?

When somebody comes to me with a problem, with palaver, I try to handle it myself. I call both parties together and we sit down, and we resolve it. We look into it. If you are wrong, we tell you, "Say you are wrong." If you are right, you must treat your brother so that your brother can be peaceful. I thank God that most of the cases that come to me are resolved. We don't want to go to the police or to court.

WHEN YOU HAVE TO GO TO THE POLICE WITH A PROBLEM, DO THEY HANDLE IT WELL?

Well, sometimes it works; sometimes it doesn't work. We all are yearning for justice, but sometimes justice is given to people who have money, not to the poor. That's how we handle justice here at times. If you are wrong and you give [the courts or the police] money, they give you the right, because you have money. It was like this before the war, too.

HAVE YOU HAD ANY INTERACTION WITH THE INTERNATIONAL COMMUNITY?

I have not really worked with the international community, but there are some missionaries, American missionaries, who come here, and I help them with their work. And we have pastoral conferences, seminars, and all of that.

I have a positive view of the international community, which is rendering some service to us. Giving us some aid for hospitals, education, medication.

IF YOU COULD ASK SOMETHING OF THE INTERNATIONAL COMMUNITY, WHAT WOULD THAT BE?

For my community, safe drinking water. To tell you the truth, we are still drinking creek water; we don't even have a hand pump around here. Everybody in this community goes to the area where the creek is; that's where we get water to drink; it's not even healthy for us. And we need more schools. Although we established one school here, the population is too big.

WHAT COULD THE LIBERIAN GOVERNMENT DO?

There are so many things. To rehabilitate the roads for us so we can carry our produce to market. Sometimes, we harvest our produce, but it goes rotten because the road condition means we can't get to market and sell it.

And we need security, because the war is over but our people are still experiencing armed robbery. We have our national army now, we have the police, but still, over the radio, you're hearing about armed robbery, armed robbery, armed robbery. The issue of security is very, very important, because it causes investors to stay out and not invest in the country. The security system in this country is not strong yet. When the [UN] peacekeepers leave, there will be chaos obviously, because our police, they are not trusted. Though I know that UNMIL [the UN Mission in Liberia] will not remain here forever, they can't just pull out. Before they can leave, I think they need to go back to the issue of security, and to help strengthen the security by having more people trained to help with the security sector.

WHAT HAS HELPED YOU THE MOST IN COPING WITH ALL THE RECENT TROUBLES IN LIBERIA?

My confidence, it's in God; in the midst of confusion, we still have God here to guide us. And also our government can help with security, and our international brothers, UNMIL. **>>**

PROFESSIONALS

We met a diverse cast of dedicated professionals who, despite often facing great danger, shared the desire to make a positive difference to their societies amid violence, trauma, and uncertainty.

For some, their own survival was very much in doubt. Take the deeply moving story of Um Mustafa, a kindergarten teacher in Iraq, who lived in constant fear that she and her family would be killed at any moment. During one of the spikes of violence targeting former regime officials, her husband, a police officer, survived an assassination attempt while she sat next to him in his car. On another occasion, the couple were kidnapped by al-Qaeda but escaped. Um Mustafa witnessed a murder firsthand and encountered dead bodies almost as a matter of routine.

Yet, Um Mustafa resolved that mere survival was not enough. She refused to be defeated, and continued to serve her community through its most challenging moments as a matter of principle and pride, strengthening the educational system as violence raged around her. She said that she needed to remain strong and set an example for the children in her classroom and her colleagues and community.

Remaining focused and positive in the face of adversity was a recurring theme of the interviews. Nearly every participant related stories of high hopes dashed and the despair that followed. Each wrestled with the fear of becoming disillusioned when things did not turn out as hoped.

Thyn Zar Oo of Myanmar (Burma) exemplified this, as she struggled to stay focused on her legal aid work, determined to help her country, even in the face of setbacks. When she was a teenager, she had watched, full of hope, as a nascent prodemocracy movement gained traction. But that hope had turned to despair when "the '88 generation," students who had taken to the streets peacefully to demand democratic change, were brutally repressed. In the wake of that experience, some activists became embittered and left the country, but Thyn Zar has never lost her desire to be of service to her people.

This sense of duty to one's country was shared by many of those interviewed. Salwa Al-Tajoury from Libya had been living in France until the revolution that ultimately toppled Muammar Qaddafi. She related how she returned to Libya because she wanted to help her country. First, she worked for humanitarian organizations, and then she turned to art—not only to help others but also for her own therapy.

Another professional who found some personal healing in her work helping others was "Oscar." During the violence that followed the US-led invasion of Iraq, Oscar took a job with the Civil Affairs Unit of the US Army, where she was responsible for maintaining a database to help Iraqi families connect with their relatives who had been detained by US forces. After the murder of her brother and the kidnapping of her cousin, the temptation to flee Iraq was nearly irresistible; however, Oscar felt that she needed to remain in her own country, working to ensure that others would not experience the same trauma she had endured. By helping others, Oscar found that she was able to gain a small bit of healing for herself.

Hasan Arzuallxhiuv, a physician from Kosovo, initially began working for the Organization for Security and Co-operation in Europe (OSCE) because it provided a job when few were available; however, he also felt a deep responsibility to his country as he went about his duties. Because of his extensive medical training, he was assigned the unenviable task of performing autopsies on murdered Kosovans found by the OSCE monitors. Serbian paramilitaries and Kosovan nationalists both tried to intimidate him, but he continued working for international organizations, committed to facilitating mutual understanding between international personnel and the local population.

Another person who used his professional skills in the fight for a more peaceful and just society was Khalid Alwafi, a lawyer from the city of Misurata in Libya. In a lull in the fierce fighting for control of the city, he and many other lawyers created an organization to collect and document evidence of war crimes against humanity from abandoned police stations and government offices. "We needed to do it right and to do it according to the law," he explained. For Khalid, who fought in the streets when Qaddafi's forces returned, it was not a matter of choice: "If you don't do this, you'll be in shame for all of your life. . . . You have to do the right thing for your people."

Sofia Montenegro, a Nicaraguan political activist and journalist who, despite coming from a family that had been close to the Somoza regime, found herself part of the movement that opposed the repressive Somozan dictatorship. Then, as now, she was striving for a very simple idea: fairness, diversity, and common ground for all. But these things don't just blossom automatically; they have to be carefully cultivated. "Democracies are a sort of gymnasium," she explained, "where one goes to do calisthenics, where people learn about political culture, discourse, debate, the building of consensus."

In his or her own way, each of the people in this chapter recognize that while passion and bravery are invaluable in the fight for justice, security, and peace, those qualities must also be complemented by expertise, hard work, and persistence. ●

Khalid Alwafi *(Libya; lawyer)*

"If you hide or run, you'll be in shame."

We began interviewing Khalid in the early morning of a Friday (prayer day) in a small hotel in Misurata. He wanted to make sure that we understood why he had acted as he had, but at the same time he was guarded, and it seemed as though he had not discussed this subject in any depth before. When he spoke about Khalid Abo Shahma being killed, his normally controlled and deliberate demeanor melted, and he was overtaken by emotions. We sat in silence for a few moments, and decided to wait until the next day to continue the interview.

<< I'm originally from Misurata. I went to school here, too. I graduated from law school in 1999. I'm married and have two children, two and six years old. When I finished law school, I went to Canada and I stayed there for a while to study English; then I came back and practiced as a lawyer for a couple of years. And then I got a chance to visit the United States, and I stayed there for a while too. I came back.

HOW WAS LIFE UNDER THE FORMER REGIME?

During the Qaddafi regime, I couldn't do anything, because if you said something against Qaddafi, or anyone associated with Qaddafi, you went to jail. There was no freedom whatsoever. We didn't have a good education system or a good health system; if you fell ill, you had to go to Tunisia to get treatment. I promised myself I would never work under a government controlled by Qaddafi. I chose to work as an independent lawyer and worked with cases dealing with companies, not government.

COULD YOU DESCRIBE THE DAYS LEADING UP TO THE REVOLUTION HERE?

We were controlled by the police and army. We watched the revolution in Benghazi on TV and saw everything. And because people in Benghazi have relatives here in Misurata and because people from Misurata have relatives in Benghazi, we talk and we know what's going on in Benghazi. We decided, "If we do not step up for Benghazi, Qaddafi will crush them." We organized over the phone and decided it was better to do something than nothing.

When we did, the army came and started shooting. And one of our guys was killed. His name was Khalid Abo Shahma. [Here we stopped the interview and continued the next day.]

WE WERE TALKING ABOUT HOW PEOPLE DECIDED TO DO SOMETHING TO HELP BENGHAZI.

Yes. We went with others to say, "We are with Benghazi, because we need freedom." We went to the middle of Misurata, and within just a few minutes, the police and army surrounded us. First they [the army] said, "If you don't go home, we'll shoot." Then right away, they started shooting randomly. People got really scared and ran to their homes. The next day, when we brought Khalid Abo Shahma to a cemetery, lots of people gathered and said, "OK, this is the time"—the time to get our freedom.

So we went to the central street in Misurata, and we saw the police and military run. The people didn't care about anything; all they had was wood and steel. But the police and military ran, because of the large number of angry people. For two days, the police stations were empty and all security forces were gone. It was really difficult.

During the first days of the revolution, we as lawyers called each other and said, "There's lots of crime taking place from Qaddafi's side. If we don't act right now, the evidence might disappear and the people won't be able to go after the criminals." So we decided on the third day of the revolution to create an association called the Human Rights Association. There were about 140 of us. Almost all were lawyers, but some were mathematics teachers and some were engineers. We lawyers told them: "You need to get evidence that will make our case strong. Don't destroy any evidence you get from the police station or the military." People gave us lots of documents they had collected when they had entered the police stations and the military bases.

YOU WERE WORRIED THAT PEOPLE WOULD DESTROY EVIDENCE?

Yes. And some of them actually set fire to the police station. So we tried to calm them down, and said, "Get us the documents."

We got papers, like orders telling the police what to do. Sometimes, "Kill, do whatever you need to just get control of the revolution." And some prisoners reported that they heard Qaddafi say, "I need to see the sea in Misurata red from blood."

But we didn't know anything about crimes against humanity or war crimes. So we sent five of our guys to Egypt for training on how to document these crimes. They stayed there for eight days, and each day they called and said, "Do this, do that." And it really helped.

[When the government institutions stopped working], we set up a local council, which formed communities to be responsible for everything: a community for old people, a community for bringing food and sharing food. I still remember people bringing big trucks with food, shelter, and everything.

And during that time, there was no Red Cross, no assistance from outside. It was a really hard time. It was the first time I saw people come together.

But later, in less than a month, a huge army came [to Misurata] and took back control of the town, the middle of the town, specifically Tripoli Street. There were many tanks and lots of soldiers. So we ran and they stayed there, in the middle of town. They had brought snipers, and put them on the buildings. The Tameen Building was the strategic base for the snipers because it is the skyline building, and enabled them to control movement across the city and to shoot in all directions. If anything moved, just [makes shooting sound]. Lots of people [were killed] everyday; some days ten people were killed, some days forty. No one could help us, so we stayed more than two months like this, maybe more

Then we decided we would fight. If we don't do anything, they will kill us all. So we gathered up all the women and children and put them in a safe place, downstairs in a building out of town and in other safe places. People used boats to bring in what we needed: food, weapons. And also people from Benghazi, they came to help us. And they showed us what to do in this situation. So we started to fight. We moved toward the middle of town, toward Tripoli Street specifically. It was . . . I'm not going to tell you exactly, but it was pretty bad because when you left your home, you said to your families, "Goodbye" because you might never come back because of the snipers. We lost lots of friends and family members.

When NATO started to target the tanks, that helped a lot, because we didn't have any weapons to take on tanks.

I forgot to mention that the security forces cut the water, so people couldn't drink, and they blocked the sewer system, which came up into the streets. And sometimes they put poison in the water. But the worst thing, and it cost lots of lives, were the snipers.

After six months of the Misurata blockade, Qaddafi's army started to withdraw. They tried to kidnap lots of civilians to use them as a human shield; they would be put in the front lines to deter attacks by NATO and the revolutionaries.

WHAT HAS MOTIVATED YOU THROUGH ALL OF THIS?

Who else would have documented crimes against humanity? We needed to do it right and to do it according to law, to have evidence. And every single man and woman from the community did their job. We have managed to collect more than a thousand documents reflecting the orders of the security forces to kill civilians, in addition to other war crimes including raping, torturing, kidnapping, and displacement.

They did what they did because you have to do whatever it takes to survive. You have to. There's no choice. If you don't collaborate as a community, you'll be in shame for all of your life. If you hide or run, you'll be in shame. You have to do the right thing for your people. To let everybody from outside know what was happening in Misurata—that motivated me a lot. **>>**

Um Mustafa *(Iraq; kindergarten principal)*

"I have to be strong; I have to be an example to follow."

*We interviewed Um Mustafa, a woman in her thirties, at her highly deco-
rated modern house. She seemed very strong and composed, but her
smile hid the terrifying side of the story. She had to try hard not to cry
when she recounted being kidnapped by al-Qaeda, and we stopped the
interview for a few minutes to let her catch her breath. When she re-
sumed, her eyes were once again full of life and hope.*

◀◀ I'm thirty-seven years old, and I've been a kindergarten teacher for
eighteen years, eight as a principal, here in Baghdad. I have a diploma from
the Teachers Institute, and currently I'm a second-year student in psychology
at college.

WHAT WAS YOUR EXPERIENCE OF THE WAR IN 2003?

My husband works in the police, so he was often away from home. I had the
responsibility of taking care of our four children most of the time. Even before the war [when there were air raids on Baghdad], we were alone at home
hearing the sound of bombing, and had no power, and heard the gossip
that Baghdad is gone and that it has been occupied. We heard many news
reports, but we did not know the truth.

In 2003, everyone left their houses, even my parents. We had no communication, no cell phones. I was worried about my husband, I did not
know where he was, I also did not know where my parents were, and three of
my children were with them.

WHY?

I heard that the residential areas would be bombed. At that time, the previous government established military areas within the residential areas, close
to schools and some houses. So these places were specifically bombed, and
these were very close to the area where we lived.

WHY DID YOU STAY AT HOME?

I was waiting for my husband. I kept my youngest daughter, who was an infant at that time, and sent the rest with my parents. The previous regime fell,
and I kept waiting [for my husband] for two, three, four days until we were
gathered again, thank God. My parents came back, too, and the situation
went gradually back to normal, until looting started.

I heard that the kindergarten was one of the institutions that was hit. I
was the assistant principal, and the principal was not present. Security-wise,
I was responsible for the building. So I went there and saw how the kindergarten had been looted by the people; it was empty, and the windows were
broken.

I talked with the students' parents and asked them, "This is your own kids' kindergarten. Why do you rob it?" And one of them answered that all the government institutions were robbed, so why not the kindergarten? After that, we tried to collect the furniture that remained, but we lost the greater part.

We contacted the Ministry of Education but received only modest directions. The situation was not stable yet. The children could not come to school, only the administrators. We were at work, but we did not even receive our salaries. We heard news that the American forces would be responsible for distribution of salaries. Sometimes we received our salaries in dollars. After that, we started to contact various bodies. The Americans visited more than once, and we started to discuss the security situation with them. However, no solution was presented, so I started seeking the assistance of humanitarian organizations.

At the beginning of the 2004 academic year, which starts in September, there was not even one chair for the teachers to sit on. Then the local councils gave us a $750 grant, which I think came from the coalition forces, to be spent on the schools. We used this to buy very basic things: carpet, chairs for the teachers. This is how we started, and children gradually started to come to school. Some of the children brought their own chairs as a donation. And then gradually we managed.

Later, we contacted an international NGO, which paid for reconstruction [of the kindergarten]. I received a threat from the chief contractor, who was under pressure from others, that I would be in trouble if I refused receipt of the building. But the construction did not meet the specifications in the tender, so I refused to sign that it did. Then a committee from the Ministry of Education visited the kindergarten and checked the defect and supported me. I transferred the tender directly to the committee, and the Ministry of Education took over and received the building.

My husband was also threatened. There were groups from the previous regime that assassinated police officers. Many were killed in our area. Someone told my husband about a group that wanted to assassinate him. The situation became intolerable; there was nothing that made us want to live in this country: no electricity, no security, not even food.

My husband went to Egypt and tried to get residence there, and my mother, the children, and I went to Syria. In the meantime, Iraqis were prevented from entering Egypt, so we stayed in Syria and transferred my children to schools in Syria. My mother stayed with the children. My husband and I would go back and forth between Syria or Egypt and Iraq. We did not quit our jobs. We are government employees; we don't have any second incomes.

On one occasion on our way back to Iraq, there was an attempted kidnapping by al-Qaeda. They [the al-Qaeda fighters] were masked and armed, and they ordered the car in which we were traveling, between Fallujah and Ramadi, to follow them. When we reached a junction along the way, God wanted to save us, and when we saw [US] planes, we started waving our hands and screaming, seeking their assistance. And the driver showed courage; he turned the car and drove.

We came back to Baghdad, which was sunk in the dark. We arrived almost at sunset. As we were driving to our house, we heard gunfire, but we did not know why and who fired. Then we learned that the area had been divided between Sunnis and Shiites. So we went to the house of my husband's uncle, who originally lived in Syria, but their son and a daughter were living in Baghdad because of the university.

Two days after our return, my brother-in-law Mohsen went out, but did not return. We kept calling but there was no response. We sent text messages. After a while, about 11 PM, someone called. With a mocking and laughing voice, he said, "What do you want? You have to forget Mohsen." We asked, "Who are you?" He replied that it was none of our business. Then we asked him what he wanted and where was Mohsen, and he replied that Mohsen is fine, and then he hung up. We could not sleep and our anxiety continued until the morning, when my husband called Mohsen's cell phone, which was answered by someone who said that they have Mohsen and demanded a ransom of five books [$50,000—a "book" is a local term for $10,000].

The phone call ended like this: "If you want your man to live, pay the ransom." Over the next ten days, we sold what we could to raise the ransom; we also borrowed money up to the eleventh day, which was the agreed date [for paying the ransom]. But we could not manage to collect the amount in full; all that we managed to get was $25,000.

They asked for someone to hand over the ransom somewhere in the Karrada district of Baghdad, next to a statue. A masked person on a bicycle came at noon, took the money and disappeared. Through the afternoon we waited, and we heard nothing about Mohsen. We lost hope of his return and said that the money and the young man had gone with the wind. Then, one hour before sunset, a taxi stopped near the house and Mohsen stepped out handcuffed and blindfolded.

We left the area and went to live with my parents.

In 2007, sectarianism increased and militias spread. We woke up in the morning to see dead bodies filling the streets. At school once, I saw people drag someone from a car trunk, and they executed him in front of my eyes. We could not utter a single word.

We went to the police, but they could not do anything because they [the gangs] were in large numbers, and the cars they were using had forged license plates, and they had forged identities, and weapons were everywhere.

After the kidnapping, we went back to Syria, and we decided not to return to Baghdad at all. We left Iraq, with my sister and mother, and went to Syria to stay with an uncle. We drove with others as part of a convoy and drove in daylight, when it is unlikely for the bandits or al-Qaeda or any other terrorists to attack us, where the area is protected by the army and police. We women traveled by road while the men were traveling by air.

After a while, we did come back to Iraq. When we came back, they tried to kill my husband. One day he came to pick me up from work. When a colleague and I got in the car, I noticed that a car parked nearby moved when our car moved; there were three people in that car. When they approached our car, I tried to warn my husband. They took out a gun with a silencer and fired on us. My husband, an officer, had a weapon and began firing at them, which caused them to flee.

After that, my husband stayed in his office all the time; he did not come home. I spent a whole month at my parents' house. The children didn't go to school, nor did I go to work.

WHAT DID YOU FEEL AT THAT TIME?

Horror and anticipation. I expected them to open the door and attack us at any moment. I suspected that someone in any car that passed near my house would aim a gun at me or my husband. I even began to think that they might harm my relatives in order to harm us.

HOW COULD YOU CONTINUE GOING TO SCHOOL?

I went every other day. Different people drove me to the college each time, and we used a different car. Sometimes I took a taxi and changed on my way, for camouflage.

These events brought us into sickness, not only psychological. This is the case with more than three-quarters of Iraqis now: anxiety, psychological strain, bad health.

WHAT HELPED YOU OVERCOME ALL THIS? WHAT MOTIVATED YOU TO GO ON?

Actually, it was the power of faith. And my responsibility to my family and my job.

IS IT HARD TO BALANCE BETWEEN YOUR WORK AND YOUR FAMILY?

I have to be strong; I have to be an example to follow. I remember the day following the incident when they tried to assassinate my husband and I was with him. I could have been dead by now. There was a graduation ceremony at the school where I work as a principal.

Afraid or not, I attended the ceremony because there were people expecting me to be there. Perhaps they [the terrorists] did not want me to be present that day. But I will not allow myself to be defeated. I must have the courage to continue my life, because if I don't, fear, terror, and murder will triumph, and I might die from fear.

Every human being has a message, and mine is to be creative until the last day of my life so that I can serve this country. **>>**

Thyn Zar Oo *(Myanmar [Burma]; legal aid manager)*

"I constantly try not to become disillusioned."

One member of our interviewing team had been working with Thyn for several weeks, so the interview was very relaxed. Thyn needed no encouragement to talk about her experiences and her life. She said it was therapeutic for her.

<< I'm forty. I'm the program manager for the Myanmar Legal Aid Network. I studied English literature and language at Yangon University; from 1999 to 2002, I studied labor relations in the US.

WHAT AFFECTED YOU THE MOST DURING THE CONFLICTS?

From around 1985 to 1987, things started happening because there was huge resentment toward corruption, toward people losing opportunities and being oppressed. High school and university students organized around entertainment and media. They made jokes—political jokes. And everybody was very into it. And it released a little bit of tension.

In 1988, when I was about fifteen years old, they really did break out. We saw leaders like [opposition leader] Aung San Suu Kyi [who had returned to the country that year]. We started hearing her [prodemocracy] speeches. We felt like we all wanted to be there. And then there is this little epiphany that we all enjoy and there's a possibility beyond this whole thing. Behind us is oppression, and there's somewhere else down the road; it's going to happen right now. We thought that it's going to happen tomorrow. Then it didn't happen. [In 1988, the military ruler General Ne Win stepped down. Mass pro-democracy protests held in August 1988 were violently suppressed, and a new military regime took power.]

And that's the first time I saw bloodshed. All our lives we'd heard on TV, in newspapers, everywhere, how bad the insurgents are; they were all bad guys. People taking arms to rebel against the government; they are just like bandits. And that's the first time the students headed to the jungles to fight with them, hand in hand, with those rebels. It was another world. That's the first time we realized that this whole reality had been created for us; it's something other than reality.

People like me, we just sit in the house, siding spiritually with these students who are our brothers, cousins, a medical student, or an engineering student, and the next day they flee to the jungles. And their families, their relatives, their friends, got interrogated, their whole environment got confiscated. So everybody is afraid to keep newspapers from seven days ago, afraid even to keep pictures of their brothers who fled to the jungles.

My cousin, a medical student, was an activist. Even before 1988, he was taken from his house when he was sleeping and put in a camp far away, and there was a lot of interrogation. When he came back, he was a hero for us, but nationally there were more important leaders than him. So when he came back, he had been tied up in rope for so long, and his health . . . for them it's nothing, but for us it's a lot.

How did you feel when he came back?

I felt happy that he didn't die, and thought how valuable he is. For me, losing him would mean a lot, but luckily I didn't lose him that time. But eventually I lost him, because he got so embittered by the whole situation: bitter toward the government and the people who let that happen. I saw it, the extent of his disillusion. He is now a very successful doctor in cancer treatment, and so is his wife. But we lost him as a doctor. And we lost him as a citizen also. He's never going to come back because he just thinks this country is—to use the rude term—a hellhole. So they left the country; they will never come back.

What does "rule of law" mean to you?

To put it bluntly—forgive me—it doesn't mean anything for me unless the law and the rule make sense for us. We've been brainwashed, and for all four decades of my life, the rule of the law doesn't mean anything to me.

What motivates you to keep doing your legal aid work?

Being able to do something about [the challenges facing the people of this country]. Everything I do on a daily basis, everything I say on a daily basis, has in one way or another an impact on my [legal aid] organization, which has some impact on this country.

I want to be able to work. But I know I can't do it by myself. So I just hope there's a job for me. Meaning that I will keep on doing something that has an impact for my country. And I constantly try not to become disillusioned. I keep looking at different perspectives and from different angles. And the worst thing I could do, the thing that I'm afraid of most, is that I will be disillusioned. So I try to stay as clear as possible. **>>**

"Oscar" (Iraq; NGO manager)

"Don't keep yourself like a chicken in a cage. You have to live your life."

We interviewed "Oscar" in Washington, D.C., while she was visiting the United States from Iraq, where she was living at the time. She was very serious, reflective, and related her experiences almost as though she were reporting what had happened to someone else.

<< I'm twenty-nine years old and based in Baghdad, Iraq. Right after the invasion, I began working with the Iraqi Assistance Center, established by the Civil Affairs Unit of the US Army. We assisted people looking for missing or detained persons. After a year, I moved to work with a US organization that was helping Iraqis manage their conflicts.

After a while, things went really upside down. It was very high tension, with killing everywhere. Sometimes, we had from twenty to thirty explosions per day. The year 2007 was the worst. In January, several friends were killed by random shootings. So was my brother. He was heading to work when a car showed up, and they were shooting people randomly. They gave him the first bullet between his eyes, and then they continued shooting him. The medical report said fourteen bullets.

Six months later, my cousin got kidnapped; they demanded a ransom of $35,000. We collected the amount from relatives and managed to release him. But while he was kidnapped, they were giving him drug injections so he would be out of his mind and could not recognize people. After they took the money, we got a message from the kidnappers that we have to leave our house and not come back.

So at that point we all moved to Syria. It's hard to be away from your country. Sometimes you get a little bit of relief, but not for long. You keep thinking about your friends and all the killings. So I decided to come back.

After two months, I came back from Syria. I stayed with relatives and went back to my job with the American organization. I tried to help women's groups working with widows. Through this project, I became aware of the increasing number of Iraqi women, specifically widows and divorced, who tend to be suicide bombers. The program helped these widows to change their attitude, because they were full of anger, full of hatred.

But I couldn't go back to the area I had lived in for my entire life, though my neighbors had taken care of the house. So many Iraqis who stayed in Baghdad were real warriors. They tried their best to protect themselves and their neighbors, even the empty houses. I know many Iraqi women who spent their nights awake; they had a small pistol or a gun, watching the street the whole night.

Also during 2007, I noticed that women were almost the only people in the streets. They were doing the shopping and acting as guards for their kids.

Many Iraqi women quit their jobs because they couldn't balance the responsibilities of protecting their kids with being productive employees.

WHAT DO YOU TELL YOUR RELATIVES ABOUT YOUR WORK?

Actually, none of my family knows where I'm working. When they ask me, I say I work for the Ministry of Irrigation. I tell some that I'm working with the UN. Generally speaking, people don't trust internationals; they believe that they are basically doing nothing, just getting jobs paid for by Iraqi petrol.

Some Iraqis realize how internationals really could play a good role. But many people, they just don't trust the internationals because of the corruption in some international organizations.

DO YOUR RELATIVES FEEL SAFE TO GO TO A STORE AND BUY FOOD?

Nowadays, we're just fed up. We don't care anymore. If we're going to die, we're going to die and that's it. I say: "You have a life. Live it or leave it." Don't keep yourself like a chicken in a cage. You have to live your life. We'll leave things to God. We have great faith in God. I don't think that we are better than the people who have been killed.

WHAT KEEPS YOU MOTIVATED?

Your voice is your own authority. So use it and don't abuse it. That's the main motivation for me. Plus, all the achievements I'm seeing. I'm seeing how widows [we're working with] have changed; instead of attempting to kill themselves, they have become these messengers helping their communities.

WHAT DO YOU THINK OF THE INTERNATIONALS IN IRAQ?

All the people I've met were committed to helping Iraqis. The only thing I would like internationals to focus on is coordination. There is lack of coordination, communication, and planning. Sometimes, despite good intentions, we end up with really bad results.

I've worked with NGOs and internationals—coordinating between the two of them and trying to reflect the local perspective in terms of dealing with specific topics. Because no one will be better [at finding solutions] than the people who are part of the problem themselves.

[Internationals make a big mistake] when they design their projects overseas without reaching out to the community and realizing what's the best way to deal with certain problems, or what types of trainings and skills are the most needed. Some NGOs spend a huge amount of money and effort on a specific project, but it's not the right timing and not the right component of the community to target.

Do two or three field visits a year to get in touch with the local people, to get a better sense of how things are going and to realize the best activities and the best methodologies in terms of dealing with the problems in the context of that community. For instance, the same methodology for dealing with conflict in Rwanda isn't necessarily of great help in terms of dealing with the Iraqi conflict. The more they study, the better they're going to act. **>>**

Salwa Al-Tajoury *(Libya; artist)*

"What I did during the revolution was paint a war car pink."

We interviewed Salwa in a museum that housed art made from weaponry. Anti-Qaddafi installation art stood outside; inside were welded statues constructed of bullets, casings, bearings, and other military hardware, including a statue of Don Quixote and his trusted donkey. Salwa was very open and direct. To begin with, she showed us some of the exhibits.

◄◄ This is Bob Marley [laughter]. It's because Ali [the artist] has a great sense of humor. During the revolution, many young people were drawing Bob Marley because he always talked about the revolution.

Everything was made from burned weapons. Ali transformed them into candlesticks, musicians, an orchestra, a woman and her baby, fishermen, a bicycle. And now that Qaddafi is dead, Ali's work is more joyful. He's started to do dancers. Tango dancers. Everything is dancing.

This used to be a missile; now it's a shark. And this is a rat. You know Qaddafi, during his speeches, he said, "You bunch of rats." Have you ever heard of a president talking like this to his people? "You are a rat"? So Ali did rats.

It's very symbolic. He never cleans the material. It's burned, it's cut, it's broken; it's a very important message for the wounded: the people who lost family members, the people who got depressed because they're very young and they lost a leg. He wanted to give them the message that even if you are broken, your life is not over.

Could you tell us about your background?

I'm a Libyan girl. I was born and lived all my life in France, and I was an activist there for women's rights and against discrimination. But my roots are here. I came back here and worked for NGOs. I was in UNICEF [the United Nations Children's Fund] initially. I discovered that even in humanitarian organizations people make money off of people's suffering. There was no action, just meetings and assessments, because with these assessments you get money out of donors. I said, "If you'll give me just a little of the money, I'll do psychosocial centers. I'll support children. I'll do the job. But you stay in five-star hotels." So I resigned, even though I had a very good salary.

When did you arrive in Libya?

On the 15th of February. I knew about the revolution from Facebook. I was an activist on Facebook. After the Tunisian revolution, we tried to make the Libyan people rise.

Can you tell us a little bit about your role during the revolution?

I thought through UNICEF I would do a lot for the children, but I didn't. To tell the truth, I wanted to do something huge, something really important, but I didn't manage it. So when Qaddafi died, I resigned from the job, and for a month I went to Misurata to distribute bread. I met the families of the martyrs. I had a grandfather crying, saying he has lost twelve of his sons. I felt so tired, so exhausted. Then I came here to the exhibition, and I saw weapons, tanks. I was so tired of it. So I asked if I could paint one of the military cars. I painted it pink [laughter]. I painted flowers on it. What I did during the revolution was paint a war car pink.

But most importantly, I was beside my people. I didn't do much, but I was here. I wanted to be here for them. I wanted to heal people by art, because I used to do theater in France. I want to make them express all the violence and all the death, because the revolutionaries got no support. No financial support, no psychological support.

Many of the revolutionaries are taking drugs now. We don't have skills for posttrauma crisis. And we have a true problem that many cannot talk about: *le prisance*; it means when you cannot make love anymore. Domestic violence has increased. The pressure. The scars are still there. The people don't know how to express all this. They are still in shock.

How do you cope?

I didn't realize it, but painting truly helped me a lot. It was my therapy. This place is my therapy. When I painted the car, I saw the smiles of the children and the people, and felt the positive energy from people.

What can be done to help people move forward?

We have to listen to the people and have a place for them, where they can have a feeling of peace. For a month we had a feeling of fear. Fear is the main thing we have to work on. Fear is a horrible weapon everywhere. In a place like this, an art place, you can sit, you can see colors, watch people create. We need to give the people a feeling of safety.

We need to develop centers where people can meet, talk, have a peaceful place, talk without being judged, because Libyans have never felt this feeling of peace. They were under Italians, then Qaddafi, and even now they feel frightened because they don't have another dictator. I want them to feel, I want them to breathe, maybe do breathing exercises, relaxations. I imagine a center with colorful things with a garden, because we don't have a lot of gardens in Benghazi and gardens are essential.

WHAT SHOULD INTERNATIONAL ORGANIZATIONS DO TO HELP?

Internationals don't meet the people; they stay in their office. They should have a translator and go to hospitals, orphanages, to the field—truly. They remain with other internationals. Meet the people—this is the first step. I witnessed a battle between the NGOs over money from donors. I met so many UN people, most of them drink, they were unhappy in their own lives. Most of them were running away from their own problems. How can you help the people if you yourself are in need of help?

WHAT MOTIVATES YOU TO MOVE FORWARD?

I'm not an organization, I'm just a woman. I'm doing what I can do with my means, like welcoming people here, trying to make a place where they can feel good. It's nothing, but this is my penny to this world.

HOW IS THE RULE OF LAW SITUATION IN LIBYA?

For the moment, we are in a transitional period. After more than forty years of dictatorship, we don't know what democracy is. We are like children trying to build a castle. Before building a castle, we have to grow up and get knowledge. Everything needs time to be rebuilt.

In Libya, all the dreams can come true; it's an empty page. In Europe, in America, everything has been done, and you have an economic crisis there, because of the capitalist system. I stay here because here I have the hope to rebuild a world that I prefer. Everything has to be rebuilt; you have so many things you can do here.

People say to me, "You could have stayed in Paris and leave us in our war, but you decided to come back and stay." I am here because this is my roots and all my family lives here. My aunts, my uncles, my cousins—this is your blood, your identity. We passed through all these traumatic events, and now I feel much more linked with this country because of this experience. I want to make sure that Libya is headed in the right direction. After that, I can go wherever I like. I mean, the world is huge; I can live wherever. But for the moment, I feel the need to be here. **>>**

Hasan Arzuallxhiuv *(Kosovo; eye surgeon)*

"My house was surrounded . . . I was inside for three months."

We interviewed Hasan—a friend of one of our team members—at a noisy, unpretentious restaurant in Prizren, where we had dinner with him and his family as well as other friends. His very young children were there, too, and it felt at times joyful, when we were celebrating friendship, and then suddenly somber, when reflecting on the war.

<< I am thirty-nine years old. I am a medical doctor, an eye surgeon. I was born here in Prizren, and I grew up here. During my education I was in different places—here in Kosovo and abroad—but I came back here to where I was born, and I continue to work and live in this town.

WHAT WAS YOUR LIFE LIKE BEFORE THE WAR?

Before the war, I was studying medicine here, but it was a conflict period. We [Kosovan Albanians] were expelled from our university in 1991. I had to take quite a long pause between 1992 and '93, and then we started the parallel education system here in Kosovo [one system for Kosovan Serbs, one for Kosovan Albanians]. I graduated in 1995. Then I went to Turkey to work in a hospital to get more practice, since we didn't have the opportunity to do that here. We were not allowed to work in the hospitals here because we were being educated in the parallel system, which was not recognized by the Serbian government at the time.

I came back from Turkey in 1997, and the political situation was getting worse and worse. And the financial situation was also very bad.

I had to find a job, and the best thing for me was to find a job at an international organization. We had this OSCE [Organization for Security and Co-operation in Europe] mission here before the war [when Serbian forces were fighting the Kosovo Liberation Army, but before NATO became militarily involved], and I found a job there as an interpreter for the human rights section. I worked with them for two to three months, and I had the opportunity to have this contact with the international community. And to see how things should be, and how we should work, and what are real human rights and democracy.

We were interviewing people who'd had someone from their family taken by police, they had been beaten, or they'd lost family members to the police. From all communities. We had Serbs also coming looking for their missing persons, not only Albanians—but mostly Albanians.

I saw so many killed. Men who were crushed by a tank, I have seen everything. But being a doctor, I participated also in the autopsies. They used me as a doctor. We went together, I explained to them where the bullet was, how the entry wound was made, and the exit wound, and everything else. There were also experts who knew how it happened, whether it was a murder or an accidental killing. One case I will never forget. One guy was sixteen years old, the nephew, and the other one was maybe thirty-four, thirty-five; and they were killed by a professional.

WHAT HAPPENED TO YOU DURING THE WAR?

During the three months of bombing [by NATO of Serbian forces], my house was surrounded by the paramilitary forces. I was inside for three months. I couldn't go out. My father—then he was seventy, seventy-one—he was the one who was going out to buy whatever was needed to keep us alive inside.

WHY COULDN'T YOU LEAVE?

Because I worked with an international organization, and they were mad at OSCE. They thought that all of us who worked with them gave them information about where the bombs should be dropped. And everything was OK until the second of June. I had a visit by the Serbian Interior Ministry force. We were all there, and when they came inside, they said to my brother, "Can you leave this room because we came to talk with Hasan?" Then I realized that they were looking for me.

Then they started. You know, "Why did you work with the international community, look what they are doing to us. They are bombing us and why have you worked with them? Do you know they are our enemies?" I said I was not the only one who worked there. I needed money, I had to work, and there were Serbs also working with me. If I am an enemy of this country, the Serbs are too.

Then they searched a little bit, but found nothing important, and they left.

WHAT DID YOU DO RIGHT AFTER THE CONFLICT?

After the war, I joined the UN mission here in Prizren and was head interpreter with the regional administrator. It was an interesting period. Internationals were popular, and the persons who were here were more or less capable. And also the nationals who were running the municipalities didn't have a lot of experience and were ready to listen.

DID YOU EVER FEEL THREATENED?

I was once threatened. I was threatened by my own people. I was coming back to my house, it was nearly midnight. There were two young guys waiting in front of my house. I saw them and I thought, if I stop, or if they see that I am scared, then I am finished. I walked straight and I came before them and just pushed them, and I started to walk to my house to the door. I thought that they could just kill me from behind and nobody would find out who killed me. And this is what they said: "Look what you are doing for your country, for your people. Why you are acting against your people?" They were part of the radical wing [of the Kosovo nationalist movement]. I turned back and said, "I am not doing anything against my people, I will never do anything against my people, and you are not the ones who can judge me." And I just went into my house.

WHAT HAVE THINGS BEEN LIKE SINCE THEN?

The international community seemed to run out of gas. And the nationals, seeing the international community withdrawing, got wilder and wilder with corruption.

We are trying to improvise a system of rule of law here, where everyone respects the law. Maybe we will have it in the future, but we don't have it now. But we don't have any problems with security and safety. It was more difficult earlier; now I think that we don't have those kinds of problems.

WHAT DO YOU WISH FOR THE FUTURE?

I would like to see a Kosovo without any problems, with rights for all communities regardless of who they are. I work in the hospital. I have two jobs, I work twelve hours a day; I would like to have a normal salary. I would like to be confident that my children could have an opportunity to live normally, to be educated normally. That's all—to live in peace with all other communities.

I love my country and that's the main thing. I would stay here even it becomes a corrupted country. This is a new country; it is being built up and we need a good tutor.

I think that this place can be brought to normal only through the help of the international community. I know they are oriented more now to Afghanistan, Iraq, but Kosovo was an experiment for the international community. As a doctor, as a scientist, when I start an experiment I want to finish it properly. I think that they should finish it properly. So they left the experiment in the middle. They started it, then they left the experiment. So when evaluating it as a success for the international community, it's the same as a scientist who starts an experiment and leaves it in the middle. Now it's a question of can you evaluate it as a success or not? **>>**

Sofía Montenegro

(Nicaragua; journalist and researcher)

"Democracies are a sort of gymnasium."

Sofía is the executive director of the Center for Communications Research, a civil society organization that studies communications, culture, democracy, and public opinion. We interviewed her in her office, in a house in a clean and tidy, mostly residential area of the Nicaraguan capital, Managua. Sofía's father had been the right-hand man to President Somoza, the Nicaraguan dictator overthrown in 1979. She smoked throughout the interview and was very open and expressive.

◄◄ I am from the north of Nicaragua. I come from a family with a long military tradition, a family of the middle to upper class. I studied journalism, and currently I direct a nonprofit association dedicated to the promotion of independent communication projects and research on the political process in Nicaragua and the development of social actors. I started to participate politically when I was seventeen years old, so practically my whole life, because I am fifty-five now.

WHAT WERE YOUR PERSONAL EXPERIENCES DURING THE CONFLICT?

I think the origins of the conflict, and the majority of conflicts, have to do with authoritarian conceptions of power. My family was linked to the Somoza regime, but in another context, all the members of my family were students at the university.

Nicaraguan universities were always like islands within all that complete control. There was university autonomy, and it had the only space for freedom—to think, to discuss—that existed. One lesson I learned was that authoritarianism and fear work only during a certain time. There comes a moment that it stops being fear and converts to rage. The rebellion is served. True? You can't live in a permanent state of terror your whole life, because the most terrorized people get to a point that they'd prefer to die rather than continue living in that condition. I have seen this several times in this country, and in other Central American countries.

This began with the first Sandinista Front and expanded. That was what finally brought the possibility of organizing not just a tiny guerrilla force but one that could convert itself into an urban movement, armed for resistance, with the whole citizenry starting to get involved. For that, they didn't necessarily need military training, but the will. The political will of the people to move. The revolution was an indispensable fact. It was legitimate, right?

There was a lot of political inexperience at that time, because, well, we were all young kids, we were teenagers, you know. I would have been twenty-two when the revolution triumphed.

There was a lack of real political experience; the country never had the opportunity to have legitimate organizations. I now think that democracy is a construct that is maintained daily—by organizations as much as civilians. Democracies are a sort of gymnasium where one goes to do calisthenics, where people learn about political culture, discourse, debate, the building of consensus. But in Nicaragua, that was an investment that was not made. Historically, the investment in building organizations that train people to learn values, attitudes, and the exercise of democracy was not done. The only training camp they left us was that of bullets. The military training camp. The other school—the public school of citizen exercise—has never existed in all the history of Nicaragua.

We came out of the struggle against the dictatorship, and the war started. Yes, the war, properly called, was what took the major portion of the decade. The way I lived it was like a process of developing conscience, like the growth of conscience—and I don't think that was just my experience, but everyone's. [This was intertwined with] the development of the feminist movement in Nicaragua. At the beginning [of the revolution], women only went to the street looking for a conscience for others: for their children, their husbands, their fathers who had been taken or otherwise disappeared. A conscience more geared to the maternal role.

Then came the armed conflict and a second level of conscience—that there was a world outside, which was not in agreement with what we wanted to do. And that brought about a radicalization of the people in relation to a second step of conscience, a nationalist conscience.

But when the military started to organize, the war began to stunt the process of democratic opening and consolidation, because the entire society militarized. By 1984, the cost—and I think women were the first to feel it in the country—was huge. People started to question if it was inevitable, this relationship between revolution and war, if revolution, that had its socialist democratic element, could be completed without having to cause a war. Me, what I know is that no war is good. And the best war is the one that doesn't occur.

The fatigue afterward, the suffering, the level of terrible loss that the population felt, wore out the foundations of consensus. And along came a paranoid leadership. Suddenly everyone started seeing counterrevolutionaries behind every tree, and this gave rise to a subsequent escalation of repression of all those who dissented.

How would you define the rule of law now in Nicaragua?

Right now in Nicaragua, nonexistent. The people of Nicaragua have made an enormous historical investment, with personal costs. There is not a single family that has not been affected by war. But the cost was consistent with the desire for freedom that the people of Nicaragua have always had. Nicaragua had never had better economic conditions than during Somoza's era. So it was not economic conditions that made the people of Nicaragua rebel. It was the absence of freedom. Today, we have a different situation. The economic conditions are bad or worse, and political space [for free discussion and action] is being closed. For this reason, I fear that this combination of factors can convert into the perfect storm. See? Because you'll have the big global economic crisis, on the one hand, and the political crisis, on the other, an institutional political crisis and the social crisis of aggravation of the conditions of poverty. When these three things come together, we are ready for everything to fall apart. And that situation is one that needs a leadership that, like a ship's good captain, maneuvers through the perfect storm. But we don't have good ship captains.

There is a feeling of urgency that all Nicaraguans have right now, to impede once again a closing of the political space, because its closure will once again open a new cycle of political conflict, and of armed conflict. I remember quite well, as if it were today, I was eighteen years old and went out in the street with [other students]; now I am an old lady of fifty-five years old going back to the street, asking for exactly the same thing.

How do you see the role of the international community in Nicaragua today?

I think the international community in the case of Nicaragua should be a lot more consistent; you have to stop peddling rhetoric with the theme of democracy. And they have poorly managed the theme of democracy, because they have used its name to intervene where it shouldn't. The same is true for its paralysis in intervention, where in fact it should have intervened.

In Nicaragua, since 1990, democracy has been the Cinderella of international investment; it is as if the [international community] didn't put any value on democracy. Here is an example: They've invested millions in the Supreme Court of Justice, the most infamous in all of Latin America. It is a highly structured system of corrupt judges, partisans, and dishonest people. In the case of Nicaragua, the assistance made to civil society was just 5 percent of all the money given to the corrupt government, from whom no rendering of accounts or democratic accountability was demanded. So the question is: "What kind of game is international cooperation playing here?" Do you get it? I believe that it is an enormous failure.

Democracy [needs] the school of the gym, where one goes to grow democratic muscles. If I don't go to the gym, then I won't have any muscles. International investment [should be in] the accelerative element of democracy: development, growth, and strength of civil societies, particularly the social movements that reclaim political rights. If you don't put a penny in social movements—a real strategic investment in organizational building toward what I call the "people's conscience"—all that you will reproduce are schools of corruption that represent the political parties of the right and left in Latin America.

WHAT MOTIVATES YOU TODAY TO CARRY ON?

What motivates me is what has motivated me since I was an inexperienced, revolutionary youth: the issue of fairness. That has been the motivating law of my life, that things should be fair for everyone. And all have to have their place. You have to give space to folks from across the political spectrum—communist, socialist, conservative, social Christian, social democrat—so that everyone feels happy and able to have a common agenda, a democratic commitment.

And you have to respect diversity. This is a multiethnic country, multilingual, and multicultural. So our model of democracy has to recognize that fact, that detail of reality. You have to respect that diversity, that richness, that difference. I think that is the secret to peace and development. Because you will be capitalizing on the energy of everyone, and you'll be able to reduce levels of conflict among everyone because everyone will be able to say, "Man, yes, there is a place for me."

All the wars of the twentieth century demonstrated to large, small, and medium societies that [taking the road to equality] is the only road if you want to have sustainable and inclusive democracy. Or, you can say: "Well, okay, let's have a poor but decent country, since this is never going to be a great and rich country, but one where everyone lives decently." I think that is a project to which we can aspire. >>

WORKERS AND SMALL BUSINESS OWNERS

Pragmatic but not cynical, more optimistic than pessimistic, and realistic but certainly not without ideals (for which many of them had risked their lives), the workers and small business owners we spoke with know what they want. And what they want is stability, security, and opportunity. They want to live in a society in which, if they work hard, they can make a good living—not a fortune, but enough to afford a good life for their families.

When asked what needed to be done to get their countries back on their feet, most interviewees mentioned the need to tackle crime, not least corruption. Yousef Ammar Shagan, who is in the coffee business, says "corruption is our major enemy in Libya." It is, he explains, not just wrong but bad for the economy: "I feel corruption is the reason for underdevelopment. If we fight corruption in Libya, we will make a shortcut to development."

Conscious how hard they have to work to make an honest living, our interviewees were scathing of those they see as prospering illegally, especially politicians who seem happy to let the chaos continue if it helps fill their pockets. "Everywhere there is chaos," said Sukraman Lama, who drives a taxi through the crazy, congested streets of Kathmandu. "And corruption. I don't think most international aid reaches the target groups: politicians come in between. They take half the aid. The corruption continues." Ferdos Hussain, a salesman in a jewelry store in Kathmandu, remembered how he had been pleased when a new king came to the throne who had been a businessman, because Ferdos assumed that he would be good for the economy and the country as a whole. But Ferdos became disappointed after the king partnered with the same old corrupt ministers and people as the previous monarch.

Bujar Isajar, who opened a café-bar when peace came to Kosovo, said that he wanted "zero-tolerance against crime to be implemented, for laws to be in line with the constitution, for all people to be equal before the law." Yet, like all the people featured in this chapter, Bujar was realistic. He didn't expect miracles overnight. "I think we are going in the right direction," he said, "slowly but steady; perhaps we are a bit impatient, but for a country emerging from a communist system, and from repression and war, it takes time to establish grounds for a functional rule of law."

Rexhep Hajdin Bobal, who had worked for "forty-five years and nine months" in Kosovo before retiring from his job as a machinist, was critical of politicians who care more for their political party interests than for the people. The people, he said, especially its more vulnerable members, not only need help from the government but deserve help. "The message to our leaders is that the elderly have been left to God's mercy. They worked so many years and contributed to society, yet they are left without pensions and are living a difficult life."

But while the interviewees don't pretend that their societies are now model societies, they also don't want to overemphasize or dwell on the challenges of the situation—especially because a return to normality could be good for business. Bujar, the bar owner, declared, "People are welcome to visit Kosovo. The situation is calm; there are no problems with security. . . . They should come and see our mountains and old towns and other historic sites. There is a lot to be seen here, and we have the capacity to welcome them, including treating them to a cold beer."

Sukraman sees hope for the future—as long as things go well and the politicians act properly. Govinda Rijal, despite having been badly beaten by police when he protested in the streets of Kathmandu for democracy, also expressed guarded optimism: "I'm definitely not pessimistic. The conflicting sides are still confronting each other. They were face-to-face in the past, but now there is a government in between them; there is a constitution in between them; there is a public between them, and there is commitment between them. They are face-to-face, but not shooting at each other."

Govinda cast an equally realistic eye on the representatives of the international community in his country. "There are some organizations that are working for the good of the people, and there are some that are here just to be here, not to do anything significant, but just to be here." Rexhep asked for the international community itself to be realistic: "I hope the international community has good intentions for Kosovo. The international community should see things more realistically; they should listen to both sides."

Above all, our interviewees want stability—stability in which they can work hard and make a living for themselves and their families. Muhammed Ali, who sells the leafy, legal narcotic qat in Yemen's dangerous marketplaces, says that he hopes for "a stronger state that can control people who are bad. A security state, a controlled state. A safe Yemen, a secure Yemen that does not allow everyone to do whatever they like. A government that rules in the market and the street."

Ferdos, too, called on the government to provide not only security but also economic opportunity, so that his sons don't have to follow his brothers and cousins abroad in search of well-paying jobs. Sukraman, whose taxi business was going from strength to strength, took a slightly different view: "If you earn a living here, you don't have to go anywhere else. People see big bucks in foreign lands, but if you work here as hard as there, you can do well." Muhammed, too, saw opportunity, even though he had to carry a gun to protect himself when he works. "Working with qat is good," said Muhammed. "Better than going into criminal activities. There are many people who live on qat proceeds."

Muhammed had been a driver before he started selling qat; Bujar had been a medical technician before he opened his bar; Govinda had worked in the hospitality industry before becoming an office manager. And that same entrepreneurial adaptability and determination had served them well in times of conflict as well as peace. Yousef, for instance, "supplied the Libyan market with coffee until the revolution broke out," at which point he promptly threw himself into the business of helping organize and publicize that revolution, becoming a media spokesman and, as a consequence, a wanted man by the Qaddafi regime. Almost all the interviewees in this chapter have similar tales to tell of risking everything for a cause they saw as just. ●

Rexhep Hajdin Bobaj *(Kosovo; machinery worker)*

"The elderly have been left to God's mercy."

We met Rexhep at his house in the village of Korisha, where a NATO air strike during the conflict missed its Serbian military target and instead killed a number of civilians. Rexhep is a village leader. The interview was conducted on the patio of his house. His wife and male family members sat in plastic chairs next to Rexhep, while three young girls, curious and very quiet and polite, sat on a colorful carpet. The entire family was very welcoming.

◀◀ I was born in 1946. I am a machinery technician by profession. I worked for a long time as a machinist until 2005, when I retired. In total, I worked for forty-one years and nine months.

WERE YOU AFFECTED BY THE WAR?

War had a lot of impact on us. We were here in Kosovo during the war. We stayed here [in Korisha] for one month, then we went to the village of Velezha. We came back here, then we left and went to [the nearby city of] Prizren, and then came back again. Then the village was burned down. The entire population of the village moved to the forest nearby to find shelter.

HOW LONG DID YOU STAY IN THE FOREST?

Two weeks. We didn't know that the KLA [Kosovo Liberation Army] was fighting [Serbian forces] in our villages. We heard sounds of weapons and artillery, but didn't know what was happening there. Conditions in the forest were miserable. The weather was very bad, too. One day it started to rain. I had an old man on my left and a younger guy on my right side in the shelter. Both died later on. Serbian forces came very close to the forest. During the night, we went back to houses to prepare food, and during the day we stayed in the forest. The old man, his name was Bajrush, said: "They will kill us all." He had started to lose his mind from the war trauma.

Serbs were approaching and noticed that we were hiding in the forest, so I told the villagers that by early morning tomorrow we would move from here. I told them that I am responsible for my wife and my daughter and I will take them and leave tomorrow. I told them, "You do whatever you think is best for you and your families." The others agreed that we all should leave. The young guy that I mentioned earlier said, "Perhaps we should move to Shpenadi village; there are some empty houses where we could rest and then continue to Albania." We all agreed and left at 1 a.m. for Shpenadi. The corridor where Serbs moved their forces and weaponry was near, and when a girl noticed the corridor, we took another route and avoided Serbian forces.

WHAT HAPPENED THEN?

As we started to leave the village, KLA soldiers noticed our movement and thought that we were Serbian soldiers. They took their positions and were ready to open fire on us. We walked for some time; there were some paralyzed old women whom we needed to carry on our backs. Anyway, we were sure we had passed the risk from Serbian forces. The girl that I mentioned was three years old. She was exhausted from walking and started to cry. At this moment, KLA soldiers, who were less than fifty meters away, saw that we were civilians. They were so close to opening fire on us. We told them who we were and that we were trying to escape to Albania. When we got to Shpenadi, we stayed until Kosovo was liberated.

HOW DID YOU FEEL IN THE FIRST MONTHS AFTER THE WAR ENDED?

It was like a revival for me. When I saw my friends and colleagues, it was like people coming out of the ground. All were crying from happiness that they had survived. It was an incredible feeling. For three months, we were in the middle of the fighting, and we had no idea what was going on, who was killed, who had survived.

Only three or four houses [in Korisha] still stood. Other houses were burned down. During the war, we looked at our village through binoculars and watched Serbian soldiers burning the houses. They left only a few houses, perhaps afraid that they might find KLA soldiers there.

War? What can you say? War is not a bad thing to everyone. But war is done by those whose minds are poisoned, by those who do not want to find other means of resolving issues. After all, even when the war happens, in the end the parties in conflict have to sit at the table to negotiate. It is better to negotiate before the war happens to save innocent civilians' lives.

HOW DO YOU FEEL TODAY?

We survived, so I feel very good. But things didn't move in the direction we had thought they would. Things are not functioning as some people had promised us. The message to our leaders is that the elderly have been left to

God's mercy. They worked so many years and contributed to society, yet they are left without pensions and are living a difficult life.

Politicians should work more for the country and not just for their political party interests. Those who do not like their country, they do not like themselves either. The state should be strengthened.

There should be more people employed. Then, rule of law should be strengthened. Our leaders will hopefully recognize the importance of educating the youth and future generations, because there will be no positive development without proper education of the youth.

How safe do you feel?

I can't complain. It's not bad. But if international forces were not present here, we would have to leave Kosovo again.

I hope the international community has good intentions for Kosovo. The international community should see things more realistically; they should listen to both sides. They can see who was right and who was wrong. Even in the international organizations, there are various people with various agendas, and I hope only good people come here to Kosovo.

They should study about Kosovo; they should know how Albanians suffered from Serbs throughout history. A cousin of mine used to say, "It is better that the devil rule this place, not the Slavs." Serbs don't want to see us prosper.

What motivated you during the war?

In the village where we took refuge there was a lady called Theresa. I had a radio and listened to the news. Theresa said that I always told them that the news was positive, but that I never told them what those reports were. I was always optimistic that things will end positively, because the enemy's intentions were bad, and they would sooner or later fail in their objectives. We had a great hope that motivated us during those difficult times. In the end, justice won.

What motivates you today?

Now we are free. If you decide now to go to Pristina, or Mitrovica, you can go freely. Before 1999, the police stopped you several times and treated you badly. Now we are free to go to Tirana, to go everywhere without fear. **>>**

Yousef Ammar Shagan *(Libya; coffee businessman)*

"We were not concerned with revenge; our concern was to build our country, make up for all the wasted years."

Yousef owns a coffee business. He roasts coffee and also has a shop. We chatted with him outside, and he was very relaxed, forthcoming, and friendly. On the day we left Libya, he asked us to stop by the shop, from which he emerged with bags of freshly roasted coffee to take home.

◀◀ I am originally from Zawiya [a city in northwest Libya]. I'm married with four children. I am an engineer. I graduated in 1988 from the Higher Institute of Electronics in Bani Walid, Libya. After graduation, I worked for a while. After military service, which was imposed by Qaddafi, I worked in vocational training, but after five years I turned to the private sector and established a company, called Issam Company. It is well known in the coffee industry. We supplied the Libyan market with coffee until the revolution broke out.

WHY DID YOU JOIN THE REVOLUTION?

I felt that my country was in a catastrophe under Qaddafi and his followers. I was born in 1966, and by the beginning of the eighties I started witnessing the deterioration of education, the daily conflicts of the economy with the government. I knew that the government never cared about the private sector, never considered us as businessmen working in the private sector but as its enemies. Their only target was oil. They did not care about the people.

My family never liked Qaddafi. We were aware of his political game. We were aware of the corrupted policies in the country. During the last years [of his regime], I used to travel a lot as a business owner. Traveling enriches your knowledge, and the satellite and Internet have made the world open in the last twenty years. We started to realize the injustice in the country, and that it was sliding toward the abyss.

In the last ten years, when Qaddafi started resolving his issues with the West, we sensed that the West had taken his side, and so we gave up. We said, "Okay, that's our destiny and we will never get rid of him." Even the attempts by activists outside Libya would be of no use with the support of the superpowers for Qaddafi—until the revolution broke out in Tunisia.

We were following what was going on not hour by hour but second by second. We used to stay up until the next day to follow the developments of the revolution in Tunisia and Egypt. I personally thought that, even if the revolution didn't break out in Libya, we would still see a breakthrough, and that breakthrough could have a positive impact on us. When our brothers in the east first started the uprising in Libya, my friends and I started meeting and thinking that this was a once-in-a-lifetime opportunity. This is our chance. Our brothers in the east made a move, and it's time to make ours.

We made our first move in Zawiya. I was an actual participant, mostly in the liberation. Around a week before February 20, all communication was by phone. My role was over on that day, when all the people in Zawiya came out and we fully took over the city, on the 20th at midday. Then another role started, and this was funding. All businessmen in Zawiya took part in funding.

I also had a small media role. I had never spoken to the media, but on the 19th or 20th, I found myself calling one of the radio shows. I used Skype because I had a laptop. I also spoke with al-Hurra [a TV channel], using my name, which caused me trouble, and with a news agency. I found out that when they broadcast the news, they disclosed the names of the eyewitnesses, and thus they disclosed my name.

On March 10, the tyrant entered the city. We were five siblings, three of us were married. Each one of us asked his wife to stay with her family. My mother was left alone in the house. We all left the house—each one of us headed in a different direction. Some of my siblings left for Tunisia; others couldn't. I personally couldn't leave because I was told that my name was on the list [of people the regime was looking for]. I was among three wanted in Zawiya. But I had a friend who lived in a neighboring village. He hid us and fed us in a room in his house for six months—when all his neighbors were supporters of Qaddafi—until we came out on liberation day [when anti-Qaddafi forces took control of Zawiya].

Of course, liberation events took place, and there were some violations of human rights. But whenever [a supporter of Qaddafi] got caught, we defended them. We were not concerned with revenge; our concern was to build our country, make up for all the wasted years, and raise awareness among the youth. And reactivate education.

WHAT DOES "RULE OF LAW" MEAN TO YOU?

Rule of law means the establishment of the state. When the state is established, there will be rule of law, respect of human rights.

WHAT DO YOU WANT FOR YOUR COUNTRY?

What we want is development. Development in all fields, especially in education and health, because these are the basics.

Currently, corruption is our major enemy in Libya. We hope that civil society organizations and the international community assist us in fighting corruption because we lack the experience. I feel corruption is the reason for underdevelopment. If we fight corruption in Libya, we will make a shortcut to development.

DO YOU MIND IF WE USE YOUR NAME AND PHOTOGRAPH?

That's no problem. During the tyrant era, I stood in the middle of Zawiya and spoke to media and disclosed my name, which caused me troubles [laughter]. **>>**

Muhammed Ali *(Yemen; qat seller)*

"I have a pistol and an AK-47. I work at night so I have permission."

We photographed Muhammed in the market where he sold qat (a leafy, mild narcotic), but interviewed him elsewhere, because it might have been dangerous for all involved to conduct the interview in the market. He chewed on a large ball of qat throughout the interview but was nonetheless ill at ease, and was not used to being asked to put into words how the conflict affected him. He was far more concerned with simply surviving amid the seemingly endless conflicts and other dangers that are part of life in Yemen. (We heard a report six months later that he had allegedly killed a person—apparently, in response to a threat of attack—and was facing criminal charges.)

<< I am a qat seller. I come from Zaraja, in the Dammar area [of southwestern Yemen]. I finished primary school. For the past eight to ten years, I've been here in Sanaa. I came here to work, to sell qat. I began as a driver, and then started selling for my father.

Working with qat is good. Better than going into criminal activities. There are many people who live on qat proceeds. There are other jobs that may not make enough money for a family, and qat provides an opportunity to save some money. You can even build up your family [fortunes].

In the morning I pick up the qat and drive to Sanaa; I sit [and sell] until sundown, then go home, calculate the money, and go to sleep at 11 p.m.

When people chew qat, they relax and stay quiet, they don't make problems. They just become peaceful. If they don't chew, they create problems; they create quarrels with their wives and children.

I work so I can save some money. I buy a piece of land; I buy a house; I provide for my children and my family. I have five children and was married three times. Three children from one wife, one from another, and one from another. I now have three wives. I am looking for the fourth.

I teach them; I educate them so that they can do a teaching job, a stable job. Because working in qat is tiring. You get stuck with bad people, dangerous things. Like sometimes you meet a thief, meet someone who wants to get qat for free by taking it from you.

What thoughts do you have on the conflicts affecting Yemen?

There have been lots of problems. Houses collapsed, roads blocked, sub-tribes fighting each other. In many parts of the al-Haddah area, there have been tribal feuds.

There is a village called al-Asha, where fighting between the Byanis and the Zaidis led to nineteen people killed on one side and twenty on the other. This issue has been going on for twelve years now, and no one has resolved it yet. Even women were killed among these people. Even animals were killed. Because of a single field. There are competing claims to own it. And they're all living in the same village.

Some people try to resolve [these disputes]. But now there is a fight among the Zaidis themselves. They fight and block the routes.

Has conflict affected your family directly?

No one in my family has been involved [in the fighting]. We are peaceful. We are just civilians. I have a dispute with my father-in-law, and I'm going against him in court. I have a lawyer. They want to force a divorce on me, but I refused. It's been a year and two months now.

Our family is in the village and they're living there. I have a building here that is rented out. So their concerns are mostly about the financial crisis rather than security. They are worried about petrol. Diesel not being available. Not enough work.

In Sanaa, all the time we are very anxious. The highway is frightening especially at night. You don't feel like you're safe at any moment. Because of the overall situation. You see people hiding in this part of the street or that side of the street. It's not about the gunshots, but you don't know what is going on.

Everybody carries his own arms and has a companion usually so that you feel safer. I have a pistol and an AK-47. I work at night so I have permission, and I worked for the government for some time. I have permission for three companions in addition to myself. I was cleaning my gun once, and it went off. I'm missing my third finger.

One morning, there was a misunderstanding between me and some people, and when I came back from work I found them blocking my way. And then what I did is I just gave them the *jumbiya* [a traditional Yemeni knife that many men wear as part of their outfit] for arbitration and said that if I did anything wrong . . . then the issue was resolved.

WHAT DOES "RULE OF LAW" MEAN TO YOU?

It's by the state. The state should apply the law against whoever is acting bad, taking control of them and detaining them, so that people stay safe. So the streets can be quiet and safe. So that work can continue.

There is no state. Everyone is acting in their own way and doing whatever they want, and there is no control. People are not educated, and the state doesn't have control.

My belief is that there will be no solution going forward. And that there might be bigger problems. A week ago there was a crisis in diesel and petrol. The locals are blocking routes. Farmers stop the diesel from Marib or from Hodeida. Some people are just a headache. Some are hijackers.

Sometimes it goes worse, sometimes it goes better. It's not stable. There is some danger. You cannot open at night. Maybe people come and block roads at night.

WHAT DO YOU HOPE TO SEE IN THE FUTURE?

A stronger state that can control people who are bad. A security state, a controlled state. A safe Yemen, a secure Yemen that does not allow everyone to do whatever they like. A government that rules in the market and the street.

Everyone in Yemen should see the right path and avoid creating a bad reputation for themselves, so that everyone respects them and honors them. That's what I ask every Yemeni to be. And again, security and stability. **>>**

Govinda Rijal *(Nepal; office manager)*

"There were four of them beating me for about ten minutes."

When we interviewed Govinda, he was already part of our team. He was working as an office manager for USIP in Kathmandu, and, aware that he had worked in the past with an American documentary filmmaker, we had asked him to join the Speaking Their Peace team during our time in Nepal. On the last day of our trip, we asked him if we could interview him. We chatted at the hotel in Kathmandu where we were staying. In fact, it turned out to be the same hotel where he got started in the hospitality industry as a clerk years back. He was, as usual, thoughtful and philosophical.

◄◄ I'm thirty years old and grew up in a village, where my parents are farmers. I did my SLC [secondary leaving certificate—the final examination for secondary school] in Kathmandu, then I started working in tourism. I worked in a hotel—this hotel—starting as a room boy, and I gradually got promoted and changed hotels.

I went to a trekking company, then went back into the hotel business, and again jumped into a trekking company. In 2006, I started working for a travel agency and stayed there for about three years. And now I am with USIP.

WHAT WERE YOUR EXPERIENCES DURING THE CONFLICT?

I got involved in politics when I was fourteen or fifteen. I volunteered for a political party during an election to prevent the polling booth from being captured by the Maoists. They put my name on their list. In 2001, while I was at my uncle's house in my village, the Maoists told me to leave the village immediately. I left my uncle's place at ten o'clock that night.

When the conflict was at its height, I worked here. I always took the transportation provided by the hotel, and every kilometer or so there would be a checkpoint manned by police, armed police, or the army. If we left our ID card at home, or back in the hotel, then we were in big trouble. We might as well get arrested.

DID THAT HAPPEN TO ANYONE?

It happened to one of my friends. He forgot his ID back in the hotel. At a checkpoint, we were told to get out of the vehicle. We were body-searched. The driver then missed the stop at the line, by an inch or so—I think the front tire touched the white line. He was made to get out, take the wheel off, carry it around the vehicle, put the wheel back on, and then drive on. That was the punishment.

SO IT WAS VERY ARBITRARY?

They could do whatever they wanted. It was not easy being here at that time. But personally I was not threatened. That was the only incident I had during that conflict.

WHAT WERE YOUR EXPERIENCES DURING THE PEACE PROCESS?

One thing I always had in my mind, I cannot live in a country ruled by a dictator or an autocrat. When the seven parties and the rebel Maoists decided to forge an alliance to fight against the autocratic regime of the king, I saw a window of opportunity that peace might prevail in the country. I wasn't attached with the political parties or the rebels, or the regime. For me, the outcome was more important than the process. When the opportunity of democratic rule presented itself, I got involved to the point that it threatened my life—at a big demonstration in Gangabu.

There were thousands of young people there roaming around with no leaders. It was a scene where an accident was waiting to happen. Everybody had their own set of opinions, not listening to anybody. The only thing they wanted to do was to fight against the security forces.

There were about fifty thousand people in the street. They had been beaten by police, and they were waiting to clash again. I was with three guys who were as frustrated as I was with the situation. We wrote slogans and split up and went into the crowd. Then we started to chant these slogans. We were able to calm the crowd and prevent people from going directly into confrontation with the security forces.

The slogans somehow got us recognized. People would come to us and say, "Let's write new slogans." "Let's do this." "Let's do that." We barricaded that area using tin roof sheets off houses. The team blocked the road and prevented the security forces from coming into the area.

On the day of the incident, one of my friends and I were sitting in a corner where an old man recognized us and said, "Tear gas is being fired from that house." We had been looking for the source of tear gas being used. When that old man told us about the house, we checked it and found it to be the source of where the shells were coming from. We saw police personnel inside, the armed police force, in fact.

A neighbor told us it was a [high-ranking] police officer's house. We went discreetly to the human rights people [blue-jacketed observers who watched and reported on human rights abuses] and told them what was happening. Thirteen blue jacket guys came with us and looked at the house. We asked the human rights people to divide into two groups, but they didn't listen; they operated in some crazy way, and then all thirteen of them left, like lambs following the mother sheep. As soon as they left the scene, the crowd started to attack the house. There was no way we could control the crowd. Soon the police started to fire from the house.

WITH LIVE BULLETS?

With live bullets. We could see the pistol coming out of the window. We could see the rifle firing at the crowd. At that moment I realized that our lives were in danger and we should leave as soon as possible. But unfortunately, about one square kilometer was totally surrounded by some four thousand police. Everyone who came between them, including women and children, was beaten, and I happened to be one of them.

I was climbing a wall to get away when I felt a stick hit my head. A bamboo stick. I didn't realize the police were right behind me. They pulled me down on the ground. There were four of them beating me for about ten or eleven minutes. The last thing I remembered was someone saying, "OK, this guy is dead, and if you hang around, you'll be in trouble. Let's leave." So to them, I was dead.

Both my hands were broken, and my head was severely injured. I remember them pulling me by my hand and leg and throwing me into a nearby ditch.

One of my classmates saw me getting beaten. He waited for the police to leave and immediately took me to the hospital. I was put on bed rest for a week. But I was very fortunate. There are some people who were not as fortunate. Five people are still missing—the government does not accept it—and up to twelve hundred people were injured. I was one of them.

But I participated in the movement again. The same three friends came to my house and said, "The king addressed the nation, but what he's said is totally wrong, so let's go to march." And I said, "My hands are in plaster, and my head is injured. I can't run. I'm totally weak. I've been living on morphine for five or six days. I don't think I can do that." But they said, "You know, even if we die, we're not leaving you. So let's go." We put plastic on top of my plaster, lots of people signed it, and then we marched toward the royal palace. I went as far as [the district of] Thamel, where police attacked the group I was in. An unknown old woman pulled all of us into her house, locked it from the inside, and saved us.

DO YOU FEEL LIKE YOUR EFFORTS WERE WORTH IT, LOOKING AT IT TODAY?

I was enthusiastic at the beginning, thinking that, although peace had prevailed, it was going to take time to change the mind-set. I'm not as optimistic now, but I'm definitely not pessimistic. The conflicting sides are still confronting each other. They were face-to-face in the past, but now there is a government in between them; there is a constitution in between them; there is a public between them, and there is commitment between them. They are face-to-face, but not shooting at each other.

HOW DID YOU FEEL ABOUT THE POLICE WHO BEAT YOU?

When I went out to march [after being beaten], I was more motivated than before, as I had a sense of revenge. When I came out in the street and saw these uniforms, a sense of revenge was there in my mind. But in the end, I didn't want these four police to be responsible for what happened to me, I wanted the institution of the police to be responsible. I wanted the regime to be responsible. In the beginning when I was injured, those four police were responsible. But in fact they weren't. They had not attacked me for personal reasons; they attacked me because of what the regime told them I was. For them, there was no difference between me and the person next to me, because the regime had identified us as troublemakers. They were doing their job, but doing it brutally.

DID YOU EVER IDENTIFY THEM?

I tried for a week. Then I thought I was stupid to pursue that, because I wanted to get this feeling of revenge out of my system.

I consulted with a friend and told him what kind of feeling I had. He convinced me that it was not these four police who were responsible. He convinced me that they were probably sleep-deprived, frustrated, pressured by higher authorities. They were having rocks thrown at them. If they were captured alone by the protesters, they would have met the same fate as I did. It was the regime that did that to me. They were just the instrument of my injury.

WHAT DO YOU WANT FOR YOUR FUTURE?

I want peace to prevail in the country. I want my family to be happy, one way or the other. For myself, I would like to complete this project, and I want to involve myself as much as possible in this work. I want to feel a part of this project.

HOW DO YOU FEEL ABOUT THE INTERNATIONAL DEVELOPMENT ACTORS THAT YOU'VE COME ACROSS?

There were lots of international actors trying to make themselves visible in every stage of everything happening. Many of them had their own personal agenda to enforce in Nepal. There were a few organizations that were always neutral, always served the proper cause, always served the necessity of the people rather than imposing their ideology on the country. That scenario has not changed. There are some organizations that are working for the good for the people, and there are some that are here just to be here, not to do anything significant, but just to be here. **>>**

Sukraman Lama *(Nepal; taxi driver)*

"Everywhere there is chaos. And corruption."

We started interviewing Sukraman as he drove us around Kathmandu in his taxi, but the honking and traffic noise, and the risk of distracting our driver from navigating through the wildly chaotic streets, made it impossible. So we drove to a beautiful Buddhist monastery on the top of a hill and sat in a tranquil, well-trimmed garden. Sukraman relaxed in the peaceful atmosphere, and gradually opened up.

<< I'm twenty-four, single, a Tamang, and come from a family of vegetable farmers. I left school after grade ten and came here to Kathmandu, where I work as a taxi driver and live with my elder brother and his wife.

HOW IS YOUR WORK?

So far, it's OK. It's adequate.

HOW WERE THINGS DURING THE CONFLICT?

Deplorable. The conflict started in 1996; before that the situation was quite good. After 1997, '98, the social situation got worse. The Maoists began to foment trouble in villages, too. Compared with that, the situation now is good. During the conflict, it was a common practice for the Maoists to torture anyone they didn't like. They used extortion and intimidation, and took others' land and property by force. And they conscripted youths into their army.

DID THIS AFFECT YOUR HOME VILLAGE?

Yes. During that period, we didn't go home. In those days we stayed in Kathmandu. When the conflict ended, we went home. Many of my friends in the village joined the Maoists, but a lot of them have already left the party. One died, too.

If you weren't supportive, they used to intimidate you and bring their militia to stay at your house. But since some of them were men from our village, I used to tell them straightforwardly, "You can stay and have food here as you like, but if you try to intimidate us, then it will not be good." I wasn't scared. They used to say, "It's fine. We'll come and stay at your home for a short time only." I used to warn them not to create problems at our home.

The government side didn't treat us like that. Once there was a raid on our village. They mistook my father for a militia member and interrogated him, but after clearing things up, he was released. So we didn't have much trouble.

WHEN THE PEACE DEAL WAS CONCLUDED, HOW DID YOU FEEL?

I didn't think it was right. With the torture and intimidation and extortion we were subjected to by the Maoists from start to finish, I didn't think it was right. The Maoists tormented us in every way, and then the people elected them and brought them to power. I have no sympathy for them, nor any hope that their system will work.

Everywhere there is chaos. And corruption. I don't think most international aid reaches the target groups: politicians come in between. They take half the aid. The corruption continues. No projects have been finished that met their objectives. Aid is being embezzled by the leaders. I wish the embezzlement would stop soon.

WHAT DOES THE "RULE OF LAW" MEAN TO YOU?

There are volumes of laws in Nepal, but they are not properly implemented. Public service workers don't arrive on time; they're always late. And yet common people are detained just on mere suspicion. That's not the rule of law.

YOU WERE DRIVING A TAXI DURING THE CONFLICT. DID YOU HAVE ANY TROUBLES?

A lot of troubles. Curfews were in effect everywhere. You could get your vehicle vandalized. Some people threw stones and lit fires at night. So people were afraid of getting into a taxi.

I gradually started to cope with the situation. My brother got another taxi, and with the two taxies, we have been getting along well. Now, I can even save a few pennies. I've been thinking of other possibilities, but we'll see what happens.

MANY PEOPLE ARE GOING ABROAD FOR JOBS. WOULD YOU?

If you earn a living here, you don't have to go anywhere else. People see big bucks in foreign lands, but if you work here as hard as there, you can do well.

SO YOU SEE YOUR FUTURE AS BRIGHT?

Yes, indeed. **>>**

Bujar Isajar *(Kosovo; bar owner)*

"For a country emerging from ... repression and war, it takes time."

We interviewed Bujar in his café-bar in Prizren, a historic and beautiful city in Kosovo. Called "Hemingway," the café-bar opened out onto a cobble-stoned plaza with a small fountain. He was full of life, and spoke passionately about his love of motorcycling and traveling. (Sadly, in 2014, while planning for a World Peace motorbike trip, he died in a crash, together with his wife, who was riding on the back of the motorbike.)

◀◀ I am forty-two years old. I was born in Prizren, I live in Prizren, and will live in Prizren forever. Before the war I worked in a hospital as a technician maintaining medical equipment. I was young, eighteen years old. I had a great time there with my colleagues, but the political situation changed, and I went abroad for a while.

Later, when the war came, there was the hope that it would be finished quickly. But it lasted seventy-eight days. Those were seventy-eight days of anxiety, of fear. We were all afraid, but we also had to make decisions for our family members. My daughter was three months old and my son was five at that time. So we decided to stay in Prizren and not leave our home, with the hope that the war would end soon. We were afraid not of NATO strikes but of Serbian paramilitary. We listened to the Voice of America and Radio Free Europe, and we knew that bad things were happening from inside [Kosovo], not from outside. There were rumors that Serbs were collecting young males, and we had to hide continuously. A time came when we got tired of hiding, and I remember once, when I was climbing over a wall in an attempt to escape, I suddenly stopped, and asked myself, "Who are you running from? From your daughter, your son, your parents?" I climbed back over the wall and went back home. My parents were surprised when they saw me. I told them we would all be together until the end.

The Serbs' logic was that they would collect young males so we could not go to war against them. Some of the youths taken by the Serbs are still missing.

The war ended; we survived. Freedom came; democracy was coming. We started our life in a euphoria. I opened my restaurant. We had the chance to talk a lot with internationals. Some of them said that the issue of Kosovo was going to be challenging until democracy and rule of law are established.

Do you think the rule of law is functioning in Kosovo yet?

I would like for zero-tolerance against crime to be implemented, for laws to be in line with the constitution, for all people to be equal before the law; basically, these are the values of democracy. I think we are going in the right direction, slowly but steady; perhaps we are a bit impatient, but for a country emerging from a communist system, and from repression and war, it takes time to establish grounds for a functional rule of law.

Gradually, the time is coming when the rule of law is going to function. We have great hopes about this. Some "fish" are being arrested, but hopefully EULEX [the European Union Rule of Law Mission in Kosovo] will arrest some "whales," too. They have very strong nets to catch the "whales."

Some other states are nowhere near having a functional rule of law, but they are already in the EU. So my wish is to accelerate this process. I want Kosovo not to be a closed place, where it is difficult to communicate with neighboring countries and EU countries. I want our state to become stronger and to enter into the EU, NATO, and democratic processes.

What do you think about those internationals that you met?

Our talks in the restaurant were mostly about politics, and the future of the new state. Some of them gave good advice; others had come to Kosovo to do their job and were not willing to discuss these issues with us. And I'm the type of person who doesn't ask what shouldn't be asked. I mind my own business.

My goal is to earn enough to travel as much possible to other countries and meet different people. Perhaps this is why I am such an enthusiastic motorcyclist. I always wanted to spend time with friends, not by myself. I worked all my life for the good of all, not only for my own good. I want to see everyone prosper.

I'm the president of Eurobikers in Kosovo. Kosovo motorcyclists have been part of Europe for a long time. When some four hundred Eurobikers came to Kosovo, they were surprised by our hospitality and the beauty of Prizren and other areas. I told them that the media write only bad things about Kosovo and are not to be trusted fully. So our perspective is tourism. We have nice places for skiing; the sea is not far from here. In short, we need to advertise our tourism potential more, because we have no potential for heavy industry.

People are welcome to visit Kosovo. The situation is calm; there are no problems with security, so they should not be concerned about this. They should come and see our mountains and old towns and other historic sites. There is a lot to be seen here, and we have the capacity to welcome them, including treating them to a cold beer. **>>**

Ferdos Hussain
(Nepal; jewelry store salesperson)

"Nowadays, even people who have a lot of money cannot live peacefully."

We met Ferdos in a jewelry store in Kathmandu's famous bustling tourist haven, Thamel. A colorful character, Ferdos was very outgoing and obviously enjoyed interacting with the customers. He was far more outspoken than most Nepalese, particularly when discussing ethnic and religious issues.

≪ I was born in Kathmandu, and I live in Kathmandu. My mother is from Patan, and my father is from Kathmandu. We are Muslims. If somebody asks us who we are, our answer is "I am a Nepalese first, not a Muslim." Our life in Kathmandu has been very nice. We have been comfortable and have felt like we do not belong to any other caste; we are Nepalese and equal. So there is not a big problem living life in Kathmandu.

We have friends from other castes, and when we were students our school friends came from all other religions. At that time, there was not so big a conflict between the religions. The Maoists slowly created caste-based groups and intensified fighting between these different castes. Now there is a big fight going on between different castes, but I believe that it will not go on for a long time.

Hindus say that Nepal should be a Hindu country, but there are more Buddhists than Hindus in Nepal. In that case, Nepal should be a Buddhist country, but Buddhists don't want Nepal to be a Buddhist country. So there should be no problem for the Hindu people if Nepal is a secular country. Like in the United States of America, if Nepal becomes a secular country, then all religious people can share their feelings and thoughts about their faith.

I am thirty-two now. When I was at school, ten or twelve years ago, I studied in a very good school, with rules and regulations. But when I jumped to the university, I found it totally different. At that time, the education environment in Nepal was very poor. When I joined a university, the environment was very bad because of the student politics; the students always fought, giving no time for study. They did not respect the teachers. So I could not involve myself in that environment. At the same time, I found that my parents wanted some help from me, as I am their eldest son. So I did not complete university. I decided to get a job.

WERE YOU AFFECTED BY THE RECENT MASS DEMONSTRATIONS IN KATHMANDU [FOR A MULTI-PARTY PEACE PROCESS AND ELECTIONS]?

There were some problems for our family. We couldn't get food and other necessary things. Kathmandu's people are not so involved in these kinds of demonstrations, but Kathmandu people helped the demonstrators by giving them some food and some places to live. Most demonstrators came from outside the valley. It was good. It was not so bad because to bring change in the country we have to sacrifice some peace. But [even though the demonstrations were successful] we couldn't get the good result. The Maoists were declared winners of the election even though the Maoists had never done good things. They made a very bad impact on the villagers and on other people in Kathmandu. They wanted donations, they troubled the tourists, and they created a very bad reputation for themselves in front of the Nepalese people.

When the civil war started, all the Nepalese people supported the Maoists, because the Nepalese people were affected by the conduct of the king's corrupt ministers. But when the Maoists later came into the peace talks, they showed their real character and created the YCL [Young Communist League], like a gang to fight with other people. Let me give you an example—this is my experience—here in the Thamel, there was a small *tanka* [a painting on cotton or silk, usually of a Buddhist deity] shop. One painter made a *tanka* for the shop to sell. One day the painter came to the shop asking for money. The shopkeeper said, "No, I don't have money right now, so you wait." And the painter said, "No, I need the money, otherwise I need my *tanka* back." The shopkeeper got a little bit aggressive, and he tore the *tanka* in front of the painter. The painter should have gone to the police, but he went to the YCL. And the YCL came there and forced the shop to close and asked for compensation for the worker [painter]. This should not be the work of the YCL; this should be the work of the police. So we found that in Nepal there are two police [forces]: one is the Nepalese police and another is the YCL police, just like two governments. So we felt very bad about that.

WHAT IS YOUR EXPERIENCE WITH TOURISTS AND OTHER FOREIGNERS?

I have always had good experiences with tourists, because my work is with tourists.

Maybe 1 or 2 percent of the tourists who came here talk bad about Nepal. Mostly, they have a problem with pollution and other things, but no problem with the Maoists or local people.

As a Nepalese, I want to say to the foreign community, the diplomats, as well as the tourists, that they should help Nepal in development, tourism, and many other things. There are many diplomats and NGOs working here, and there should be more coming. Overall, the international community wants Nepal to develop more and be a peaceful country. Like in Vietnam after the big conflict, the country was going down, but many NGOs worked there and a lot of the foreign community also worked together. As a result, now Vietnam is more developed than Nepal. So we are also hopeful with regard to the foreign community.

But I found that the last American ambassador [who was ambassador during the mass demonstrations] was too involved in Nepal politics. Sometimes his statements were so bad that they affected the local people here.

WHAT IS YOUR HOPE FOR THE FUTURE?

I want a peaceful Nepal for me, my family, and for my children.

One of my cousins lives in Texas; my brother lives in Melbourne [Australia]; my other cousin lives in Germany. They all say, "We'd like to come back to Nepal." They are studying there, working there just because here in Nepal there is less opportunity for earning money. In the future, my children should not have to do the same thing that my brothers and cousins did. The Nepalese government should give opportunities for the people to live here peacefully. I want Nepal as it was ten or twenty years before, when my mother was a housewife and my father was a shopkeeper. My father had a shop renting bicycles, and he earned 200 to 500 rupees [a few dollars] per day. He felt that that was a very peaceful time. Less money but a happy life.

But nowadays, even people who have a lot of money cannot live peacefully. They always fear what will happen tomorrow, and that makes people get diseases like diabetes. My mom has diabetes because of worrying too much about the future.

My parents had a very nice life in the past. Even in the nighttime. If they wanted to go someplace at midnight, they didn't need anyone for protection. They could go freely anywhere. At that time, the population of Kathmandu was very small. People feared ghosts, evil spirits. But now there is a big population in Kathmandu and people are scared of people. This is the difference from the past. So that's why I want Nepal to be like it was before. **>>**

INTERNATIONALS

Why do people leave their own country, more often than not a country at peace, to work in another country, one where violent conflict is raging or where the local population is struggling to rebuild their society, economy, and government? Do these people find what they expected? How are they affected by what they discover? How do they see themselves and the people they work with "in country"? What advice do they have for others who are thinking about becoming an "international," the term often used to designate those who work for international organizations, nongovernmental organizations (NGOs), and aid agencies in conflict and postconflict zones? These are the questions that the internationals discussed in their interviews.

The motivations for engaging in conflict-related work abroad varied among those we interviewed, but all shared at least two ambitions: to see the world and to help it. Fiona Mangan traveled a lot as a child and was struck by "how different things could be" in the developing world; she became determined to return in the future and "do something"—something concrete—to contribute to a better life for others. "You can do research," she remarked, "but you really can't contribute unless you get to these places and really understand them." "Ashton," a US diplomat, was born in Libya and grew up in very different parts of the world. He was inspired to pursue a career that would take him abroad by the example of his father, a US government official, and also by his own "love for interacting and for learning about other cultures and other people, and looking for ways to be constructive and to help." "Sterling," a soldier who has worked for the United Nations, was driven by a combination of a sense of adventure "and a very strong sense that one has to do something for your country or for society."

Béatrice Pouligny was searching for the answer to some of life's big questions, such as how to find meaning in a world that can seem so violent and inhumane. Her intellectual curiosity intersected with a spiritual search for understanding and with a desire to serve. She didn't just want to know why humans can be so violent and cruel to one another. She also wanted to find an answer to the question, "How can we heal and move from there?" She started working early in her life as an intern for an NGO, and then built a career working for the United Nations and various NGOs and research institutes.

For others, it was a choice that came later in their careers. Ali Chahine studied business in war-torn Lebanon, and didn't start working as an international until he was thirty. David Marshall was an established lawyer when he started on the path that led him from doing pro bono work for Amnesty International to working for the United Nations. Mohamed Abdulaziz Ibrahim had been working as a prosecutor and then as a judge in Egypt before he began working on rule of law with the United Nations.

Once involved, the sense of service and the personal goals that propelled the internationals into their careers did not go away, though they did evolve in different ways. Ashton encountered a turning point in his career when he was working in the Balkans and realized, "Holy Smokes, there's nothing we [US diplomats] can do here that's good" without working very closely with local partners. Ali discovered that sharing, say, a language or religion with the local people did not necessarily make his job easier; indeed, "sometimes it back-fires. . . . If you want to get more credibility, don't use your [personal] affilia-tions. You want to show them that you are a real professional, that you believe in what you are doing—this works better than starting out saying, 'I'm like you, I'm a Muslim.'"

David found that his expectations "about what we, the international com-munity, can deliver" lowered, and he came to see the United Nations as "a very slow-moving ship," but, he pointed out, "there's no other game in town." Sterling expressed a similar view, explaining that "intellectually, I knew that the UN was going to be a far more difficult organization" to work for than the army, "because it's much more bureaucratic. But the scale of the difference was a bit of a shocker." He learned to work within the system, but he has yet to change his opinion of the way the United Nations is managed.

Most of the internationals we spoke with were candid about the short-comings of the international community. Some, like Sterling, identified the problems of "large, cumbersome organizations" and "political interests" that "always trump reality." Beatrice, too, recalled that sometimes "nobody wanted to hear" about uncomfortable political realities.

Such obstacles, however, did not undermine the internationals' sense of purpose and duty, nor did the mortal dangers involved in fulfilling that duty. David was in the UN building in Baghdad when it was bombed and his col-leagues murdered. He said that he couldn't overcome the trauma, but he did learn to put it in "the bigger context [of the vast scale of the] death and de-struction" in Iraq. Fiona pointed out that an international can sometimes be overcautious and imagine dangers that don't actually exist, but she also spoke of taking "calculated risks," and recalled being in a hotel in Libya when a bomb blew in the windows. The contrast between the insecurity often experienced in country and life at UN Headquarters or another relatively tranquil Western setting can be startling and disconcerting. Returning home from a war zone, said Ashton, can be a difficult transition: "For months after I returned from Bosnia, I felt like a whirling dervish trapped in a slow-motion world."

What keeps the internationals going seems to be a stillness, or at least a conviction, at the center of that whirlwind: an abiding belief in the value of trying to make the world a more just, humane, and peaceful place. This is not a question of professional vanity but of personal commitment. "I don't go [to a country] with the intention of leaving a mark or doing something in their life," said Ali. "I go to be human, to treat [the local population] with human-ity and respect; to sympathize and acknowledge." Or as Mohamed explained, "I deeply believe that there will never be peace without justice, and having a certain knowledge of justice, I can go there and start to make a difference." ●

Fiona Mangan *(Ireland)*

"You can't really contribute unless you get to these places and really understand them."

We interviewed Fiona, a colleague at USIP, in a restaurant in Washington, D.C. Her passion for and commitment to the work she does abroad, and the people in those countries, were evident in her tone and words.

<< I'm from Dublin in Ireland. I've been living in the US for a number of years now. I went into law as an undergrad, but I don't think I ever had the sense that I was going to practice law in the traditional sense; I was more interested in legal philosophy and how law can shape society. When studying in Spain, I had the opportunity to take classes that were a little broader than just law—international relations, international development theory, political science, etcetera, and that led me to branch out during my master's [degree], studying war and the drivers of conflict, security, and development. I thought I'd left the law behind me, but the discipline had stuck. It was in combining the two that led me into the rule of law world.

WHAT LED YOU TO WORK OVERSEAS?

A number of things, I suppose. My parents traveled with us and exposed us to a lot. When I was ten or eleven, we went to Kenya and Egypt. And then, when I was fourteen, we took a long trip around India. Through both of those trips—combined with the type of schooling I received, my family background in Northern Ireland—there was an awareness of how different things could be. In a young and immature kind of way, I wanted to go back and do something. My first work overseas was just after I finished my undergraduate [studies]. I spent the summer working in India, in Delhi. I worked at a center for street children. Then, while pursuing my master's, I decided to do my thesis on Somaliland's case for international recognition and got it in my head to do field work. I was twenty-two and a grad student working alone but scrounged up funding and went all over the country and did interviews. In order to be allowed to travel around, I had to have special protection unit security officers—which the government assign to any internationals who leave the capital—so I had these loosely uniformed guys with dodgy AK-47s to take care of me. And, of course, they were chewing qat the whole time. Looking back, it's hilarious.

BUT THE RISKS, REAL OR IMAGINED, ARE WORTH TAKING?

You can do research, but you can't really contribute unless you get to these places and really understand them. What is the point of doing this kind of work if you do not make that commitment? And doing so involves some risk. But they are calculated risks.

There was this amazing group of academics in Hargeisa, the capital of Somaliland, who got together every once in a while to chew qat and talk politics. And this lovely man who'd been helping me with the research invited me along, noting, "I just want to let you know that it's at doctor something's house this weekend, and it's a little bit outside town. I can give you a lift." And I had built a relationship of trust with him, but I remember thinking, "I am going to take a car with this man that I've known for a couple of weeks and go to a house full of men at night. Am I mad?" But I just told a lot of people where I was going, and they knew the people involved very well and knew when to expect me back. I took the risk, and it was one of the most wonderful evenings I had there. This group of intellectuals and academics allowed me into their set, and the amount of seriousness and deliberation they gave to my project was remarkable. They had bought me, I will never forget, a little box of Pringles, because that's what they thought they should invite me to have.

It sometimes seems awful that we have to doubt, for security reasons, such genuinely wonderful people. But you do. And yet, at the same time, it's nice to be able sometimes to take a bit of a chance, as often it pays off.

YOU CURRENTLY WORK ON PRISONS, AMONG OTHER TOPICS. HOW DID YOU GET INVOLVED IN THAT?

I met someone who worked with Lawyers Without Borders and greatly influenced me, bringing me in on some work for them in Liberia. We were there to assess the impact of some training they had carried out for public prosecutors and defenders. It involved a lot of court observation, which I loved, and while I was on that job I got a call asking, "Any chance you could do prison visits?" I remembered some coursework I'd done, spent hours at night downloading articles and guides over a slow Internet connection, and took the chance. After that beginning, rule of law work took me to the Irish Department of Justice, back to school, to a series of organizations, and eventually I found myself at USIP.

I had just started at USIP when I was brought in on a conversation with the Libyan deputy minister of justice—in the postconflict chaos the country was struggling to know who was running the prisons, what condition they were in, and the extent of ministry control. He wanted us to do an assessment to understand the state of the prison system. So a colleague and I headed out, traveling around the country to almost all of the ministry-held prisons operational at that time, and to militia-run detention centers.

DON'T YOU EVER FEEL CONCERNED FOR YOUR SAFETY?

There are always some safety concerns involved in prison visits, and you have to manage them. Just to give an example, at one prison, in spite of precautions we had taken, we observed after entering the cell areas that the prison director had a weapon concealed under his shirt, tucked into his belt. He was former militia with no background working in prisons and his inexperience contributed to the already dangerous environment. Not only was he carrying a firearm—which should never be brought into cell areas—but he allowed himself to be drawn into a screaming match with some of the prisoners in a cell. Things were escalating, and we just withdrew.

There have been other incidents, too. Perhaps a year after that incident, a bomb blew in the windows of a hotel where my translator and I were staying in southern Libya.

These things take their toll but they also further strengthen my belief in the importance of not allowing these to become forgotten places. This is particularly clear in prisons, where I'm very aware that the work we do allows us a just a tiny window into prison life but that these are the everyday conditions and dangers for prisoners and prison guards. Things may happen on a visit, but I get to leave. They stay. **>>**

"Ashton" (United States)

"It's not about us; it's about them."

We interviewed "Ashton" in his apartment in the Chelsea neighborhood of New York City, home to many art galleries and artists. The apartment was on one of the top floors of the building and had floor-to-ceiling windows that looked out over the city. Full of energy, he spoke quickly but also precisely about his upbringing and his work as a US foreign service officer.

<< My father was a government official, so I spent about half of my life overseas, growing up in different countries. I was born in Libya; as a child, I lived in a lot of different places, but the real formative years for me were spent in Australia and Laos. I spent three years in Laos, from age eight to eleven, when we [the United States] were in the middle of a hot war there. So from a young age, I was very interested in the outside world, I was very comfortable in foreign cultures. I was happy as a kid, even though I had some rather traumatic experiences in Laos. When we moved from Vientiane to Vienna, imagine the polar opposites between those postings.

WHAT KINDS OF TRAUMATIC EXPERIENCES?

Well, one example was when I almost drowned in an open-air sewer. Like most kids in Vientiane, we played outside all the time. My family lived next to a *klong*, a combination wetland, cesspool, and watershed. One day while climbing on the masonry fence between our property and the *klong*, I fell in and still remember the feeling of sinking and being trapped underwater. It seemed like an eternity, but an adult neighbor eventually pulled me out after diving in himself.

Another example was when my dad arranged for me a couple of times to fly with him to an airbase in northern Thailand, Udorn, so that I could watch air operations from the flight line. One of my visits to Udorn co-incided with the North Vietnamese Army's launch of its 1973 winter offensive. Suddenly, it seemed like out of nowhere, all kinds of cargo aircraft were converging on the base, and taxiing at high speed to our corner of the facility. They came to a quick stop, then spun around. I watched as the rear ramps of the aircraft opened up, and it looked like Armageddon. Looking into the cargo bellies of the airplanes I could see there were American kids in there—you know, nineteen-, twenty-, twenty-one-year-old soldiers, just ripped to shreds. They were lying on gurneys and strapped to the aircraft in various ways. The wounded were hauled off by medics, transferred to ambulances right in front of me. I guess no one thought twice about the ten-year-old kid standing nearby watching the whole procedure. So there I was, watching all these guys dressed in battle fatigues but wrapped in gauze and blood everywhere, blood everywhere. It was a poignant experience, needless to say.

Later in my teenage years, we moved to Vienna, Austria. I loved Vienna for very different reasons and it was a nice, calm, civilized contrast to Laos.

After that, we came back home, and I did high school in the United States. And then the day after graduation, Dad packed up the family again and we moved back to Asia. I wound up falling in love with East Asia all over again. I later went to college in Virginia, got a degree in Asian studies and eventually got a commission as a Foreign Service Officer in the mid-1980s. I spent tours in Asia, Germany, and Scandinavia. Then I came back to Washington and wound up completely serendipitously going to Sarajevo for almost a year, and thus began my engagement with the Balkans. It turned out to be the highlight of my career. I later returned to Europe, and, like a whole lot of USG [US government] officials, eventually wound up in Iraq. Probably as some kind of reward, I was given the New York City posting towards the end of my career.

HOW DID YOU FEEL ABOUT WORKING IN THE LOCAL COMMUNITIES AS AN OUTSIDER?

I loved the opportunity to go to Sarajevo. I was horrified by what I read around '94, '95 about what was going on in Bosnia [the violent breakup of the former Yugoslavia, which was accompanied by many atrocities], and just couldn't believe it was happening a few hundred miles from where I was in Europe at the time. And when the opportunity arose, I thought, "My god, this is my opportunity to go; I've just got to contribute." I had a lot of interaction with the local government officials in terms of joint projects we were doing: capacity building, capability building, and such. That was an extremely satisfying thing for me. I just loved working with the Bosnians. I loved the fact that I was there, helping the underdog.

WHEN YOU CAME BACK TO THE UNITED STATES, WAS IT HARD TO MAKE THAT TRANSITION?

The hardest thing about returning home from war zones is coming down off of what's a months-long adrenaline rush. It was in Bosnia that I first became an adrenaline junky and I was hooked immediately. I was in Bosnia the first time during the summer of 1998 when IFOR [the NATO-led Implementation Force] was transitioning to SFOR [the Stabilization Force] and the internationals in country had their hands full keeping a lid on what was still a roiling, precarious situation. The presence of the US and other militaries had stopped the worst of fighting and the killing, but distracting the parties, getting them to focus on coexistence, peace, and prosperity, was a major undertaking. It took a lot of people working long hours to keep the antagonists apart and to demonstrate that they had more to gain by moving in a different direction than resorting to fighting. The scale of the challenge was overwhelming. Just to add a little external pressure to the situation, the summer of 1998 was when our embassies in Dar-es-Salaam and Nairobi were bombed by al-Qaeda. For months after I returned from Bosnia, I felt like a whirling dervish trapped in a slow-motion world.

WHAT ADVICE WOULD YOU GIVE TO INTERNATIONALS IN WORKING WITH LOCALS?

It's not about us; it's about them. You're there not to do things, but rather to help them learn how to do things. You have to provide some sort of technical or other expertise. You have to educate, you have to convey something that may not necessarily be monetized but can be transformed into something that is useful. That utility can be very different to a ministry of education, a ministry of interior, or a ministry of foreign affairs, but in almost every case, with every skill set, something useful needs to be conveyed. Internationals are sent to postconflict or postcrisis zones for pretty specific reasons; there's always a broad spectrum of need and everyone deployed to a Bosnia, an Iraq, or a Banda Aceh has something valuable to impart.

And you have to have empathy. Plain and simple. Sensitivity to local conditions and other people and an ability to get along.

WHAT MOTIVATED YOU TO DO THIS WORK?

My dad, mostly. I acquired an interest in the outside world, in traveling and experiencing new things from my dad and the places around the world his career took me to. But it was actually my own experiences, you know, in the foreign field, where I developed a love for interacting and for learning about other cultures and other people, and looking for ways to be constructive and to help. The guy who pulled me out of the *klong* in Laos was an Israeli neighbor, so I've always had in my mind the need to reach out to the rest of the world. Having found an opportunity to make it part of my career has made me very happy. It turns me on to be part of some solution.

WAS THERE A TURNING POINT FOR YOU?

The Balkans. When I got to Sarajevo, what I realized was, "Wow, you can actually get a lot of things done if you have an effective partnership." I used to go down and spend six hours a day at some of our local government counterparts' offices, and we would have maps spread out, spilling over conference tables, and a parade of people filtering through the meetings, each contributing something, each offering some insight or expertise. Those meetings—that engagement—resulted in an incredible back-and-forth. And when I left those offices and got back to my office, I would spend the next six hours of my day documenting the sessions, packaging tidbits for various other partners in Washington, D.C., and other places around the region. I realized, "Holy Smokes, there's nothing we can do here that's good, nothing that will ultimately be effective without these guys. This is their neighborhood, they know this place, and anything that we want to accomplish will have to be done with them through an iterative process." If you're effective, respectful, and constructive with local partners, they will start to look to you—and the partnership they have with you—as their solution. And that's been fun.

HOW DID YOUR LOCAL PARTNERS FEEL ABOUT THE RELATIONSHIP?

When they see that sort of dedication and commitment and investment in grey matter, they realize, "This is our friend, this is our partner, and we have got to invest in this guy because we're getting stuff done." And they would turn on CNN and see the results of our mutual efforts, the impact of our investments. Then they would come back the next day and say, "OK, let's do more." Enthusiasm is an infectious and a wonderful thing. **>>**

Béatrice Pouligny *(France)*

"For me, it was the biggest question: How can we do that to each other?"

I interviewed Béatrice on the balcony of her apartment just outside Washington, D.C. We looked out over leafy trees and a walking trail winding through a peaceful park. Béatrice was deeply reflective, measuring her words to ensure clarity.

<< I am forty-nine. I was born and raised in France. I was raised in an environment with a lot of violence, which led me, early on, to ask about violence in the world. When I was six or seven, I began investigating things in political terms. I made that connection very early for unknown reasons.

HOW OLD WERE YOU WHEN THIS WAS GOING ON?

One of my first outbursts was when a group of Palestinians took [Israeli athletes] hostage at the Berlin Olympics, in 1972; I was seven at the time. I watched the TV, the news, intently, and I remember saying, "But there is a reason why they are doing this." I couldn't know why, and I had all these questions in my head. So very early on I was driven to find meaning in what was happening, while the events and violence in my own life did not make any sense.

Up to my teenage years, I was very spiritual and artistic, which was for me, I think, a way to survive. I was into all kinds of artistic stuff, including dancing. I remember that, even through my dancing, I wanted to do things to help the world understand and transform the pain.

I was made to become a secretary, so I did that and started working when I was seventeen. I had to fight to be able to work on a cause that made a difference. My family, my mother in particular, was opposed to it and wanted me to work in a bank. But with the support of my teachers, I started an internship and then began working for an NGO that worked on international issues and supporting projects in different parts of the world.

THIS WAS BEFORE YOU WENT TO COLLEGE?

This was after the French baccalaureate. I actually never went to college. I had a professional diploma as a trilingual administrative assistant. I was working with an NGO, and they didn't make me do any secretary stuff. I organized big meetings and did various things for the secretary general of the organization. And they said that I should continue to study. They told me about the Institute for Political Studies in Paris. I had never heard about it. So I asked for an appointment for [acceptance] and received special authorization to take the exam, as I did not have the usual profile or any of the credentials you need to enter that school. As a consequence, I graduated with a master's at twenty-one.

I started working with Amnesty International, mostly on human rights violations in South America, but I was recruited a year later as a UNDP [United Nations Development Programme] junior professional officer. It was a series of unusual circumstances that led me to be interviewed and recruited. I was sent to Niger, where I worked on rural development issues and with civil society. I was often in a fight for what I was doing, as it was often considered close to crossing the borderline of UNDP's mandate. But the head of the UNDP in Haiti saw one of my reports and said he needed somebody like me. So that's how I arrived in Haiti.

I worked in different programs whose objective was to have people from different sectors working together. I also worked on human rights and the democratic transition, including the preparation of elections. I then transferred [in late 1990] to the first UN mission in Haiti. At the same time, I had started working with a group of Haitian friends on justice issues and we founded a local organization. After the first democratic government was formed, I did a little bit of go-between for the international community and the Haitians, and helped put in place that organization. We were working at different levels of the society but also with grassroots networks all over the country.

And then the 1991 coup happened, and I decided to stay. I worked underground for two years, mostly human rights work and communications, supporting the nonviolent resistance, working 24/7 and living a life I did not even know existed. That's probably one of the most intense experiences of my life. I have seen the best and the worst of humanity there.

WITH THE UNITED NATIONS?

No. I had quit. Now, I was with a local organization. When I was in the UN, I was threatened to be pulled out of the mission almost every day by the general who headed the military side of the mission. He thought I had a bad influence on his guys, because I had them learn creole, and go on foot to meet with people and try at least to be there, to make a difference. I was also warning of a military coup coming and of the need to tackle some of the most critical issues facing the country. But, at the time, nobody wanted to hear it. They recognized it afterwards.

After four very intense years in Haiti, I needed a break and I asked to go back to Sciences Po Paris. I did a PhD on how local populations and local actors interact with UN missions and what their strategies are; it was in six countries. I really wanted to show a different face of peacebuilding. In parallel to my field research, I continued doing other field work and community training. I also started teaching in Paris and in other countries, and I started working as an advisor to some international organizations and governments. I was recruited as a tenured researcher before I even defended my PhD.

It was still intense, and my work was not always understood, in particular in my own institute. Because I was a lot into trying to understand people's experiences and resources, so we can better help them. So it was a bottom-up perspective integrating people's own voices, and integrating different disciplines. It was also an action-oriented research, which was really a no-go for many of my colleagues. But, for me, it was a matter of ethics. I wanted the work I was doing to directly serve people, first, before my own publications as a researcher. I wanted to acknowledge the fact that the stories I was telling, the knowledge I was helping gather, was theirs. Many of my colleagues did not always understand what I was doing. The fact that I received many grants and awards did not help.

At the time, I was mostly working on war situations and then I started working more in situations where massacres and genocides had been committed. For me, it was the biggest question: How can we do that to each other? And how can we heal and move from there? And that's how I started working on that and designing a program on four continents with multidisciplinary teams, international researchers supporting local teams.

YOU WERE IN FRANCE AT THAT TIME?

I was based in France from late 1999 to 2006, when I burnt out and moved to the US, but 90 percent of my time I was abroad, spending weeks at a time in countries, and returning to them time and again. I have worked in about thirty war zones on all continents between 1986 and today.

WHAT ADVICE WOULD YOU GIVE TO PEOPLE COMING INTO THIS WORK?

[What is important is] clarity about who you are, why you do the work you do and the ethics around that, how you connect with people, what your relationship with violence is, and how you conceive your role as an outsider. Also, clear your body and clear your space on a regular basis so you can continue to embody a different energy for people who can't because they are in the middle of a war, in a very difficult situation. We cannot build peace from the same energy as the one that has created war. **>>**

"Sterling"

"We had a dead Taliban fighter and a crying five-year-old girl."

We interviewed "Sterling" on the balcony of the home in which he grew up. It was a peaceful venue that looked out over the water and was nestled amidst large trees. He was on a much-needed vacation from the realities of preparing for or conducting combat operations as a noncommissioned officer. Sterling is a member of his country's special operations force, whose mission is primarily counterterrorism. Sterling was both matter-of-fact and reflective, and careful not to reveal any operational details.

<< CAN YOU TELL ME ABOUT YOUR BACKGROUND?

I grew up largely on a little island, but before that I had moved around with my family. And there is a lengthy family history of military service. When I left high school, I decided to join the army to see if I liked it, and I ended up staying in. I joined because I had a very strong sense that one has to do something for your country or for society.

While I was in the army, I spent six months in Somalia, during the 1993 humanitarian intervention there. I was in my early twenties; it was my first time in an impoverished country. I adapted to it well. Intellectually, I knew that people were poor and life is hard in places, but to see it in such a stark example made a difference for me for the rest of my life.

A COUPLE OF YEARS LATER YOU JOINED THE SPECIAL FORCES? HOW WAS THAT?

The Special Forces is a different type of soldiering for a different type of people, who are far more independent, given a lot more leeway, and given a lot more responsibility.

The more I worked in different environments, the more I realized the world is a complex place. There are very few goals you can achieve by yourself.

HOW DID YOU GO FROM THE SPECIAL FORCES TO THE UNITED NATIONS?

I was going to have to go back to the regular military, which didn't appeal to me. I got into the UN the same way that probably most people get into it: I knew somebody. He was working in Kosovo. I began working as a UN security officer in Kosovo.

Intellectually, I knew that the UN was going to be a far more difficult organization to deal with because it's much more bureaucratic. But the scale of the difference was a bit of a shocker. Some of the most professional people I have ever worked with were working at the UN. But they were all paddling upstream against a system that was not very professional; it was not very well managed overall.

As I gained more experience, I realized how to work within the system better and how important personal relationships were to getting work done. But my views of the UN didn't change.

I think somebody in the international community needed to be able to step in and provide some kind of governance, some kind of stability to give both sides of that conflict an opportunity to step back and figure out their own solutions to it. I think the main thing is to expect some results, but expect a lot of difficulties in trying to bring all that together. [The UN mission] could have been run better for sure, but, that said, it's a giant bureaucracy from a lot of different countries, so the main thing is just don't expect too much.

AFTER THE UN, YOU WENT BACK INTO YOUR COUNTRY'S MILITARY. WHY?

It was mostly 9/11. When that happened, I was in a room in Kosovo with an Australian, a South African, and a Brit. We saw that on the news and all of us thought that, well, this is no surprise. You can be shocked, angry, whatever, but it's no real surprise. And I thought I would regret it if I didn't go back. That was something that I had spent my entire professional career training for, and my friends back in the military were going to be in harm's way, and I would regret not being there with them.

I ended up doing four tours of Afghanistan. I did close protection on my first tour, then the other three tours were combat tours in one capacity or another: interdicting Taliban, disrupting the chain of supplies for improvised explosive devices, disrupting their sort of chain-of-command networks by capturing or killing their commanders. And doing the intelligence gathering to try and build up enough of a picture on somebody that we could then capture or kill them.

Nobody really likes doing close protection. The job that people want to do over there is what we call direct-action missions, where you are going out with a much more targeted approach.

ARE SOME PEOPLE NATURALLY IMMUNE FROM THE STRESS THAT GOES ALONG WITH SUCH WORK?

No. The Special Forces puts people through a very rigorous process and selects for specific attributes that translate into somebody who's resilient to do that job. We have psychologists that help, and training absolutely helps. The military is very good at training realistically and that really helps you deal with the situation you are in because it's not the first time you've seen it.

And then there are other things that you're not going to be able to train for. I remember on one operation where an Afghan combatant was killed. It couldn't be avoided; he was armed, he was fighting us, and he was killed. But he was killed in a family compound with his niece of about five years old there to see her uncle being killed. That doesn't change the fact that that person was a combatant, that he was lawfully killed, that he was a threat and somebody needed to kill him to defend themselves. None of that changes the fact that that was just her uncle. We had a dead Taliban fighter and a crying five-year-old girl. We obviously took her away as quickly as we could and put her with her other relatives. But you could really see how that affected all of us. She was put into those circumstances through no fault of her own and is going to have to deal with that for the rest of her life.

How do you feel about working with international organizations?

They are organizationally very different than the military, obviously, and to work with them you need to understand them. There's a lot of people on both sides—the security field and the development field—who really don't understand each other.

Where do you see the security threats or conflict threats coming from?

The real problem is there are people who either feel disenfranchised or don't feel that they are getting fair access to resources in their country, who don't think that they are being represented well by their government or their leaders, and that creates situations that are ripe for conflict.

I can't fault somebody in Somalia living a subsistence life for wanting to ransom an oil tanker to get some money. The international community needs to enforce laws against piracy, but from another point of view, whether it's right or wrong legally or morally, it shouldn't be unexpected.

What does "rule of law" mean to you?

The ideal that I think of is simply that there is an accepted norm, and that everybody is held accountable to the same degree to that norm. The key factor is fairness or evenhandedness in the application of the laws.

How could the international community do a better job?

I think that there needs to be a better coordinated, more preventive sort of diplomatic and development-focused way of dealing with conflict in order to avoid having to use military force. I think that's the best way of dealing with things. But realistically I don't see a huge change in how countries are going to deal with problems. People, countries—they don't want to be proactive. They don't want to spend the money on the ounce of prevention; they would sooner wait and spend the money on a pound of cure.

Do you see any big changes on the horizon?

I don't see the big picture of things changing a whole lot. Governments and politicians and bureaucracies and militaries are all going to be the same large, cumbersome organizations that they have always been. Political interests will always trump reality and political realities will trump what should be done. You have to deal with the circumstances that you are working in.

What about you? How do you see your future?

I'm quite happy. I guess I shouldn't say I'd like to retire, but if I really wanted to retire I would have retired, because I can. I think that I'd like to just lessen the pace of work in my life. I've had a pretty busy career so far.

I'm forty-five, and I joined the military when I was eighteen. I'd like to slow the pace a bit, although I would miss a lot of the fun and exciting stuff in the military, because I think my brain's still probably nineteen. I see myself sticking around the military for a few more years, and then doing something more part-time but still working internationally. **>>**

Ali Chahine *(Lebanon)*

"I don't go with the intention of leaving a mark ... I go to be human."

We interviewed Ali in Tripoli, Libya, in 2012, when we were there to facilitate a workshop on dealing with crimes in the transition from the Qaddafi regime. Ali could be very businesslike at one moment and then funny and mischievous the next. He never took himself too seriously. But he is a brilliant facilitator, able to gain people's trust very quickly. One could tell that he loved doing what he does.

<< I was born in 1970 in Beirut to a middle-class family, three brothers and one sister. I studied engineering, then did my MBA. I have a background in volunteerism; I was a volunteer as a youth in many NGOs in Lebanon during the [civil] war.

When I was thirty [in 2000], I started working for the ICRC [International Committee of the Red Cross]. My first postings were to the former Yugoslavia for one year—capacity building, communication—and then in the same capacities in Somalia and Kenya, and then in southern Africa, in Zimbabwe, and neighboring countries.

DID YOUR OWN EXPERIENCES OF WAR IN LEBANON AFFECT YOUR VIEW OF THOSE COUNTRIES?

It helped me to see things from [the local people's] perspective. When there were displacements, shortages of food, threats, I could associate that with what used to happened in my country.

WHAT DO YOU RECALL MOST STRONGLY ABOUT THE WAR IN LEBANON?

I lost some relatives because of this war. I lost my grandfather, who was shot; my aunt's husband was killed in bomb shelling. We had some injuries, but overall it brought us together. I remember when I applied for the final exam at high school, there was really heavy fighting in Beirut, and my family was in the South [of the country] in the village. My mother and father came with me. They came to Beirut while there was fighting, and the night before the exam we didn't sleep until four in the morning, and we slept in the basement because of the shelling, and then we went for the exam. There were very few students during the final exam to graduate. And when we were working on it, suddenly there was a bullet, sniper bullet, it entered, and all of us were still sitting on the chairs, our heads down, glass was broken. And then we looked up and the teacher said, "OK, continue." And we continued with the exam. We were so happy that we were able to do our exams and finish because other schools couldn't.

How old were you when all this was going on?

When the war started, I was seven. The first time I recall hearing bullets and shelling, I think I was six, and it continued since that time, because actually it never finished even after the '91 war. There was another war in '96, then in 2006. But I was eight to nineteen or twenty when most of the fighting took place.

What kept people in Beirut?

People kept going on. What was destroyed at night they start to build up during the day.

We didn't have anybody from the family kidnapped or killed until the end of the war. One time, I was ten years old, a mortar entered the wall of our five-room apartment. Seven of us were in the house, none of us was injured; it was really a miracle. It was sunset; we were on the seventh floor, and there were armed people on the roof of the building on the ninth floor. So the other faction fired an RPG rocket that hit the seventh floor, not the ninth. It passed through the whole house, to the neighbors' building. But luckily, it went [through] the east side of the house, and we were on the west side of the house. There was a lot of dust, and my father went to open the apartment door and it didn't open. He was just begging, and the neighbors from outside were also trying to break the door, and then finally it opened.

Then my father died in '95 [of natural causes]. I was the eldest, and I was responsible for the family. Responsible to make decisions, it's a huge burden. This was really a horrible feeling, to feel that you are responsible, to decide either to flee or to stay, and to flee to which part. So I could imagine what burden my father had when he was alive; all these seventeen years of civil war, he was carrying it.

What motivated you to carry on?

There was always hope. Always. Every day you wake up, you find there's hope, there's something beautiful in life. Even in this difficult time there's something beautiful.

DID YOU ENCOUNTER INTERNATIONAL ORGANIZATIONS OR INTERNATIONAL NGOS IN LEBANON?

When I was about twenty or twenty-one, I had a positive perception about them. I saw them trying to help with their noble cause, and having a lot of stories to tell and to learn from.

Actually, I now do trainings and facilitation [of meetings in countries recovering from conflict], and that's because of one workshop I attended back then with an international organization. A lady—half-French, half-Algerian—she told me the basics of trainings and how to treat and respect people's views, and this is always what I keep in mind when I do my own training and facilitation: respect your trainees, your participants, and be passionate about the topic.

DOES IT HELP YOU IN YOUR WORK IF YOU SPEAK THE SAME LANGUAGE OR HAVE THE SAME RELIGION OR ETHNICITY AS THE LOCAL PEOPLE?

Actually, sometimes it backfires. When I was in Serbia, for example, it was easier for me to communicate than in Kosovo, even though in Kosovo they always called me "Brother Muslim," "our Muslim Brother." That doesn't give an advantage. If you want to get more credibility, don't use your [personal] affiliations. You want to show them that you are a real professional, that you believe in what you are doing—this works better than starting out saying, "I'm like you, I'm a Muslim."

WHAT DO YOU HOPE TO ACHIEVE WHEN YOU GO ON A MISSION?

I don't go with the intention of leaving a mark or doing something in their life. I go to be human, to treat [the local population] with humanity and respect; to sympathize and acknowledge. Also, when it comes to helping, I have to be focused, and 99.9 percent of the people you meet will ask you for help directly or indirectly. This is human nature, and they expect something from you, either moral or material. So you cannot just say, "How can I help you?" You have to be focused. What helps me to be focused is a program, a mandate, an objective, a one-year plan.

I had a boss at my first mission in Belgrade who told me, "When you go on mission for a year, for the first three months just learn, listen, and talk to people; observe. Otherwise you will spend the remaining months correcting the mistakes you made in the first three months." **>>**

Mohamed Abdulaziz Ibrahim *(Egypt)*

"For us, it's not only a job, it's a mission, and it's an obligation."

Mohamed was interviewed in New York, where he had come from Sudan for a UN meeting. He was animated and passionate about his work, especially about explaining the tenets of Islamic law, human rights, and justice. He was keen to share his deep knowledge of these subjects and thus bridge misunderstandings that can hinder peacebuilding efforts. (He spoke in a personal capacity, and the views he expressed are his own and do not reflect those of the United Nations.)

<< Could you tell us something about your background?

I'm a justice at the Cairo Court of Appeal. I'm on secondment with the United Nations, as the director of the rule of law section with the UN Mission in Sudan. Before that, I worked for three years in Afghanistan helping with rule of law. In Egypt, I joined the legal system at the age of twenty-one as a prosecutor. As soon as I reached the age to be a judge [thirty], I got my master's degree in international criminal law in the United States, and then I returned to Egypt and worked as a judge. My doctoral degree covered international human rights, comparative with Islamic law.

By coincidence, I came to study in the US in the wake of September 11, and everyone was speaking negatively about Islamic law. I tried to build bridges while I was here; I made presentations and lectures, and I enjoyed it, so I said to myself, Why not specialize in that?

While I was doing my doctorate, my supervisor, who was the Special Rapporteur in Afghanistan for Human Rights, was asked if he knew of an expert in Islamic law. So I found myself in Kabul working with the UN mission there. The first month, I discovered that I was the first one with an Islamic law background working with the mission. And that I had to help the Afghans, because the human resources had been diluted by wars and there was no good expertise. Ten percent of the judges didn't know how to write and read, and 30 percent had only a high school education.

Once, I was giving a presentation about human rights and sharia for the thirty-nine mullahs of the provinces in Afghanistan. I was in a very formal suit. As soon as I took the floor, about nine of them raised their hand and said, "Sir, before you speak, why are you wearing your tie?" And I said, "Why not? Judges in my country wear ties as a way of looking decent and distinguished, resembling justice." They said, "If you come to Kandahar with this tie as a Muslim, you can get slaughtered and killed immediately." And I asked, "Why?" One said, "This is the sign of infidels." And I said, "Well this is the first time I've heard this. Would you let me know why legally?" He said, "The tie looks like the cross, and the cross is the infidel's sign." I said, "You're judges and I'm a judge; let's deliberate. I know the etymology of ties, and it doesn't have anything to do with the church. And you cannot say that Christians and Jews are infidels because in the Qur'an they are mentioned as People of the Book, so they are monotheistic believers like Muslims and thus they are different from people who don't believe in God. So all of us are monotheistic believers, and even our prophet married two Jewish women and one Christian woman to set the example that these are our family. So you cannot say, 'They are infidels and I will kill them.' You have to be very careful with the terms you use. I know the Qur'an, and there is no single verse saying that believers shouldn't wear ties."

Sudan is a different beast. You have the Southern Sudanese judiciary educated in a common and civil law system in Arabic, and suddenly the law is all in English. When I first started working in Sudan, they had ninety-plus cases with death sentences. Most of them hadn't had lawyers to defend them, and most had been subject to trial for a law they didn't understand because it's in English. You could imagine how fair a trial or due process could be in a system like that. In the North, it's a political challenge, because the government became reluctant to deal with the UN. They look at the UN and the ICC [International Criminal Court] as one entity, and they look at us as informers for the ICC, so they said, "Stop walking. You cannot even go to the court." In North Sudan, we approached the judiciary with political restraint. It's the same country, like Dr. Jekyll and Mr. Hyde. I go to the North, I have to deal in a certain language and a certain approach; I go to the South, different language, different approach.

Sudan for me is another emotional thing, because my father worked there as a prosecutor when he was young; at that time, Egypt and Sudan were still one country. So I felt really emotionally that I have to do something, not only because my father was there but I deeply believe that there will never be peace without justice, and having a certain knowledge of justice, I can go there and start to make a difference.

WHY IS SEEING JUSTICE BEING DONE IMPORTANT?

In the Middle East, where I come from as a Muslim, "Justice" is one of the names of God. Divine justice is different from human justice; but as judges, we try to aim for perfection in our decisions, not to reach divine justice but aiming to understand it. For us, it's not only a job, it's a mission, and it's an obligation. In the Qur'an, more than one verse says that we are entitled to do justice, so it's not at the discretion of a judge to do justice, it is part of our religion to be just and fair. Accordingly, we have this approach in Islamic human rights: we don't have rights in Islam, we have duties. It is my duty to enforce justice, to protect life. This is what the Qur'an is saying. If you look at this positive approach for human rights, an individual person is the core establishment of society.

WHAT MOTIVATES YOU TO FIGHT FOR JUSTICE?

When I was young, my father was a judge. He always came from work and was like a student spending all the night searching books, writing and rewriting. Later, I started liking the work, not just because my father did it; I really enjoyed it. Normal people think that they have lost their rights, and just by a word I give it back to them. Doing justice is something that is really valuable on this Earth, and that's why most prophets in the monotheistic religions, most of their duties as prophets are to apply justice and work as judges.

WHAT'S YOUR INTERPRETATION OF JUSTICE BASED ON SHARIA LAW?

It is the main foundation of the sharia legal system, of course.

BUT ISN'T THE QUR'AN INTERPRETED IN DIFFERENT WAYS IN DIFFERENT COUNTRIES?

But the notions are the same: justice, equality. I can cite tons of verses in the Qur'an saying that all human beings originated from one human soul, which is the notion of equality. So you cannot say that men are more than women, or less than women, or white is better than black or yellow. We are all one race, coming from one God, and the message is one—coming from different messengers but the same message. >>

David Marshall *(Canada)*

"Working on justice issues is adult-only viewing."

We interviewed David in his office at the United Nations, overlooking the East River in New York. The early morning sun was streaming through the small office window. David was welcoming and freely shared his experiences and views (views that, he emphasized, were his personally and did not reflect those of the United Nations).

◄◄ I'm forty-eight. I work here in New York at the Office of the High Commissioner for Human Rights [OHCHR]. I was born in the UK but raised in Canada; I was educated in the UK and the US as a lawyer.

COULD YOU DESCRIBE SOME OF THE PEACE OPERATIONS YOU'VE BEEN INVOLVED IN?

In 1998, I was doing pro bono work for Amnesty International, and part of that was doing trial monitoring in the US and Europe. I was asked to go, on behalf of the International Bar Association, which contacted Amnesty, to be seconded to OHCHR to monitor trials in Sierra Leone, the treason trials in 1998. So that was my first engagement with the UN. Later, I was seconded by my government in Canada to go to Kosovo to work with the Organization for Security and Co-operation in Europe, and since then I've been doing a number of missions, to Iraq, Afghanistan, West Africa, Sudan, and Nepal.

WHAT EXPERIENCES STAND OUT FOR YOU?

My first real engagement with the UN was monitoring the treason trials in Freetown. There had been a military coup against the democratically elected government, and the persons involved in that coup were put on trial. There were two sets of trials, one civilian and one military; I monitored both. It was a very emotionally fraught event because the trials brought out some of the crimes that took place by those involved in the coup. So, sitting in Freetown in October of 1998 in a courtroom with no air conditioning hearing witness testimony after witness testimony of the most horrific crimes. Old ladies coming in and testifying about how their sons were taken by the rebels and then in front of them beaten, tortured, dismembered, hearts cut out, with pieces placed in the mouth of the mother, arms chopped off, heads chopped off, and I have to say it was the most grim testimony I've ever heard. And in the military trial, those persons were convicted, and they were in a matter of days executed in the soccer stadium by machine gun. Working on justice issues is adult-only viewing; do not show your children the rebuilding of criminal justice systems.

In 2003, the UN building in Iraq in Baghdad was bombed, and our colleagues were murdered. I was in that building at the time. What was most profound about that event was that, notwithstanding that attempt to destroy the role of the UN, there was still a call—by national stakeholders, civil society, and governments—for the UN to continue to help and rebuild the justice system, however painful that was for us. Anyway, 2003 had the most profound effect on me, about the role of the UN and what we can and can't do, but also about the centrality of law, about rule of law and how important it is.

Is it hard making the transition from mission to home?

Yes. [Coming home from] Sudan and Afghanistan were the most profound [transitions]. The poverty there is chronic, the health issues are chronic. You're trying to help people who are incredibly poor, in a culture where there's no respect for legal actors, legal institutions, or law, and then you get in a plane and you're in Frankfurt and New York within ten hours. It's humbling because you recognize that most of the rest of the world is poor. Most of the world is dealing with dysfunctional institutions. But I'll never forget someone in Kandahar [in Afghanistan] in 2002 was still talking about the need for justice for the murder of her child by the mujahedin [guerrillas] in 1983.

How did you overcome the trauma of the bombing of the UN compound in Baghdad?

I don't think you do. I don't think I have overcome it. I think you live with it for the rest of your life. But I put it in context. In the sense that, since 2003, thousands and thousands of Iraqis have been murdered, thousands and thousands of civilians have been murdered; so that day was a horrible day for us and for the victims and their families and friends, but the bigger context is the death and destruction in that country.

What does the term "rule of law" mean to you?

It's changed. Ten years ago it was quickly building a fair and effective justice system that would deliver justice. That was a naive view. My expectations have been lowered about what we, the international community, can deliver. One important thing is that we've never really discussed what the end goal is, what we are trying to achieve.

WHAT DOES "SECURITY" MEAN TO YOU?

If there is organized violence or use of excessive force, there will be a meaningful state response to investigate and punish. So it means physical security, but it also means a sense of institutional, cultural security that the state will take on.

WHAT WERE YOUR EXPERIENCES WORKING WITH LOCAL STAFF, OFFICIALS, AND CIVIL SOCIETY?

[Although it may sound] somewhat corny, I think the engagement with local stakeholders is what makes this work worth doing right. I value building those relations. It takes years to build those relations, but it's the most valuable thing, for me, for this work.

You must move humbly. You need to understand the cultural dynamics at play, but I think the most important thing is just walk quietly.

WHAT'S IT LIKE WORKING FOR THE UNITED NATIONS?

It's a large bureaucracy. It's a very slow-moving ship, the UN, and at times it's painful to watch its engagement, but there's no other game in town. But it's a very proud organization to work for, tears and all. One of the frustrating things is this disconnect from the field; we're so far away and our world here [in UN Headquarters in New York] is the political sphere. So there is a sense of great distance from the impact of the policies we're developing.

I think that we, the international community, not just the United Nations, really need to get our act together around issues related to impact. What do we mean by helping states develop a rule of law, a sense of justice? It's about lowering our expectations, lowering the international stakeholders' expectations about what can be achieved, but we still need a conversation about what it should look like; we need to explain to the stakeholders, to the citizens, what we're trying to achieve for them.

HOW WOULD YOU DEFINE "IMPACT"?

You want a system that has integrity, accountability, effectiveness, and is performing well and has sufficient capacity. It's those sorts of general themes I think everyone needs to rally around. Those are your master messages.

Separately, in terms of practical solutions, you need systems that will produce competent people, so you need competent law schools, competent bar associations, some competent training centers, competent oversight entities, competent laws, and a competent national human rights institution. **>>**

PART III

THE *SPEAKING THEIR* PEACE PROJECT

THE *STP* TEAM

Each member of the *Speaking Their Peace* (*STP*) team was crucial to the success of the project as a whole. Each brought his or her own unique skill set to our joint endeavor, allowing us to explore more widely and more deeply the transition from conflict to peace. What we shared in common were the qualities that made *STP* possible: abundant curiosity, respect for our interviewees, a fascination with the stories they related, and a readiness to follow wherever an interview might lead.

The *STP* team grew as the project evolved. As we added new countries to our portfolio, we recruited new members, usually from among colleagues at the United States Institute of Peace, which supported the project. We did not use interpreters, so we needed people who were fluent in the host country's language and sensitive to its culture. We also needed people who knew the country's history, geography, and social and political scene, and who had networks in the country that they could tap to find people to interview.

For Kosovo, I turned to my colleague Teuta Gashi, who is originally from there, to help me set up the interviews. Teuta drew up a list of potential interviewees, to which I added the names of some people with whom I had worked in Kosovo in the late 1990s and early 2000s. Teuta and I traveled to Kosovo together to conduct the interviews.

In Nicaragua, the team included Suzanne Wopperer and Lelia Mooney. Suzanne was living there and drew from her networks to identify interviewees or people who could recommend people to interview. Lelia, who had worked there on a variety of projects, did the same. Both spoke Spanish, and the three of us conducted the interviews, some of which were with people we met as we traveled.

In Peru, Lelia and I did the interviews together. To find interviewees, Lelia was again able to tap into her existing network, and I consulted with a colleague at USIP, who put me in touch with some of his relatives living in Peru.

In Nepal, the interviews were conducted over the course of two trips that I took for other work-related reasons. On the first trip, Govinda Rijal and Morgan Miller worked with me; on the second trip, our team consisted of Govinda, Anil Kochukudy, and me. Shobhakar Budhathoki assisted in the selection of interviewees and sat in on a few of the interviews.

In Libya, as in Nepal, I was there to work on other projects, but I made the time to conduct interviews, some of which were with people I had already met, but most were entirely new encounters. A local colleague helped me set up a few interviews. Libya was still reeling from its revolution, and the Qaddafi regime had left people wary of speaking candidly, especially to foreigners, so it was critical that our interviewees already knew me or my Libyan colleague. Najla Elmangoush did the Arabic interviews with me.

Originally, I had planned to be part of every interview in every country, but as the list of countries expanded, that plan had to be revisited. I had traveled to Liberia, Yemen, and Myanmar (Burma) for other projects, but had not had the opportunity to conduct interviews. So, when I heard that my colleague Tim Luccaro was going to Liberia, I suggested that Morgan, who had already conducted interviews in Nepal, go with him. Tim conducted interviews by himself in Sudan while he was there for another project. Erica Gaston was a frequent traveler to Yemen, and Leanne McKay was working for a few months in Myanmar (Burma), so I asked each of them if they could conduct interviews for *STP* while they were in those countries I briefed them on our project's goals and process, and they returned with fascinating interviews.

Afghanistan did not work out as I had hoped. We arranged for a number of interviews to be conducted by colleagues in Afghanistan, but the interviews turned out to be less expansive than we were looking for. So we had to take another approach, which included Anil and me interviewing Afghans while they were in the United States.

Khitam Al-Khaghani conducted the interviews in Iraq. She selected people who she knew had personal experience with the violent conflict there, and who were varied in terms of their education, location, age, ethnicity, and gender. She had no problem finding people to interview, because of the deep networks USIP has in Iraq. Although some people were reluctant at first to recount their harrowing personal experiences, she convinced them to do so by explaining that one goal of the *STP* project was to inspire personal healing and social reconciliation in other countries that had been wracked by war.

The interviewing process itself was a profound and moving experience for the entire team. For most of us in the peacebuilding field, traveling to conflict zones is nothing new. However, when we do so, we usually focus on a much broader level of conflict mitigation, where we are looking for institutional and countrywide solutions. When we meet with individuals, it is generally in this context. We do not usually dive beneath the surface and delve into personal stories, as we did for this book.

Several of the interviewers on the *STP* team have themselves experienced the trauma of conflict, so their participation often meant reopening old wounds. But in many ways, this project was as therapeutic for us as we hope it was for those we interviewed. It gave us as *STP* team members the opportunity to bear witness not only to the stories but also to the healing and resilience in the testimony of those we interviewed.

In the following pages, each team member offers his or her own brief reflections on the experience of conducting the interviews presented in this book: the challenges involved, the surprises encountered, the insights absorbed, the inspiration felt, and, sometimes, the transformation experienced. ●

Teuta Gashi

Teuta was born in Kosovo. She earned a degree and became a schoolteacher. In 1998 and 1999, she worked with an international mission to monitor a cease-fire agreement. The mission documented many human rights violations. When international forces took over Kosovo, Teuta worked with them to help rebuild Kosovo's educational system. Subsequently, she studied for a master's degree in the United States and then worked at USIP. She now works for the International Financial Corporation.

<< Traveling back to Kosovo to conduct interviews was a difficult trip for me to make. After experiencing so much hardship, death, and destruction, and after losing so many people who were so close to me, I knew returning would open many fresh wounds. But I also knew that I owed it to my friends, colleagues, and family to help them get their stories out for their own healing. By allowing their stories to be told, they would be able to get a sense that their loss and sacrifice were not for naught—that by hearing about their painful experiences, someone else would be motivated to work toward ensuring such an unspeakable tragedy never happens again.

The interviews really highlighted the importance of empathy. The ability to listen, sympathize, and foster trust are attributes that are in short supply these days. Yet, after listening to the harrowing tales of the widows from Junik, it is impossible not to be empathetic. That they have been able to carry on is a testament to their fortitude and courage.

I was particularly impressed by Nekibe. During our interviews, she wept openly and expressed the unimaginable scope of her losses and the trauma she endured. Yet, despite such immense personal challenges, she was able to channel the power behind the myriad of those emotions to help build Kosovo's justice system from the ashes of war. She was a truly remarkable soul, and her resilience and compassion should be a lesson to us all. **>>**

Leanne McKay

Leanne was born and raised in New Zealand. Leanne's studies in international law and her work with refugees fueled a fascination with the complexity of conflict and peace and a belief that there can be no peace without justice. She joined USIP after spending eight years living and working in conflict-affected Muslim majority states, including Sudan, Somalia, Indonesia (Aceh), Yemen, the West Bank and Gaza, and Pakistan.

<< In our work, it's easy to get caught up in a project, running from meeting to meeting, dealing with e-mails and reports. People crowd your day, but sometimes you just forget to really see them. The interviewing process gave me the opportunity to stop and listen. To add depth to newly formed relationships. To be reminded of why I love what I do, and to be inspired by stories that reflected loss, pain, struggle, hope, strength, and belief that things can and will be better.

The process went both ways. It also gave people who themselves are busy, managing projects, juggling work and family commitments, dealing with authorities, and so on, a chance to reflect, for just a short while, on why they do what they do. One interviewee took long pauses before answering questions, deeply reflecting, and articulating to himself and me, the essence of his belief in humanity. It was my privilege to share that experience.

Everyone has a story, and we will never know those stories if we don't take the time to listen. If the law and the rule of law are ultimately about people and society, then surely we should be spending as much time trying to understand people as we do poring over legal texts and trying to figure out how institutions work. **>>**

Khitam Al-Khaghani

Khitam was born in 1980, right at the beginning of the eight-year-long Iran-Iraq War. She was raised in Baghdad, and in 1991 witnessed the terrifying attacks on the city during the Iraqi-Kuwaiti War. She also experienced the economic embargo on Iraq that turned daily life into "mission impossible." After the fall of Saddam Hussein's regime in 2003, Khitam worked at the Iraqi Assistance Center established by the US Army to support the Iraqi people. The following year, she joined USIP. In 2007, Khitam's brother was killed during a random shooting by a group of terrorists, making her even more determined to help people escape the horrors of violent conflict.

<< When you interview people in a conflict zone like Iraq, and especially when you meet people from the hot spots, or what the security forces and media used to call "the Triangle of Death," you expect to wade into an endless river of sadness, to walk along an endless dark path. It is such a challenging task, but what provides a bright light is the willingness of people to share their stories and have their voices heard clearly by people in other conflict zones, hoping that others will learn the same lessons sooner and will think a million times before falling over the precipice into war and winning only the lose-lose prize!

I consider myself very lucky to be given the opportunity to listen to, learn from, and support victims of conflict. I always begin an interview feeling guilty that I am asking people to open their wounds—and not just to open them but maybe to add salt to them. But, by the end of the interview, I see a completely different look in their eyes, looks that are full of hope and proud to be the way they are, and proud to be finding solutions that don't include being involved in conflict or trapped in a victimhood cycle.

Some people say, "Create the healing out of the disease." I'm a victim of conflict and war myself, and I learned from the braveness of others to move on bravely. And I learned how to forgive, because only God can judge people for their bad deeds. **>>**

Anil Kochukudy

Anil was born in upstate New York and raised near New York City. When he was four years old, he and his sister were sent by their parents to live in India for a year and half with relatives, and he became accustomed to moving between cultures. Anil got his first taste of peace and conflict work in New York, serving as a community mediator. He moved to Virginia to study peace operations and then started working for USIP on conflict management training and rule of law programs.

<< Though I have studied peace and conflict in graduate school and have visited conflict-affected countries, my life has been relatively free from war and threats and acts of violence. I found the interviews a window into another world and a reminder that war is by no means just about statistics. Hearing someone describe how they had to flee because of threats, or how they were beaten by police and left for dead, is hard to forget. It makes you acutely aware that behind the statistics of displaced persons and victims of violence are countless personal stories.

The interviews also helped me fully appreciate the courage shown and trauma experienced by those who decide to remain in conflict areas. I expected that for some interviewees the retelling of their stories would be retraumatizing, opening up old wounds. But I discovered that my interviewees were happy to share their experiences. **>>**

Erica Gaston

Erica was born and raised in New Orleans. She was always interested in international issues and studies, and after 9/11 she grew particularly interested in issues of security and justice. After graduating with a degree in international relations, Erica wanted to experience the challenges of living in a developing country and took a fellowship position in Egypt. She has since lived in Afghanistan, Pakistan, and Ethiopia, among other countries, working on civilian protection, education, and victims' rights for organizations such as USIP and the Open Society Initiative.

≪ As a human rights researcher, I have conducted many interviews with conflict survivors and victims of conflict trauma in many different contexts. The people I interviewed in Yemen seemed less emotive about or less touched by the conflict that has happened around them. They have taken it as part of the life that was given to them to live. Others I've interviewed in other countries have shown greater fear, greater anxiety, and greater trauma. Perhaps it is because conflict in Yemen is so persistent, yet low level, that it has been normalized. Or perhaps Yemenis are simply more philosophical about it.

I found all three of the people I interviewed in Yemen inspirational, albeit in different ways. The shaikh was an intellectual and a philosopher, but he had a light spirit, a sense of humor, and a bit of a twinkle in his eye. Jamila has a natural charisma that draws intellectuals, activists, and all sorts of characters to and around her. Despite being a woman in an incredibly difficult environment, despite being someone vulnerable to being targeted, she charges into spheres of controversy without hesitation. The qat seller was not used to reflecting on how conflict affected him; he was simply surviving, responding to threats or dangers as best he could. ≫

Morgan Miller

Morgan was born in Paris and grew up in France, the United States, and Jerusalem. The three years she spent as a child living in East Jerusalem exposed her to both sides of a deeply rooted conflict and sparked her interest in pursuing a career in conflict prevention and peacemaking. She spent two years working as a program specialist at USIP. She then studied at New York University and is now a practicing lawyer.

<< I was struck by the complexity and resilience of humanity. Our interviewees refused to be reduced to sad stories of lives impacted by conflict. Law students extolled the virtues of the law while bemoaning the status of the court system. Farmers linked the rule of law to a steady food supply. They didn't want to talk just about their experience with the conflict; they wanted to talk about the future.

As a member of the international community working in a country impacted by conflict, one usually strives to be distanced, impartial—an observer. The fluid structure and settings of the *STP* interviews forced me to seek a personal, human connection to the people I was interviewing.

Some of my most successful interviews in Liberia were those I conducted with young people, like myself. I could relate to their struggles for professional success and their frustrations with their government's shortcomings, even if our circumstances were very different. Ultimately, the experience reminded me of the importance of acknowledging the human connections, biases, and preferences that underlie all our work, no matter how impartial we may think we are. **>>**

Govinda Rijal

Govinda grew up in a remote village in Nepal before moving to the capital city, where he pursued his education and worked in the tourism and hospitality industry. Growing up amid civil unrest, Govinda experienced firsthand the injustices of the political system. On one occasion, he was left with two broken wrists and thirty-three stitches after being beaten by the police. Since then, he has worked with USIP and other organizations, facilitating dialogue between police and civil society.

<< Every conflict victim has his or her part of the story of the conflict, and it is the most important story for that person to share. Every time there is an incident reported in the media or a story recited in a conversation, the victims are reminded of their own experiences and of the suffering of their family members. To be able to share their personal stories, with the hope that sharing it may help prevent others from suffering a similar fate in the future, is an honor for them and made them proud.

Some of the interviewees enjoyed expressing their views with us, some were fearful, some were emotional, some were excited, some were unsure and confused, and a few of them could not stop crying. But I could always feel a sense of comfort in those interviewed at the end of the interview. Whether or not they were satisfied with what they had just told us, there was this sense: "At least someone cared about us. At least somebody asked about our sufferings. At least somebody came to ask about our future plans." They felt they were important.

For example, we interviewed a woman selling small tourist items in a big bamboo plate on a staircase. By asking her conflict-related questions, and by listening patiently to the answers, we give her respect and acknowledged that she had suffered in the past. She felt proud, empowered, and respected.

I consider myself a conflict victim, and sometimes in retrospect I think how horrible those moments were for me. Now, after these interviews and listening to the stories of other victims who have suffered so much and yet moved so far ahead through their own efforts, I think that what I suffered was nothing compared with the suffering the others went through. **>>**

Lelia Mooney

Lelia is a governance and rule of law, development, and diversity professional with over twenty years of experience designing, managing, and evaluating complex governance, rule of law, social inclusion, sustainability, multistakeholder engagement initiatives, and local capacity development projects across sectors (public, private) in Latin America and the Caribbean, Asia, and Africa.

◄◄ The trips to Nicaragua and Peru to interview people were transformational for me. For the first time, my task was not to write reports with recommendations or evaluations that needed to be delivered on tight deadlines. Quite the contrary. My job this time was to listen to what different individuals coming from different sectors of society and representing different points of views had to say about what the rule of law meant to them, in real life.

Promoting the rule of law, democratic governance, social inclusion: we use these buzzwords when we're designing bold projects intended to generate changes across societies. However, how much time do we really spend thinking about the recipients of these reforms? How willing are we to discover and accept the fact that sometimes these initiatives tend to fail precisely because we do not listen to those on the receiving end of the assistance? The *STP* project reinforced the importance of letting all sectors in society voice their experiences to facilitate a transition to healing, forgiveness, and social transformation. The stories the interviewees told us were powerful because they represented their direct experiences with conflict, their self-resilience, and their efforts to rebuild their lives and communities.

I was deeply moved by the group of women from Huanta, who walked for hours to meet with us to tell us their story of suffering and their constant search for closure and reparations. While they were well aware that we had no answers or solutions for them, they wanted to be listened to. **►►**

Suzanne Wopperer

Suzanne grew up in Buffalo, New York. Before earning a degree in international relations, she was an intelligence analyst with the US Marine Corps. Her work led her to question sources of conflict and approaches for its resolution. She later joined USIP, where, among other things, she digitized the database and brought voices from conflict zones into the public spotlight. Currently, she is the principal at La Biósfera Reserve & Retreat, a multidisciplinary educational center in the mountains of northern Nicaragua.

<< I had been engaged with Nicaragua in one way or another since the mid-1980s. The *STP* interviews I conducted with veterans of the revolution and the civil war echoed many of the sentiments I had heard twenty-five years before.

Nicaraguans have a huge capacity for love and a desire to inquire. I was as impressed with their animated and articulate ability and desire to recount their stories as they were to have an eminent and transparent peace-oriented institution funded by the US government recording them. Where one might see the desolation of hopes dashed and plans derailed, I saw the energy of faith and a certain glimmer of enthusiasm for the future. The interesting thing was their general consensus (young, old, Contra, Sandinista, unaligned) about what was needed, for their society and for their future.

I genuinely empathized with all interviewees, as varied as their perspectives were. From the think-tank and advocacy *capitalinos* to the battered veteran *campesinos*, all were eloquent, thorough, and passionate. I particularly enjoyed Sofía Montenegro's frank and pointed observations, and Henry Ubeda's humorous treatment of hinterland chaos and how it shows that war is often a series of random acts and knee-jerk decisions. I was motivated by the youths' determination for positive change. I was undone by the highland folks' good humor in the face of the battering they took, and by the lowland coastal folks' faith, still, in the revolutionary spirit. **>>**

Najla Elmangoush

Najla was born in Cardiff, Wales, but her family, which was originally from Libya, moved back to Benghazi when she was just six years old. She was the oldest of four children, and her parents stressed the importance of a good education. After earning a law degree, Najla practiced for three years and saw firsthand the corruption in the judicial system. She decided to go into academia and teach at Benghazi University. Following the revolution, she worked with USIP on various Libya projects. Currently, she is a Fulbright Scholar studying conflict transformation at Eastern Mennonite University. She is a single mother to two daughters.

◄◄ I'm really happy and excited about this book because it highlights the stories and experiences of so many people. For me, what was surprising when I conducted interviews was how asking some of these questions affected me. You're asking people questions about specific events or traumatic moments they've have been through, and sometimes, I felt it was extremely difficult to have this conversation. For me, personally, there are so many memories when it comes to Libya, so asking people these questions made me feel like I was reliving my own memories. It would make me feel sad or introspective. At the same time, as a Libyan, I understood the interviewees' feelings and exactly what they were talking about, and so I felt like we shared these experiences. **►►**

Tim Luccaro

Tim was born in the small town of New Hope, Pennsylvania. He spent his formative years in the community steeped in the Quaker tradition on nonviolence and inclusion. He first began working with refugees affected by conflicts while working for Habitat for Humanity in North Carolina. He later went to graduate school in Washington, D.C., where he began working with the World Bank and USIP. He moved overseas to help USIP find enduring solutions to intractable conflicts in such places as Liberia, the two Sudans, and Afghanistan.

<< Being asked to capture the stories of those who have suffered through the tragedies of war is an opportunity both to document the personal, historical narratives of particularly turbulent moments in our global history and to offer individuals an outlet to share their suffering. In my mind, the latter is often the more important of the two.

In almost every area I traveled or worked, people often seemed excited, or perhaps more accurately relieved, to have someone listen to their stories or those of their families and how they had survived or struggled through the violence that defines or defined their nation. Perhaps they wanted to talk because we have yet to provide adequate psychosocial counseling and trauma healing in conflict-affected populations. Or perhaps they felt they could talk to us, people from outside their community, in their homes because the physical and psychological wounds of the war are still too sensitive to be discussed in public.

Your hope is that asking people to tell their experiences offered them in some small way a catharsis or a chance to heal, or at the very least gave them the sense that someone cared about their experiences and was willing to give their voices and their struggles a chance to be heard—and that it might serve a larger purpose.

Perhaps no moment sticks out more clearly for me than that of a driver in Liberia who worked with us during a trip a colleague and I took to document stories for this book. A thirty-year-old man, he had suffered through much of the violence with his family in a small community just outside the capital of Monrovia. For a week he'd been working with us, driving us from town to town around the country, helping to translate, and listening to the stories of other people's experiences. As we passed over a bridge on the outskirts of the city, he turned in his seat and asked us if we would listen to his story. He proceeded to tell the story of how he often had to cross the very bridge we were on, which had been set up as a checkpoint by one of the many fighting factions at the time, manned by a group of child soldiers. He described a particular instance in which a young man, no more than fourteen, pulled him aside as he crossed the bridge. High on drugs, high on the power of being armed with lethal weapons as a pubescent boy, the checkpoint leader took our driver over to the side of the bridge, made him kneel on the ground, put a gun to his head, and told him to beg for his life. Somehow, through prayer or divine intervention, the young soldier eventually let our driver go on his way, sparing his life in a moment of completely pointless violence. Nearly every day since, our driver had had to cross that bridge. >>

THE *STP* WEBSITE

The *Speaking Their Peace* website—SpeakingTheirPeace.org—gives visitors the opportunity to explore a wide array of audio, video, and unpublished material and to say what they think about the issues that lie at the heart of this book.

STP Videos and Extra Photos

SpeakingTheirPeace.org presents an array of fascinating videos and colorful photos related to the *STP* project. Visitors can watch videos that combine clips and photos from many different interviewees to create short, visually and intellectually arresting films that are sure to stimulate ideas and discussion. There are also videos of some of the interviewers, who explain how the *STP* project unfolded, the challenges they faced, the emotional impact on them, and the inspiring power of the people they interviewed.

Visitors to the website can also explore a wide selection of photographs taken on location. The photos, almost all of which are in color (unlike the black-and-white images in this book), include portraits of interviewees, behind-the-scenes shots of the *STP* team preparing for and conducting interviews, and evocative views of the cities and countryside of the countries that the team visited.

Additional Interviews

We didn't have room in the book for all the interviews we conducted. Some of those that we couldn't fit in can be found on the website.

Free Teaching and Discussion Guides to Download

Educators can download free teaching guides customized to different learning environments. One guide is designed to be used by high school teachers. Another guide is tailored for use by college professors. Both guides identify key themes that students can explore, outline teaching ideas, present questions for discussion and writing assignments, and suggest activities for inside and outside the classroom. The guides help educators enable their students to see the connections between the political and the personal, the individual and the universal, the local and the global, and the interviewees' lives and the lives of the students themselves.

For more teacher resources, visit USIP's Global Peacebuilding Center at www.buildingpeace.org.

Book club members can download a discussion guide that will generate lively conversations not only about how individual interviewees coped with trauma and nurtured hope but also about universal themes such as the relationships between corruption and conflict, law and stability, revenge and forgiveness, and peace and justice.

Ongoing Conflicts and Peace Processes: Data/Links

For readers who want to learn more about the conflicts featured in this book and about other, ongoing conflicts and efforts to resolve them, SpeakingTheirPeace .org provides many useful links to other websites. Hosted by international organizations, nongovernmental organizations, and various other bodies, these websites offer background information and news about countries trying to escape the clutches of conflict and make the transition to peace. Links are also provided to published materials, such as USIP reports, that feature material from the *STP* project

Speak Your Own Peace

Visitors to SpeakingTheirPeace.org are invited to speak their own peace by contributing—in writing or on video—their thoughts about the issues and themes at the core of this book.

Visitors can take the part of an interviewee and post their answers to the same questions we asked the interviewees featured in this book: "What motivates you to carry on when you face extreme challenges or violence?" "What does 'rule of law' mean to you?" "Do you think international intervention is helpful?" "What do you want people to know about your country?"

Visitors can also offer their own comments on any aspect of the book and how they have used the book. For instance, a reader could describe his or her own ideas for helping reconcile former enemies; or educators and students could explain how they used the book and what ideas or projects it sparked.

These ideas, comments, and feedback can be posted on the website in writing by contributing to the website's blog or via video. The website explains how to upload your videos. Visitors will be able to see their own contributions (written and video) on the website, as well as what other visitors have contributed.

Meet the Author

SpeakingTheirPeace.org provides up-to-date details of where and when Colette will be speaking about the book, signing copies, and answering questions. A video features Colette answering questions about the project and the book.

The website also provides the text of and links to book reviews, author interviews, and other media coverage of *Speaking Their Peace*. ●

ABOUT THE AUTHOR

Colette Rausch is committed to participating in efforts to help bring peace and stability to war-torn societies, but her own life has been anything but orderly and ordinary.

Her adoptive father (a musician who learned to play performing for silent movie audiences as he traveled across the country with his father) and mother divorced when Colette was eight years old. She and her brother sometimes found themselves with no roof over their heads, living in other people's homes or, when they could afford it, in motel rooms. Colette started working at a McDonald's at fourteen and was the restaurant's manager by sixteen.

She began taking college courses as a senior in high school and moved herself into a college dorm. She worked her way through college, including a stint running the night shift in a funeral home. She dealt blackjack at a Reno casino after she earned a degree in journalism from the University of Nevada Reno. At first, she thought of becoming a war correspondent. But her love for justice won out, and she earned a JD in law from Santa Clara University.

Around this time, she found her birth parents; her mother was living in the United States, and her father in Germany. They have remained in close touch ever since.

After practicing law for a large firm, Colette joined the State of Nevada's Attorney General's Office, where she first was the lawyer for the Consumer Affairs Division and later director of the telemarketing and consumer fraud unit. Her successes there led her to join the US Department of Justice (DOJ), where she worked in both the white-collar crime and the violent crime units as a federal prosecutor in Las Vegas.

Colette quickly earned a reputation for being a tenacious litigator, successfully prosecuting prominent white-collar crime and consumer fraud cases. She also prosecuted the state's first case under the federal Violence Against Women Act, and the first case involving the federal anti–church burning law. Later, she became a federal public defender for death row inmates.

In the 1990s, as some Eastern European countries struggled to make the transition to democracy, Colette's career took a new direction. She was appointed by the DOJ as its legal adviser, first in Hungary and later in Bosnia. In Hungary, she worked on the development of a crime task force. In Bosnia, she worked with local justice officials on law reform. She then returned to Washington, D.C., as the DOJ program manager for Central and East Europe, establishing criminal justice development and training projects in Albania, Bosnia, Croatia, Kosovo, and Macedonia.

From there, Colette took a position with the Organization for Security and Co-operation in Europe, working closely with the United Nations to focus on strengthening rule of law and adherence to human rights standards, training judges and prosecutors, defense counsels, and revising laws and establishing systems for monitoring human rights.

Today, Colette serves as associate vice president of Governance, Law, and Society at the United States Institute of Peace, an independent, nonpartisan organization funded by Congress that works to prevent and resolve international conflict. Focusing on justice, security, and peace, she has worked in numerous countries embroiled in or emerging from conflict, including Afghanistan, Myanmar (Burma), El Salvador, Guatemala, Iraq, Liberia, Libya, Nepal, Nicaragua, and Yemen.

Colette has built a formidable reputation, both at home and abroad, for her commitment, integrity, inventiveness, and effectiveness. ●

CREDITS

Poem: "When It Is Calm Again" was published in *Dirges for My Homeland: A Collection of War and Other Poems* by Saah Charles N'Tow (2004); © Saah Charles N'Tow.

Photographs: Unless otherwise noted, the Endowment of the United States Institute of Peace holds copyright on these photographs.

Colette Rausch: photographs on pages 3 (bottom left), 15, 46, 54, 57, 66, 69, 73, 77, 80, 81, 84, 90, 94, 111, 135, 149, 164, 187, 190, 207, 217, 223, 238, 244, 250, 253, 256, 262, 263, 264, 265, 268, 269, 270, 271.

Morgan Miller: photographs on pages 3 (top left), 41, 49, 60, 61, 88, 98, 106, 118, 140, 152, 154, 167, 180, 185, 211, 227, 272.

Tim Luccaro: photograph on page 3 (top right), 267.

Govinda Rijal: photograph on page 3 (bottom right).

Patrick Dunn: photograph on page 44; © Patrick Dunn.

Teuta Gashi: photographs on pages 91, 93, 95, 96, 102, 120, 137, 157, 204, 214, 230, 235.

Lelia Mooney: photograph on page 108.

Dafina Beqiri: photograph on page 114; © Dafina Beqiri.

Leanne McKay: photographs on pages 143, 177, 197.

Samia Al-Hadad: photograph on page 146; © Samia Al-Hadad.

Suzanne Wopperer: photograph on page 159.

Anil Kochukudy: photographs on pages 161, 174.

Fahd Al-Abssi: photographs on pages 170, 220, 266.

Vivienne O'Connor: photograph on page 201.

Shobhakar Budhathoki: photograph on page 232.

Khitam Al-Khaghani: photograph on page 276.